A more complete list of Willmaker reviews—

A+ Magazine (November 1984), *Press-Telegram* (March 30, 1985), *InCider* (September, 1985) *HALT* (May 1985), *Express* (May 10, 1985), *Press Democrat* (April 28, 1985), *Co-op Newspaper* (June 10, 1985), *Computer Currents* (June 18- July 2,1985), *Journal American* (June 7,1985), *Changing Times* (July 1985), *Copley News Service* (April 19, 1985), *Macazine* (May 1985), *Macintosh Buyer's Guide* (Fall 1985), *Penapple* (November 1985), *Uncle Jam International* (September 1985), *American Bar Association Journal* (November 1985), *MacUser* (January 1986), *Family Computing* (January 1986), *Boston Computer Society* (January/February 1986), *Personal Computing* (November 1985), *P.C. Letter* (December 1985), *Family Computing* (January 1986), *Legal Information Alert* (February 1985), *Oakland Tribune* (December 30, 1985) , Fortune (February 17, 1986), *MacNaught Syndicate* (January 27, 1986), *Minneapolis Star Tribune* (January 16, 1987), *Software Reviews on File* (February 1986), *Atlanta Journal and Constitution* (January 27, 1986), *San Francisco Chronicle* (February 12, 1986), *Productivity Digest* (February 1986), *Seybold Report on Professional Computing* (January 20, 1986), *WholeEarth Review* (Spring 1986), *MacWorld* (April 1986), *Random Access Guide* (March 1986), *Philadelphia Enquirer* (March 9, 1986), *InfoWorld* (March 10, 1986), *Nibble* (April 1986), *Santa Clara Valley TIPC User's Group* (March 1986), *Peter McWilliams* (March 1986), *RUN Magazine* (April 1986), *Times-Tribune* (April 1, 1986), *Los Angeles Times* (April 17, 1986), *Arizona Republic* (March 14, 1986), *Adweek* (April 15, 1986), *New Products Rundown* (April 1986), *InfoSystems* (March 1986), *Litchfield County Times* (March 21, 1986), *Sonoma Business* (Spring 1986), *BYTE* (May 1986), *PC World* (May 1986), *Bay Area Business Magazine* (May 1986), *Gazette Telegraph* (May 15, 1986), *Dallas Times Herald* (April 27, 1986), *St. Louis Computing* (May 1986), *School and Home Courseware* (February 5, 1986), *inCider* (June 1986), *Macazine* (June 1986), *Lawyer's P.C.* (June 1,1986), *Macbriefs* (May/June 1986), *Commodore* (July/August 1986), *Directions* (June, 1986), *The Journal* (July 25, 1986), *New York Times* (July 29, 1986), *Industry Week* (August 1986), *Baltimore Sun* (April 23, 1986), *North Coast Users Group* (July 1986), *Oakland Tribune* (August 4, 1986), *Commodore Powerplay* (October/November 1986), *Mac Magazine Reports* (October 1986), *Lawyer's P.C.* (December 1986), *Computer Reseller News* (October 27, 1986), *Commodore Powerplay* (October/November 1986), *Management Accounting* (January 1987), *Louisville Courier Journal* (January 5, 1987), *Trenton Times* (December 28, 1986), *Lawyer's P.C.* (November, 15, 1986), *San Jose Mercury* (February 8, 1987), *Family Computing* (February 1987).

WILLMAKER

(formerly WillWriter)

WillMaker Program by Legisoft
WillMaker Manual by Nolo Press

Illustrations by Mari Stein

NOLO PRESS • 950 Parker Street, Berkeley, CA 94710

Printing History

Nolo Press is committed to keeping its books up-to-date. Each new printing, whether or not it is called a new edition, has been completely revised to reflect the latest law changes. This book was printed and updated on the last date indicated below. Before you rely on information in it, you might wish to call Nolo Press (415) 549-1976 to check whether a later printing or edition has been issued.

New **"Printing"** means there have been some minor changes, but usually not enough so that people will need to trade in or discard an earlier printing of the same edition. Obviously, this is a judgment call and any change, no matter how minor, might affect you. New **"Edition"** means one or more major, or a number of minor, law changes since the previous edition.

License Information

WillMaker is sold solely for the private noncommercial use of its purchasers. It is a violation of United States copyright law to duplicate the WillMaker disc (except for the backup copy).

First Edition (1.0)	September 1985
Second Edition (2.0)	April 1986
Second Printing	August 1986
Third Printing	October 1986
Fourth Printing	May 1987
Fifth Printing	November 1987
Third Edition (3.0)	April 1988
Second Printing	June 1988
Third Printing	March 1989
Fourth Printing	September 1989
Fifth Printing	December 1989
WillMaker Program	Legisoft (Jeff Scargle & Bob Bergstrom)
WillMaker Manual	Nolo Press (Stephen Elias & Jake Warner)
Illustrations	Mari Stein
Production	Stephanie Harolde & Glenn Voloshin
Book Design	Keija Kimura
Packaging Design	Carol Pladsen
Index	Sayre Van Young

ISBN 0-87337-107-0 (IBM 3 1/2)
ISBN 0-87337-063-5 (IBM 5 1/4)
ISBN 0-87337-065-1 (Macintosh)
ISBN 0-87337-064-3 (Apple)
Library of Congress Card Catalog No. 84-63151
© Copyright 1985, 1986 and 1988 by Nolo Press

Important

Please Read This: We have done our best to give you useful, accurate and up-to-date software and written information to help you write your own simple will. But please be aware that laws and procedures in the various states are constantly changing and are subject to differing interpretations. Also, we have no control over whether you carefully follow our instructions or properly understand the information contained on the WillMaker disk or this manual. Of necessity, therefore, neither Nolo Press nor Legisoft makes any guarantees concerning the use to which the WillMaker program or manual is put, or the results of that use. In other words, any will you write using WillMaker is yours and it's your responsibility to be sure it carries out your intentions. If you want a legal opinion regarding the legal effect of any will you write using WillMaker, have it reviewed by an attorney in your state who specializes in wills and estate planning. Also, if you become confused by any aspect of WillMaker or the manual, we recommend you talk to a lawyer before further use.

Nolo Press does offer several services which update all of our self-help law books and software on a regular basis. This includes the Nolo News, a quarterly self-help law newspaper that updates all of our books and software and contains many helpful self-help law articles. In addition, and more specifically, our free WillMaker User's Service provides all registered WillMaker purchasers with notice of any necessary program upgrades and law changes, as well as notification of other Nolo self-help law software as it becomes available, for a two-year period. **To receive the Nolo News and the WillMaker User's Service, complete and mail the card found in the disk packet.**

Working Together

The creative and cooperative work of many people—lawyers, programmers and friends—made WillMaker possible.

Bob Bergstrom and Jeff Scargle of Legisoft were primarily responsible for the WillMaker program. Steve Elias and Jake Warner of Nolo Press coordinated writing the manual. However, in many ways both manual and program are the product of the cooperative and creative efforts of all four.

Daryl McKibbin, Roger Scargle, and Mark Terrell aided Legisoft in the programming. Carla Holt, Sharon Sittloh, Linda Ross, Deanna Hisaw, Bill Hennessy, Peter Noerdlinger and Steve Nerney contributed to Legisoft in various valuable ways.

Jackie Clark, Denis Clifford, Stephanie Harolde, Toni Ihara, Keija Kimura, John O'Donnell, Carol Pladsen, Mary Randolph and Glenn Voloshin of Nolo Press contributed much valuable labor to creating the manual. In addition, the efforts of Kate Thill, Barbara Hodovan, John O'Donnell, Julie Christianson, Jack Devaney, Amy Ihara, Renee Rivera, Susan Quinn, Alison Towle, Ann Heron, David Cole, Claudia Goodman-Hough, and Albin Renauer have helped market and support WillMaker.

Finally, we are grateful to the many people who helped us test the preliminary versions of the WillMaker program and to all those users who suggested ways WillMaker could be improved.

Table of Contents

PART 1

Introduction to Wills and WillMaker

Welcome to WillMaker, a computer program and accompanying manual which permits the average person to efficiently prepare his or her own legal will. WillMaker is designed for use by residents of all states (and the District of Columbia) except Louisiana[1]. It allows a typical adult American citizen to pass all of his property to family, friends and charities.

WillMaker allows you the following options when making your will:

• You may make up to sixteen separate specific bequests of cash, personal property, or real estate to your spouse, your children, your grandchildren, and/or any other relative, friend, partner, person, charity or institution of your choice;

---

[1]Louisiana has several legal rules and procedural requirements different than those called for by WillWriter. If you live in Louisiana and inadvertently purchased this program, please return it directly to Nolo Press and we will promptly refund your purchase price.

• You may leave the rest of your property to whomever you choose;

• You may forgive debts;

• In the event a beneficiary named to receive your property fails to survive you by 45 days you may choose to have the property go to the beneficiary's living children, or to other beneficiaries (if any) named to receive the same property, or to one or more of the alternate beneficiaries that WillMaker permits you to name.

• You may name a guardian to care for the person and property of your minor children until they reach 18 in case there is no natural or adoptive parent to assume this role.

• You may create a trust for property you leave to one or more of your children to take effect when you die. Under the terms of the trust, you may stipulate that the child receive the money or property left in the trust at any age from 18 to 30, for the purpose of having them receive the property when they are sufficiently mature.

• You may include children in your will who were born or adopted during an earlier marriage, or when you were not married, as well as those born or adopted during a current marriage;

• You may name a personal representative (executor) to handle your estate without having to post a bond;

• You may specify how you want your personal representative to pay your estate's debts, expenses and taxes;

• You may disinherit anyone (except your spouse in most states) by not leaving them any property. WillMaker automatically leaves one dollar to each of your children (and in some cases your grandchildren) that you name in order to prevent them from claiming that you accidentally overlooked them.

In short, WillMaker and the accompanying manual enable the user to produce a basic will sufficient for the needs of most adult American citizens and permanent residents. However, some people will want to go beyond WillMaker when planning to dispose of their estate. And, for a very few, WillMaker will be of little value. Let's take a minute to review the types of situations for which the use of WillMaker is either not advised or should be supplemented with other estate planning techniques.

If your anticipated estate is large enough to warrant estate planning (that is, the art of keeping your estate taxes and probate fees to the minimum), you should not totally rely on WillMaker for disposing of your property. For these larger estates, you should make a will, but only as part of a more general estate plan which includes limiting the amount of property subject to probate. This might include owning some property in joint tenancy, establishing a living trust, etc. Estate planning is discussed in some detail in Part 6 of this manual. For now, it's enough to realize that if your anticipated estate is worth more than $75,000 or so, you may wish to supplement your will with some estate planning techniques designed to minimize the value of the property passing through probate. In addition, if your estate, or the combined estate of you and your spouse, is worth more than approximately $600,000,[2] you will want to familiarize yourself with estate planning techniques designed to reduce taxes. We discuss tax planning in Part 6(C) of this manual.

Part 9 of this manual provides a number of examples of what can and cannot be accomplished with WillMaker, taking these estate planning considerations into account. Please remember, however, that you are writing your own will and that WillMaker is only a tool to help you. You must take responsibility for the result.

Joint Will Note: WillMaker is intended for use by individuals and cannot be used to create a joint will (one document disposing of the property of two people). For the reasons discussed in Chapter 9(B) (What WillMaker Cannot Do), we believe that joint wills are both unnecessary and likely to create practical and legal problems.

Warning: If your estate is larger than $1,000,000, it makes sense to use WillMaker only as a stopgap measure until you can develop a comprehensive estate plan with the help of a lawyer. Once you reach the million dollar level, good tax planning becomes both subtle and tricky and you can and should seek competent legal and accounting help to supplement your own study of various probate avoidance and tax-saving techniques.

Sample Will

Before you plunge into the rest of this book, why not take a moment to see what a will produced using WillMaker looks like. Here is a short sample will made out by Thomas Hobsbaum.

---

[2]We use the $600,000 figure because it is the amount that is exempt from federal estate tax.

WILL OF Thomas Anthony Hobsbaum

I, Thomas Anthony Hobsbaum, a resident of the state of VERMONT, county of Caledonia, declare that this is my will. My Social Security Number is 573-67-8999.

FIRST: I revoke all wills and codicils that I have previously made.

SECOND: I am married to Justine Ferris Hobsbaum.

THIRD: I have one child now living, whose name is: Cecilia H. Hobsbaum.

FOURTH: I hereby leave $1.00 to Cecilia H. Hobsbaum This bequest is in addition to and not instead of any other gift, bequest, or devise that this will makes to this person.

FIFTH: I give my residuary estate, i.e. the rest of my property not otherwise specifically disposed of by this will or in any other manner, to Justine Ferris Hobsbaum. However, if the beneficiary named in this section to receive this property fails to survive me by 45 days, that beneficiary's living children shall take the property, in equal shares. If the beneficiary named in this section to receive this property fails to survive me by 45 days and leaves no children of his or her own, the property shall go to Fred Hobsbaum.

SIXTH: If any beneficiary under this will in any manner, directly or indirectly, contests or attacks this will or any of its provisions, any share or interest in my estate given to the contesting beneficiary under this will is revoked and shall be disposed of in the same manner provided herein as if that contesting beneficiary had predeceased me without issue.

SEVENTH: If my spouse and I should die simultaneously, or under such circumstances as to render it difficult or impossible to determine who predeceased the other, I shall be conclusively presumed to have survived my spouse for purposes of this will.

EIGHTH: If any person not my child who receives property under this will is a minor at the time of distribution, I direct my personal representative to distribute the property to the minor's custodian under the provisions of the Uniform Gifts to Minors Act, or the Uniform Transfers to Minors Act, enacted by the state of VERMONT, if either is applicable.

NINTH: Any bequest or devise made in this will to two or more beneficiaries shall be divided equally among them, unless unequal shares are specifically indicated.

WILL OF Thomas Anthony Hobsbaum

TENTH: I name Justine Ferris Hobsbaum as personal representative (executor) of this will, to serve without bond. If this person or institution shall for any reason fail to qualify or cease to act as personal representative, I name Fred Hobsbaum as personal representative (also without bond), instead.

ELEVENTH: I hereby grant to my personal representative the following powers, to be exercised as he or she deems to be in the best interests of my estate:
1) To retain property without liability for loss or depreciation resulting from such retention.
2) To dispose of property by public or private sale, or exchange, or otherwise, and receive and administer the proceeds as a part of my estate.
3) To vote stock, to exercise any option or privilege to convert bonds, notes, stocks or other securities belonging to my estate into other bonds, notes, stocks or other securities, and to exercise all other rights and privileges of a person owning similar property in his own right.
4) To lease any real property that may at any time form part of my estate.
5) To abandon, adjust, arbitrate, compromise, sue on or defend and otherwise deal with and settle claims in favor of or against my estate.
6) To continue or participate in any business which is a part of my estate, and to effect incorporation, dissolution or other change in the form of organization of the business.
7) To do all other acts which in his or her judgment may be necessary or appropriate for the proper and advantageous management, investment and distribution of my estate.

The foregoing powers, authority and discretion granted to my personal representative are intended to be in addition to the powers, authority and discretion vested in him or her by operation of law by virtue of his or her office, and may be exercised as often as is deemed necessary or advisable, without application to or approval by any court in any jurisdiction.

TWELFTH: Except as otherwise specifically provided in this will, I instruct my personal representative to first pay all my just debts, and all expenses necessarily incurred after my death, from the following assets in the order listed: -NOT USED-.

THIRTEENTH: Except as otherwise specifically provided in this will, I instruct my personal representative to first pay all my estate and inheritance taxes assessed against my estate out of the residue of my estate.

FOURTEENTH: I direct my personal representative to take all actions legally permissible to have the probate of my will done as simply and as free of court supervision as possible under the laws of the state having jurisdiction over this will, including filing a petition in the appropriate court for the independent

Page 2 Initials:_____ _____ _____ _____ Date:_____

WILL OF Thomas Anthony Hobsbaum

administration of my estate.

    I, Thomas Anthony Hobsbaum, the testator, sign my name to this instrument, this _____day of _____, 19___.
    I hereby declare that I sign and execute this instrument as my last will, that I sign it willingly, and that I execute it as my free and voluntary act for the purposes therein expressed.
    I declare that I am of the age of majority or otherwise legally empowered to make a will, and under no constraint or undue influence.

_____
(Signed)

    We, the witnesses, sign our names to this instrument, and do hereby declare that the testator willingly signed and executed this instrument as the testator's last will.
    Each of us, in the presence of the testator, and in the presence of each other, hereby signs this will as witness to the testator's signing.
    To the best of our knowledge the testator is of the age of majority or otherwise legally empowered to make a will, and under no constraint or undue influence.

    We declare under penalty of perjury, that the foregoing is true and correct, this _____day of _____, 19___

_____residing at:_____

_____residing at:_____

_____residing at:_____

PART 2

About Wills Generally

The WillMaker program enables you to write your own simple will. Before you begin, however, you may wish to know a little about what a will is and why you need one. As you surely know, the purpose of a will is to insure that your intentions about your property and your minor children are carried out after you die. A will is one way you can officially "speak" after your death.

A.   What Makes Wills Valid and Effective?

There are two basic aspects to every will:

• Is it valid?

• Is it effective?

Any will that is properly and voluntarily signed in front of witnesses (who also must sign) by a person having the legal capacity to do so is considered valid.

Any will that brings about the result the person making it desired is effective. The effectiveness of a will depends on the clarity of the language used, the absence of ambiguities, and the observation of a few simple rules that apply to spouses, children, and (occasionally) grandchildren.

WillMaker has been carefully designed with these considerations in mind.

B.   Your State of Residence

Because WillMaker is attuned to important differences in state laws, it requires that you indicate your state of residence. For most people, your legal residence is where you now live and intend to go on living for the indefinite future.

1. If You Live in More than One State

But for some people—students, politicians, and members of the armed forces, for example—things aren't always so simple. If you maintain homes in two states, deciding which state is your legal residence can sometimes be tricky. As a general rule, the state in which you vote and pay state income taxes is your legal residence, even if you spend much of your time in another state.

If you can't decide which state is your legal residence, you will need to get advice from an attorney before using WillMaker.

State Death Tax Note: If you aren't sure what state is your legal residence, and you know that one of the states has a much higher death tax than the other (for instance, New York has a high death tax while Florida does not), consult an attorney before declaring your state of residence in WillMaker. See *Plan Your Estate* by Denis Clifford (Nolo Press) for a summary of state death tax statutes.

2. If You Live Overseas

If you live overseas because you're in the armed services, normally your residence is the state you lived in before you received your assignment, the state where your parents live, the state where you now maintain a permanent home, or the state in which you are registered to vote. The more ties you maintain with a state while out of the country, the surer you can be that it is your state of residence. If you have contacts with several states and aren't sure what state to claim as your residence, get some advice from the military legal authorities.

If you live overseas for business or education, you may well still have ties with a particular state—for instance, you were born in New York, lived there for many years, are registered to vote there, and you receive mail in care of your parents, who still live there. If so, that's your residence for the purpose of using WillMaker. However, if you don't maintain continuous ties with a particular state, such as voting, receiving mail or maintaining a home there, see a lawyer to find out what place will be considered your legal residence. This is also true if you maintain homes both in the U.S. and in another country.

C.   What Law Governs Your Will?

Your will's validity is determined by the laws of the state where you sign and witness it. Wills produced by WillMaker are valid in every state except Louisiana. Therefore, if you move to another state (other than Louisiana), your WillMaker will remains valid. (You should, however, review and update it, as described in Part 12 of this manual.)

However, when you die and the provisions of your will are interpreted, any questions involving ownership of property will be controlled by the laws of the state that is your legal residence when you die. The only exception is questions about real estate, which are usually controlled by the laws of the state where the real estate is located.

D.   Who Can Make a Will?

To make a will you must either be:

• 18 years of age or older; or

• Living in a state which permits younger persons to make a will if they are married, in the military, or otherwise considered "emancipated." Also, Georgia law permits people 14 years or older to make a will.

In addition to the age requirement, you must also be of sound mind to prepare a valid will. The fact that you are reading this manual is some evidence of your mental soundness. However, the usual legal definition of sound mind is that the person making the will:

• Has the capacity to understand the relationship between herself[1] and those persons who would normally be provided for in the will (the "natural objects of her bounty");

• Has the ability to understand the nature and extent of her property;

• Has actual knowledge of the nature of the act she is undertaking; and

• Has the capacity to form an orderly scheme of distributing her property.

If you have any serious doubts of your ability to meet these rules, consult a lawyer.

E.   What Happens If You Don't Make a Will?

If you don't leave a will or make some alternative estate plan, the law of each state causes your property to be distributed to your spouse, children or other relatives (if you have no spouse or children) as provided by statute. This is called "intestate succession." If you die without a will, you are said to die "intestate."

---

[1]We use "he," "she," "his," "her," "him," and "her" more or less interchangeably throughout the book. While this may not be a perfect solution to the gender issue, we feel it is less awkward than the "his/her" construction.

Relying on the laws governing intestate succession may be satisfactory for a few people, because the property division mandated by state law is similar to what they would have done in their will anyway. But, because state intestate succession laws simply divide all property between a few close relatives according to a statutory formula, and completely exclude more distant relatives, friends, and charities from receiving property, they do not meet the needs of most people. This certainly goes double for all people with children who want to specify someone to care for them should this ever become necessary, as intestate succession laws do not deal with this important area at all.

F.   Why Make a Formal Will?

Initially, it would seem to be the easiest of tasks to write a simple will. Why can't you just write something in your own handwriting, such as, "I want my kids to get half of my property, except for the family house, which I want my spouse to have, along with the other half of the rest of my property— except for the gold statuette in the living room, which I want to go to my Aunt Clarissa."[2] In fact, some states do allow the use of handwritten ("holographic") wills. Unfortunately, there is often a catch. What you intend by your informal language may not be what your heirs end up with when lawyers finish picking over your words. In addition, it can sometimes be difficult to prove that a non-witnessed handwritten will was really signed by the person whose name appears at the bottom. Consequently, most states require formal witnessed wills. And even in those that don't, it is clearly the best approach.

Reliance on formal wills with precise language isn't necessarily bad. It is a convenient way to make sure you achieve predictable results. It is also true, however, that attorneys have benefited from, and promoted, overly convoluted will-drafting techniques designed to make people jump through precise (and in some cases, silly) legal hoops in order to control the process of passing money and property from one generation to the next.

---

[2]The French philosopher Rabelais accomplished the task of writing a one-sentence will, as follows: "I have nothing, I owe a great deal, and the rest I leave to the poor."

In addition to containing formal language, wills must be signed and witnessed in a ritualistic manner. The reason for this is obvious. As people become older, they sometimes run the risk of being heavily influenced by friends, relatives and organizations determined to get their property when they die. Requiring a will to be witnessed helps to reduce the risk of coercion and undue influence. Witnesses can also establish that the person whose name is on the will really signed it. In many states, there is also a requirement that the witnesses be "disinterested"—that is, not receive any property in the will. We discuss witnesses in more detail in Part 11, Section A.

WillMaker is designed to provide you the tools and information necessary to do your own simple will. In doing this, WillMaker follows accepted procedures and uses clear, well-accepted language. The program itself and this manual explain all of these in detail. Our goal is both to have WillMaker help you make a good legal will and to have you understand the reasons for all the terms and procedures you use. In addition, we repeatedly emphasize the additional steps that many of you will want to take to maximize the property left to your intended beneficiaries and minimize the amount collected by the government in estate taxes and by lawyers in probate fees. This is generally done by limiting the property left by the will to items of lesser value and disposing of the large ticket items (e.g., real estate) by alternative estate planning techniques. The more typical of these techniques suited to moderate-sized estates are described in Part 6.

G.   How Can You Explain Provisions in Your Will?

In addition to disposing of their property, some people want to use their will to explain the reason they are making particular gifts, express feelings about those they leave behind, and state their preferences for funeral arrangements. To keep things simple, WillMaker does not allow you to accomplish any of these tasks in your will. However, we believe that all can be effectively handled in an accompanying letter, which we show you how to prepare in Chapter 10(C).

PART 3

Computer Wills:
Are They a Good Idea?

At this point, you may be wondering whether computers are really a valuable tool to help you prepare your own will, or if computer wills are just another technological fad. At first blush, wills and computers would seem to have little in common. Traditionally, wills have been associated with rumpled-suited lawyers, antique offices and quill pens, not with the high tech hum of a thinking machine. However, the times are definitely changing. It's not so easy to find a friendly, reasonably-priced family solicitor whom you can trust these days. And, as it turns out, the computer is an ideal tool for assisting you to make a simple will. So helpful, in fact, that a great many lawyers routinely use computers to store many of the same type standardized words and phrases that are utilized in the WillMaker program.

Why do computers and wills work together so well for both lawyers and non-lawyers? Fundamentally, a will consists of collecting answers to certain well-defined questions developed over hundreds of years. Doing this isn't difficult once you get to it. Unfortunately for many of us, there is a good deal of initial resistance to overcome when it comes to confronting what will happen when we die. As you probably know, it's easy to put off writing a will until tomorrow, or better yet, the day after. But, once you acknowledge your tendency to procrastinate, and decide to confront it, WillMaker can prove an invaluable aid to writing your simple will.

Like that rumpled-suited lawyer of old, WillMaker's program helps you focus on the questions you must ask to write a sound legal will. Thus, WillMaker asks for information about your property, family and friends, as well as your wishes for disposing of your property. It then stores your answers, and produces a will tailored specifically to your circumstances. In terms of the questions and answers relevant to the simple will prepared by WillMaker, no attorney, old-fashioned or not, could do better. In fact, when you consider the ease with which you may update your will, the privacy you gain by making your will in your own home, and the money you save in the process, WillMaker offers several advantages as compared to the old lawyer-drawn will. Of course, you will be wise if you supplement WillMaker by reading a good estate planning book, such as *Plan Your Estate*, by Denis Clifford.

How does the WillMaker program work? Once you get it up and operating, it provides you with some introductory messages and explanations on how to interact with the program. (Part 14 of this manual provides detailed guidance on the computer end of WillMaker.). After these preliminaries, the fun begins. In a step-by-step process, you are asked to:

1. Provide basic information, such as your name, the state and county you live in, your social security number, and your spouse's name;

2. Make choices as to whom will inherit your property;

3. Identify the property you want each person or charity to receive;

4. Specify any debts that you wish to forgive;

5. Choose persons to care for your minor children if this becomes necessary (i.e., appoint your children's "guardian");

6. Decide whether to establish a trust for property left to your children (often used to specify an age older than 18 when children receive the property);

7. If you establish a trust, name a trustee for any property left to one or more of your children in trust;

8. Choose persons who will administer your estate (in legal phraseology, your "personal representative");

9. Decide how your personal representative should pay your debts and taxes, if any.

After you enter each piece of information or answer each question, your answer is displayed on the screen for your verification.[1] In addition, once all appropriate information and your choices have been gathered by the computer, you will be provided another opportunity for careful review of your responses. Finally, after you have double-checked everything and made any necessary changes, you can direct WillMaker to print your will, ready to sign. The cover sheet to your will tells you what to do next. This, of course, involves signing your will in front of witnesses. In most states, it also may make sense to attach a notarized statement to your will which can be used by your personal representative to speed your will's admission into probate, although this is not legally required. We discuss these procedures in detail in Parts 11 and 12 of this manual.

Many computer programs allow the user to move around from one part of a program to another with relative ease. However, this jumping around is somewhat restricted in WillMaker. The program takes you through the steps in writing your will in a definite order. The main reason we impose this logical sequence is that your answers to questions at one point in the program often affect what questions you need to answer later. For example, if you answer "yes" to the question of whether you have children under 18, you are later provided the opportunity to name a personal guardian for them. However, if you say "no" when you are asked if you have minor children, you obviously have no need to name a guardian to care for your non-existent minor children and WillMaker skips this step.

This sequencing is an important advantage of computers in self-help law. Using a program such as WillMaker, you are presented only with the choices that are relevant to your particular situation... you don't have to deal with options that don't apply to you. Simply put, WillMaker decides in accordance with programmed logic paths what material should be presented and what should be skipped based on your responses to questions.

---

[1]The verification feature can be turned off and on at your option. However we encourage its consistent use as a means of making sure your will accurately reflects your intentions.

In this same vein, the language of your will is pre-set, depending on your choices. We don't provide you with access to this language for word-processing purposes for the simple reason that we know our language will work, whereas yours may not.

By now you have probably gathered that the WillMaker manual is a crucial part of this package. We urge you to read it before you fire up the program and take it for a spin.

While making a will is not difficult (people managed to do it for centuries before computers were invented), we want you to carefully focus on a number of important considerations. These include making an accurate determination of exactly what is in your estate (i.e., what you own for purposes of leaving it to others in a will), how best to minimize taxes and probate fees, and how best to use wills in the context of a larger estate plan. Please pay particular attention to Part 4, just below, which provides an overview of the rest of the manual, as well as specific recommendations for what parts you should concentrate on, depending on your situation.

PART 4

How to Use the
WillMaker Manual

The rest of this manual is divided into eleven parts, as follows:

This outline incorporates the basic analytical steps we think you take as part of preparing your will. In other words, your first task, covered in Part 5, is to inventory your estate, or "survey your bounty," as the *olde tyme* lawyers used to say. This means determining not only what you own, but also (if you are married) separating your property from your spouse's. It also means determining what belongs to you but cannot be transferred by a will, such as property owned in joint tenancy. Obviously, if you are not married, your job is easier. For purposes of this manual, it means you can safely skip Part 5, Sections B and C.

After you have inventoried your estate, you are ready to read Part 6, where we discuss common estate planning techniques designed to minimize the expense and hassle involved in transferring your property to your intended beneficiaries (the people you want to inherit it). Of course, avoiding probate and saving on estate taxes won't help you directly—but it will help insure that your relatives and friends get as much of your property as possible at your death, by avoiding needless payments to governments and lawyers.

Next, in Part 7, we discuss several special considerations that will affect you if you have children. You can skip this section if you are not a parent. If you have children, however, whether they are natural, adopted, or born out of wedlock, Part 7 is essential reading.

Then, in Part 8, we deal with several typical problem areas, such as what happens if your will leaves more or different property than you own when you die, who inherits a bequest in the event the beneficiary fails to survive you by 45 days, and how you should instruct your personal representative to pay your debts, expenses of your estate and estate taxes, if any. This is followed by Part 9, where we provide specific examples designed to illustrate how WillMaker can and cannot be used. You might want to skim Part 9 now.

In Part 10, we provide a checklist for making out your will. It should help you determine if you have forgotten any major property or have inadvertently overlooked a person you want included in your will. Part 10 also tells you how to print your will and how to prepare an optional letter to accompany it. This is appropriate if you wish to explain your reasons for making particular gifts, express your feelings about your loved ones, or specify your desired funeral arrangements.

Part 11 discusses what to do when your will is complete. This involves the process of signing, witnessing and storing your will.

Part 12 alerts you to situations when updating your will is appropriate.

In Part 13, we give you a brief explanation of each major provision you will find in your will once you print it. Of necessity, some of these contain some legal gobbledygook, and you will want to be sure you understand exactly what they mean. Indeed, as you read and understand your will line by line, it's even possible that you will be motivated to make changes in the manner we describe in Part 12.

In Part 14, we tell you how to use WillMaker on your computer. While the WillMaker program can be used without reading this portion of the manual, many readers will want to consult these specific explanations and instructions.

Finally, in Part 15, we provide definitions of the legal terminology that appears throughout this manual and in the WillMaker program itself. We encourage you to consult it whenever you become uncertain about the meaning of a particular word or phrase.

Some of you may now be thinking something like this: "Wait, I just want to make a will leaving Aunt Matilda my small savings, my teapot, and the rest of my property, except of course the things I want to leave Uncle George and Nephew Fred. I don't care how much my property is worth, and I don't really want to learn about estate planning." Others may be thinking: "I only want to appoint a guardian for my kids, not deal with all of my property. Do I really have to go through all of this?"

Our answer to both these questions is "yes." You really do need information on a number of areas, such as how to determine the extent of your property, the effect of your death on your children, probate alternatives, etc., to be able to write an effective will within the context of a sound estate plan. If, despite this admonition, you still want to skip reading what follows and get on with it, we strongly encourage you to also see a lawyer or someone else with a sound knowledge of wills. Remember, you are writing your own will and it's your responsibility to learn enough about the process to ensure the result will fully meet your needs.

PART 5

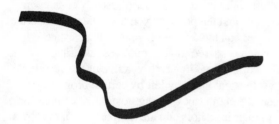

What Is In Your Estate?

Before you actually use WillMaker to help you make your will, you need to know what you own, what it is worth, and what you owe. This is called "determining your net estate." Why is this important? There are two reasons. First, you obviously can't leave property to your loved ones if you don't own it. And, second, before you can think sensibly about using any estate planning devices, you need a good handle on what your property is worth.

For example, if the value of your net estate is over $600,000, you should give some thought to planning to minimize inheritance taxes.[1] To do this, you will need more specific information and advice than we provide here. You will find this in *Plan Your Estate*, by Denis Clifford (Nolo Press). And, as we said in the introduction, if your estate is worth more than $1,000,000, you should almost certainly have your estate plan reviewed by an expert. But, even if you conclude you need more help, WillMaker will generate a good interim will until you get it.

---

[1]As we mentioned earlier, $600,000 worth of property is exempt from federal estate tax. The recent Tax Reform Act does not affect this exemption.

A. Identifying Your Probate Estate

In Section F of this part, you will be asked to compute the value of your net estate by listing all your assets and liabilities. Don't worry, this isn't difficult. First, however, it's necessary to introduce you to the concept of "probate estate." This is simply the portion of your total property which will be subject to the probate court process when you die. Because property left under the terms of a will usually ends up in probate, your probate estate and the property you leave by will are often the same.[2] In the event you don't make a will, your probate estate includes the property which is passed to your relatives under the intestate succession laws of the state in which you live or the state in which your real estate is located. Property left by certain probate avoidance devices, such as joint tenancy, living trusts, and savings bank trusts, passes directly to their inheritors and are not part of your probate estate.

As we discuss in more detail in Part 6(B), making sure you only leave a modest amount of your property by your will is one of the basic principles of planning your estate to minimize probate fees. To repeat this important point, property left in a will must normally go through probate, and probate costs money. Because many of the fees (e.g., attorney and court fees) involved in the probate process are established by taking a percentage of the total value of your probate estate, it follows that the more of your property you can leave in ways that avoid probate, the smaller these fees.

---

[2]There are exceptions to this rule for very small estates. State law differs on this point, but many states exempt property left by will from probate when the total estate is less than between $30,000 - $60,000. A few states set this exemption level somewhat higher. In addition, several community property states, including California, allow one spouse to leave property to the other by will, free of formal probate.

Net Estate and Probate Estate Defined

• Your net estate is everything you own minus everything you owe;

• Your probate estate is the portion of your net estate that will be subject to the probate court, either because you leave it in a will or die intestate. In many states, the total value of this property determines the amount of the probate fees.

Figuring out what is in your probate estate is a three-step process:

• First, catalog everything you own;

• Second, identify the property that for one reason or another will be automatically transferred to someone else upon your death, and therefore will pass outside of probate;

• Third, deduct the property passed outside of probate from the rest of your property. What is left is your probate estate, the value of which will probably determine the amount of probate fees payable by your estate.

Basically, the following types of property will *not* be in your probate estate:

• Real estate (generally termed "real property") held in joint tenancy or tenancy by the entirety;

• Joint tenancy tenant checking, money market, brokerage or other financial accounts;

• Life insurance with a named beneficiary that is not specifically left to your estate;

• Property held in trust, including simple savings bank trusts and living trusts.

• In some states, small amounts of property left by will, and property left by one spouse to the other.

See Part 6(B) for more about these probate avoidance devices.

B. Property Ownership Laws

Now that we've reviewed the types of property that pass outside your will and therefore avoid probate, we turn to the important task of cataloging what you own. If you are unmarried, this will be easy. You own what you own, period. If you are married, however, your property ownership waters can become as muddy as the mighty Mississippi in springtime. Why? For two reasons. First, your spouse may own some property you believe you have the right to leave in your will. Second, your spouse may have the right to inherit at least a minimum share of your property, whether you like it or not. In both situations, the laws of your state will determine what is yours to leave by will, and what is not. This means that if you are married (this includes everyone who has not received a final decree of divorce), it's important that you have—or get—some information about:

• The laws of the state where you are residing on a permanent basis; and

• The laws of any state in which real estate you own is situated.

Fortunately, for most people this isn't difficult, as states can be broadly divided into two types for the purpose of deciding what is in your estate when you die—community property states and common law property states. (See the chart on the next page to identify your state.) With some exceptions (inheritance and gifts are the main ones), community property states presume that property and income received by either spouse during the marriage is jointly owned, whereas common law states do not make this presumption. Both of these approaches are fully discussed in Subsections 2 and 3 just below.

After you refer to the chart to determine the category to which your state belongs, turn to Subsection 2 below if you are married and live in a community property state, and Subsection 3 if you are married and live in a common law state. If you are not married, you can skip to Section D of this part of the manual. If while married you moved from a common law state to a community property state (other than California or Idaho), you will need to read both Subsections 2 and 3[3].

---

[3]Why? Because the property you acquired in the common law state may be governed by one set of rules and the property acquired in the community property state by another. However, if you moved to California or Idaho from a common law state, only community property concepts will be used to determine the portion of your property you own, as well as that owned by your spouse. We discuss this more below when we talk about moving from state to state.

Marriage Note: A surprising number of people do not know whether they are married or not. Problems with making this determination commonly occur in three circumstances:

• Many people have been told, have heard, or somehow believe they are divorced, but have never received any papers to confirm this fact. If you are in this situation, call the court clerk in the county where the divorce was supposed to have occurred and get the records. If you can't track down a final decree of divorce, it's best to assume you are still married;

• A great many people believe they are married by common law. Most aren't. Common law marriages can currently only be formed in the following states and Washington D.C.:

Alabama	Montana
Colorado	Ohio
District of Columbia	Oklahoma
Florida	Pennsylvania
Georgia	Rhode Island
Idaho	South Carolina
Iowa	Texas
Kansas	

AN UNCOMMON-LAW-MARRIAGE

Even in these states, you must intend to be married; merely living together isn't enough to create a common law marriage.

• Some people don't know if their divorce is legal. This is particularly true of Mexican and other out-of-country divorces where only one person participated. This is a complicated area and beyond the scope of this manual. If you have any reason to think that your former spouse might claim to be still married to you at your death, see a lawyer. In the meantime, assume you are still married.

Community Property States

Community Property States	Common Law States
Arizona	All other states
California	
Idaho	
Nevada	
New Mexico	
Texas	
Washington	
Wisconsin[4]	

---

1. Community Property States

In community property states, what you own typically consists of your separate property and one-half of the property owned as community property with your spouse. Obviously, then, it's extremely important that you know what property falls in the community property category and what is legally classified as your separate property.

---

[4]Effective January 1, 1986, Wisconsin changed its marital property law to closely resemble those found in community property states. This law indicates that it covers all property owned at the time of a person's death even though the property was accumulated prior to 1986. Therefore, Wisconsin should be treated as a community property state for the purpose of assessing what you own when you die.

a. Community Property

• All employment income received by either spouse during the course of the marriage.[5] The one major exception to this rule is that all community property states, except Washington, allow spouses to treat income earned after marriage as separate property if they sign a written agreement to do so and then actually keep it separate (as in separate bank accounts). Most people don't do this, but it does happen;

• All property acquired with employment income received by either spouse during the course of the marriage (but not during permanent separation);

• All property which, despite originally being separate property, is transformed into community property under the laws of your state.

This can occur in a number of ways. The two most common involve one spouse making a gift of separate property to the community (e.g., putting a separately-owned home in joint tenancy), and a spouse who owns separate property allowing it to get so mixed together with community property that it's no longer possible to tell the difference (lawyers call this "commingling").

Example: John has $10,000 in the bank when he marries Elsie. This is his separate property. Over the next several years, John deposits numerous paychecks in this account and regularly withdraws money to pay bills. The account balance fluctuates from a low of $2,000 to a high of $20,000. The separate property money in this account has been so commingled with community property that it is all now community property.

---

[5]This generally only refers to the period when the parties are living together as husband and wife. From the time spouses permanently separate, most community property states consider newly-acquired income and property as the separate property of the spouse receiving it.

b. Separate Property

• All property owned by either spouse prior to marriage, or property the spouse receives after marriage by gift[6] or inheritance, as long as you keep this property separate from community property and don't commingle the two. As we mentioned, if commingling occurs, separate property may automatically turn into community property.

The community property states differ slightly on what is classified as community property. One of the biggest differences is that in Texas and Idaho, income derived from separate property is considered community property. In California, Arizona, Nevada, New Mexico and Washington, any income earned by separate property is also separate property.

For most couples who have been married a number of years, determining what is community property and what is separate is relatively easy. The lion's share is community, as any property owned before marriage is either gone or commingled. Probably the major exception to this "all community" generalization is property one spouse receives by gift or inheritance and keeps separate. In some situations, determining whether particular property is separate or community can be more difficult. Here are several potential problem areas:

Businesses: Family-owned businesses can create difficult problems, especially if they were owned before marriage by one spouse and grew later. The basic problem is to figure out whether the growth

---

[6]Community property can be transformed into separate property and vice versa by means of gifts between spouses. Further, one spouse's separate property can be given to the other spouse as his or her separate property. The rules for how to do this differ from state to state.

value is community or separate property. If you plan to leave your share of the business to your spouse, or in a way your spouse approves of, you have no practical problem. However, if your view of who owns the business is different than that of your spouse, and you don't see eye to eye on your estate plans, it's important to get professional help.

Monetary Recovery for Personal Injuries: As a general matter, personal injury awards are the separate property of the spouse receiving them, but not always. For example, the determination as to whether it's separate or community property can vary when the injury is caused by the other spouse. In short, there is no easy way to characterize this type of property. If a significant amount of your property came from a personal injury settlement, you will want to check the specifics of your state's law.

Borrowed Funds: Generally, all community property is liable for debts incurred on behalf of the marriage (i.e., the community), while a spouse's separate property is responsible for that spouse's separate debts. Unfortunately, it isn't always easy to determine whether a particular debt was or was not incurred for the benefit of the community. Further, under some circumstances, a spouse's separate property may be liable for debts such as those for food, shelter and other common necessities of life incurred by the other spouse. Whether this is true depends on the law of each state, as well as the circumstances. The point is that it is sometimes difficult to say what debts the community property (and sometimes the separate property) left in an estate will be responsible for.

Pensions: Generally, money received in the form of pensions, at least the proportion of them attributable to earnings during the marriage, are considered to be community property. However, some federal pensions are not considered community property because federal law considers them to be the separate property of the employee earning them. At present, Railroad Retirement Benefits and Social Security Retirement Benefits fit within this category. Military and private employment pension payments, on the other hand, can be considered as community property to the extent that they result from work done during the marriage.

One question you may be asking at this point is: "So what? If I leave everything to my spouse—what difference does all this information make?" It can make a big difference if you want to keep your probate estate to the absolute minimum. Remember, as we discussed above, all your property (this includes your one-half of community property), along with your separate property, is included in your probate estate[7] if not placed in joint tenancy, an inter vivos trust, or one of the other probate avoidance devices. And remember, too, that the higher the value of your probate estate, the more money your estate must pay in probate fees. However, if particular property is already your spouse's, it is not in your estate at all, probate or otherwise, and you don't need to worry about it. The point, of course, is this: To take full advantage of the probate avoidance techniques discussed in Part 6, you must have a good idea of what you do and do not own.

---

[7]If you do not use any probate avoidance techniques, your net estate and your probate estate will be the same (except that your probate fees will be based on the total or gross value of your property, whereas your "net estate" is measured after your liabilities are deducted from your assets.)

2. Community and Separate Property Division—Examples

The discussion in the previous section may have left you shaking your head. If so, you aren't alone. Thousands of lawsuits are fought over these issues every year by lawyers who are all supposed to understand them. For most people of good will, however, categorizing separate and community property isn't difficult in most circumstances. Here are some examples to help you and your spouse better understand how community property principles determine what is in your "probate estate."

Example 1: You are living in a community property state and your property consists of the following:

• A computer inherited by your spouse during marriage;

• A car purchased prior to marriage;

• A boat which is owned and registered in your name but which was purchased during your marriage with your income;

• A family home which you and your wife own as "husband and wife" and which was also purchased with your earnings;

• A community property loan[8] which your brother still owes to you and your spouse.

Your net "estate" (all your property) consists of the car, one-half of the boat, one-half of your equity in your family home, and one-half of the debt owed by your brother. Why? Your car was yours before the marriage and is thus separate property; the boat was purchased with community property income (i.e., income earned during the marriage); the home was both purchased with community property income and title is held as husband and wife; and the loan to your brother was made from community property funds. The computer, on the other hand, was inherited by your spouse and is therefore her separate property. You can leave all the property in your net estate in your will (and forgive one-half the debt, thus leaving this amount to your brother), or you can adopt one or more of the probate avoidance devices discussed in Part 6(B).

---

[8]Debts owed to you by others (accounts receivable) are a form of personal property and must be tallied up as part of your estate.

Example 2: James is married to Sue Ellen. They have three minor children, Peter 15, Sharon 12 and Pilar 10. James and Sue Ellen live in Arizona, a community property state. They own approximately $50,000 equity in a house (with a value of $150,000) as "husband and wife" and a joint tenancy savings account containing $15,000. James separately owns a fishing cabin in Colorado worth $12,000, which he inherited from his father, and an Austin Healy sports car worth approximately $10,000, which he purchased before he was married. In addition, James owns $100,000 worth of separate property stock in a blue-chip corporation.

Note: Remember, gifts or an inheritance received by one spouse after marriage are the separate property of that spouse.

Using WillMaker, James makes the following property disposition:

› His one-half interest in the community property home to Sue Ellen ($25,000, or one-half of the equity[9]);

• His fishing cabin to Sue Ellen;

• His Austin Healy to his brother Bob;[10]

• One-third of the stock to his daughter Sharon;

• One-third of the stock to his daughter Pilar; and

• One-third of the stock to his son Peter.

James makes no provision for his share of the joint tenancy savings account since this passes to Sue Ellen because of her "right of survivorship."

In addition, James uses WillMaker to appoint his sister-in-law, Karen, as a "personal guardian" for the children in the event Sue Ellen is unable to perform this task. But because Karen is notoriously "loose" when it comes to money, he appoints his father-in-law, Ned, to act as trustee for the children to handle their shares of stock until each turns 25.

---

[9]James would also be wise to at least consider the several common techniques for transferring valuable property to others outside of a will, and thus outside of probate. It is often particularly advisable to do this with mortgaged real property, because if the property is left by will, in many states, the entire value of the decedent's property (in this case, half of $150,000, or $75,000) will be counted when computing probate fees. See Part 6(B).

[10]Joint ownership techniques such as joint tenancy or the use of an inter vivos trust can be used for personal property as well as real estate and would accordingly accomplish this same result outside of the will, and thus outside of probate.

3. Common Law States

Before we plunge into the ins and outs of property ownership in common law property states, let us remind you that you really do not need to know this information unless you are married. If you are not married, you can leave all your property as you see fit.

In common law property states, the property you own consists of:

a. Everything you own separately in your name if it has a title slip, deed or other legal ownership document; and

b. If there are no title documents, everything you have purchased with your separate property and/or separate income. Thus, in these states the key to ownership for many types of valuable property is whose name is on the title. If you earn or inherit money to buy a house, and title is taken in both your name and your spouse's, you both own the house. If your spouse earns the money but you take title in your name alone, you own it. If title is in her name, she owns it. If there is no title document to the object (say a new computer), then the person whose income or property is used to pay for it owns it. If joint income is used, then ownership is joint (generally considered to be a tenancy-in-common, unless a written agreement provides for a joint tenancy).[11]

---

[11]Despite the general rule stated here, the courts in most states will not allow a manifest injustice to occur. Thus, if property paid for by one spouse ends up in the other spouse's name, the courts will usually find some way (called "using their equity powers") to straighten the matter out so that

Here are two examples illuminating property ownership rules in common law property states.

Example 1: Wilfred and Jane are husband and wife and live in Kentucky, a common law property state. They have five children. Shortly after their marriage, Wilfred wrote an extremely popular computer program which helps doctors diagnose a variety of ills. Wilfred has received annual royalties averaging about $100,000 a year over a ten-year period. During the course of the marriage, Wilfred used the royalties to purchase a car, yacht and mountain cabin, all registered in his name. The couple also own a house as joint tenants. In addition, Wilfred owns a number of family heirlooms, which he inherited from his parents. Over the course of the marriage, Wilfred and Jane have maintained separate savings accounts. Jane's income (she works as a computer engineer) has gone into her account and the balance of Wilfred's royalties has been placed in his account (which now contains $75,000).

HARE LOOMS

justice is done. Put another way, many judges will bend over backwards to see that parties only own what they should own.

In this situation, Wilfred's property (his net estate) would consist of the following:

• One-hundred percent of the car, yacht and cabin, since there are title documents listing the property in his name. Were there no such documents, he would still own them because they were purchased with his income;

• One-hundred percent of the savings account because it is in his name alone;

• The family heirlooms;

• One-half of the interest in the house.[12]

Example 2: Martha and Scott, husband and wife, both worked for thirty years as school teachers in Michigan, a common law state. They had two children, Harry and Beth, both of whom are grown with families of their own. Generally, Scott and Martha pooled their income and jointly purchased such items as a house, worth $100,000 (in both their names as joint tenants), cars (one in Martha's name, worth $5,000 and one in Scott's, worth $3,000), a share in a vacation condominium, worth $13,000 (in both names as joint tenants), and some of the household furniture. Each maintained a separate savings account (approximately $5,000 in each), and they also had a joint checking account with a right of survivorship, containing $2,000.

Scott spent several thousand dollars equipping a darkroom he built in the basement. Hoping that son Harry would take up his photography hobby, Scott placed the entire contents of the darkroom in a revocable living trust which passed them to Harry upon Scott's death, but which left Scott in control during his life. The remaining property consisted of antiques and heirlooms which both Martha and Scott had inherited from their respective families.

Scott used WillMaker to make a will leaving his real estate to Martha and the rest of his personal property to Beth. Because the real estate was held in joint tenancy, including it in the will was unnecessary; Martha already owned it as a surviving joint tenant. To repeat, where property is in joint tenancy, you cannot use a will to leave

---

[12]Although the house is in Wilfred's net estate, it would go to Jane outside of the estate because of its joint tenancy status. In short, the house is in Wilfred's net estate, but not in his probate estate. However, if the house was in Wilfred's name alone, it would be his property, even if purchased with money he earned during the marriage, or even if purchased with Jane's money.

it to anyone other than the other joint tenant(s).[13] For the same reason, the joint checking account with an automatic right of survivorship went to Martha outside of the will and free of probate. Harry received the darkroom equipment outside of probate directly under the terms of the trust. Beth received Scott's savings account (regardless of the source of the funds) and the specific heirlooms and antiques which Scott left to her in his will.[14]

C. Family Protection in Common Law States

If you plan to leave your spouse one-half or more of your property in your will, you can skip this discussion and proceed to Section D. Otherwise, read on for important information.

At first glance, it would seem there is no problem for married people in common law states when it comes to deciding what property they can leave and to whom. If one spouse's name is on the title document, or the property was acquired with his funds in the absence of such title, that spouse owns it and can leave it by will to the beneficiary of his choice, right? No, not when it comes to disinheriting a spouse. Suppose, for example, one spouse owns the house, the car and most of the possessions, including the bank accounts, in his name alone and leaves it all to a stranger (or worse, a lover). The stranger could then kick the surviving spouse out of the house, empty the bank accounts, and so on. Of course, this rarely happens. But just in case, all common law property states have some way of protecting the surviving spouse from being completely, or even substantially, disinherited.[15] While

---

[13]However, in many states you can unilaterally (by yourself, without permission from the other joint tenant) terminate a joint tenancy prior to death and then leave your share of the jointly-owned property as you see fit.

[14]If any antiques were owned by Scott and Martha jointly without specific terms indicating a joint tenancy, Martha would be entitled to one-half of them (or one-half their value) with the other half going to Beth. This is because Martha and Scott would have each owned one-half of the antiques as tenants in common, without a right of survivorship.

[15]Some states in both categories (common law and community property) provide additional, relatively minor protection devices such as "family allowances" and "probate homesteads." These vary from state to state in too much detail to discuss here. Generally, however, these devices attempt to assure that your spouse and children are not totally left out in the cold after your death, by allowing them temporary protection, such as the right to remain in the family home for a short

many of these protective laws are similar, they do differ in detail. In fact, no two states' laws are exactly alike.

A SMIDGEN OF HISTORY

Hundreds of years ago, the English courts, confronted with the problem of a few people disinheriting their spouses, developed the rules called "dower" and "curtesy." These are fancy words for the sensible concept that a surviving wife or husband who is not adequately provided for in a spouse's will automatically acquires title to a portion of the deceased spouse's property by operation of law. "Dower" refers to the interest acquired by a surviving wife, while "curtesy" is the share received by a surviving husband. When the United States was settled, most states adopted these concepts. To this day, all states except those that follow the community property ownership system still retain some version of dower and curtesy, although some states have dropped the old terminology. These, of course, aren't needed in community property states because each spouse already owns one-half of all the property acquired from the earnings of either during the marriage.

In most common law property states, a spouse is entitled to one-third of the property left in the will. In a few, it's one-half. The exact amount of the spouse's minimum share often depends on whether or not there are also minor children and whether or not the spouse has been provided for outside the will by trusts or other means (see Section 3 below).

What happens if the person making the will leaves nothing to her spouse or leaves less than the spouse is entitled to under state law? In most states, the surviving spouse has a choice. He can either take what the will provides (called "taking under the will"), or reject the gift and instead take the minimum share allowed by the law of the particular state. Taking the share permitted by law is called "taking against the will."

---

period, or funds (most typically while an estate is being probated). Accordingly, they should not prove unwelcome to any of you.

Example: Leonard's will gives $50,000 to his second wife, June, and leaves all the rest of his property, totalling $400,000, to be divided between his two children from his first marriage. June can elect to take against the will and receive her statutory share of Leonard's estate, which will be far more than $50,000.

When a spouse decides to "take against the will," the property which is taken must of necessity come out of one or more of the gifts given to others by the will. In other words, somebody else is going to get less. In the above example, the children will receive much less than Leonard intended. You should understand, therefore, that if you do not provide your spouse with at least his statutory or "intestate"[16] share under your state's laws, your gifts to others may be seriously interfered with.

Put bluntly, if you do not wish to leave your spouse at least one-half of your estate, and have not either generously provided for him or her outside of your will, or arranged to have your spouse legally waive his or her rights, your estate may be heading for a legal mess and you should see a lawyer.

1. The Concept of the "Augmented" Estate

In many common law states, the share that the surviving spouse is entitled to receive is measured *both* by what that spouse receives under the terms of the will and outside of the will by transfer devices such as joint tenancy and living trusts. The total of both of these is called the "augmented" estate.

Example: Alice leaves her husband, Mike, $10,000 and her three daughters $70,000 each in her will. However, Alice also leaves real estate worth $500,000 to Mike by a living trust. The total Mike receives from this augmented estate, $510,000, is more than one-half of Alice's total property, so he has nothing to gain by taking against the will.

While the augmented estate concept is actually rather complicated (we've simplified it here), its purpose is clear and easy to grasp. Basically, all property of a deceased spouse, not just the property left

---

[16]As mentioned in Chapter 2, a person who dies without a will is said to have died "intestate." When this happens, there are a whole set of rules in each state about who gets what. The share that someone gets under these rules is their "intestate share." As mentioned above, in most states, a surviving spouse's intestate share depends on whether or not there are children. It typically varies between one-third and two-thirds of the probate estate.

by will, is considered in determining whether a spouse has been left his statutory share. This means that in determining whether a surviving spouse has been adequately cared for, the probate court will compute the value of the property the spouse has received outside of probate, as well as counting the value of the property that passes through probate. This makes sense because many people devise ways to pass their property to others outside of wills, to avoid probate fees.

TAKING CARE OF FAMILY, FRIENDS & CHARITIES

2. Chart of Family Law Protection in Common Law States

The following chart provides a cursory outline of the basic rights that states give to the surviving spouse. We do not attempt to set out the specifics of every state's law here. Also, please realize that many states' laws are quite complex in this area. Once again, if this issue is significant to you (that is, you don't plan to transfer at least one-half of your property to your spouse), see a lawyer.

I. SURVIVING SPOUSE RECEIVES RIGHT TO ENJOY A PORTION (USUALLY ONE-THIRD) OF DECEASED SPOUSE'S REAL PROPERTY FOR THE REST OF HIS OR HER LIFE

Arkansas	Kentucky
Connecticut	Ohio
District of Columbia	Rhode Island

II. SURVIVING SPOUSE RECEIVES PERCENTAGE OF ESTATE

a) Fixed percentage

Alabama	1/3 of augmented estate
Alaska	1/3 of augmented estate
Colorado	1/2 of augmented estate
Delaware	1/3 of estate
Florida	30% of estate
Hawaii	1/3 of estate
Iowa	1/3 of estate
Maine	1/3 of augmented estate
Minnesota	1/3 of augmented estate
Montana	1/3 of augmented estate
Nebraska	1/2 of augmented estate
New Jersey	1/3 of augmented estate
North Dakota	1/3 of augmented estate
Oregon	1/4 of estate
Pennsylvania	1/3 of augmented estate
South Carolina	1/3 of estate
South Dakota	1/3 of augmented estate
Tennessee	1/3 of estate
Utah	1/3 of augmented estate

b) Percentage varies if there are children (usually one-half if no children, one-third if children)

Illinois	New Hampshire
Indiana	New York
Kansas	North Carolina
Maryland	Ohio
Massachusetts	Oklahoma
Michigan	Vermont
Mississippi	Virginia
Missouri	Wyoming

D. Moving from State to State

What happens when a husband and wife acquire property in a non-community property state but then move to a community property state? California and Idaho treat the earlier acquired property just the same, as if it had been acquired in the community property state. The legal jargon for this type of property is "quasi-community property." The other community property states do not recognize the quasi-community property concept and instead go by the rules of the state where the property was acquired.[17] Thus, if you and your spouse moved from any non-community property state into California or Idaho, all of your property is treated according to community property rules (see Section B, above). However, if you moved into any of the other community property states from a common law state, you will need to assess your property according to the rules of the state where the property was acquired.

The opposite problem exists when couples move from a community property state to a common law state. Here each spouse generally retains their one-half interest in the property accumulated while they were married in the community property state. However, the reasoning of the courts in dealing with the problem has not been totally consistent. Accordingly, if you have moved from a community property state to a common law state, and you and your spouse have any disagreement as to who owns what, you will need to check with a lawyer.

E. Gifts to Charities

This topic has hung on from times past. It used to be that gifts to charitable institutions (e.g., churches, hospitals, educational institutions) could be successfully challenged if they were made 1) within a certain time prior to death (e.g., within a year), or 2) in excess of a certain percentage of a total estate. This was primarily to discourage churches and other charitable organizations from using unfair means, such as promising you a place in heaven, to fill their own

---

[17]Interestingly, California, Arizona and Texas recognize quasi-community property for dissolution (divorce) purposes. However Texas and Arizona do not recognize quasi-community property for will purposes, while Idaho does. Consult an attorney to find out the rule for Wisconsin.

coffers at the expense of a surviving family. While most states have entirely done away with these restrictions, seven have not: District of Columbia, Florida, Georgia, Idaho, Mississippi, Montana, and Ohio. If you are in one of these states, you should check with an attorney if you desire to leave a large part of your estate to a charitable institution, especially if you believe your spouse or children will object, or you believe you may not have too long to live.

F. Checklist for Deciding What Is in Your Net Estate

Now that you have an overview of what property you do and don't own, it is time to return to the central point of this chapter, which is to estimate the value of your net estate so you will know what you have to leave and whether estate planning is appropriate. To assist you in this endeavor, we provide a worksheet on the next page. Just put down your best estimates as to what your property is worth—precise numbers are not necessary. You will probably be surprised at the total. Remember, if you and your spouse own community property, only one-half of its value and one-half of any debts owed on it belong to you. Similarly, if you own property in joint tenancy, tenancy in common, partnership, etc., you should only list your share.

Living Trust Note: Include in the following list all property which you have placed in a living or savings account trust. Although that property will not pass through probate, it will be counted as part of your estate for determining potential estate tax liability.

THE NET VALUE OF YOUR ESTATE[18]

I. *ASSETS* (Add up what you own)

A. Personal Property

1. Cash _____

2. Savings Accounts _____

3. Checking Accounts _____

4. Money Market Accounts _____

5. Brokerage Accounts _____

6. U.S. Savings Bonds _____

7. Precious Metals _____

8. Other Bonds _____

9. Stocks _____

10. Money Owed to You _____

11. Interest in Profit Sharing
   Plan, Stock Options,
   Limited Partnerships, Etc. _____

12. Automobiles, Boats, etc. _____

13. Household Goods _____

14. Works of Art _____

15. Jewelry and Clothing _____

16. Miscellaneous _____

TOTAL VALUE OF
PERSONAL PROPERTY _____

B. Real Estate (repeat for each piece of property you own)

Current Market Value _____

Current Market Value _____

Current Market Value _____

[18]As you complete this form, it may occur to you that your property, ownership documents and other important papers are spread all over the place. If so, we strongly recommend *Your Family Records,* Pladsen and Clifford (Nolo Press).

C. Business/Property Interests

Value of any Partnership, Sole
Proprietorship, Share of Small
Corporation You Own   _____

D. Value of Any Patents, Copyrights,
and Royalties   _____

E. Value of Life Insurance[19] (face value
minus amount borrowed, if any)   _____

TOTAL VALUE   _____

TOTAL THE VALUE OF ALL THE
ASSETS LISTED ABOVE   _____

II. *LIABILITIES* (add up what you owe)

A. Mortgage debts (include all money you
owe on real property listed above   _____

B. Personal property debts: (loans, total
car payment obligations, other debts _____

C. All taxes owed   _____

D. Any other liabilities   _____

TOTAL   _____

III. *NET WORTH*   _____

FROM TOTAL ASSETS: _____

SUBTRACT TOTAL LIABILITIES: _____

NET ESTATE   _____

Probate Estate Note: Now that you've determined your net estate, you may want to know what your probate estate consists of. We tell you how to figure it out in Chapter 6(B)(7), which follows, when we introduce you to the common probate avoidance techniques.

---

[19]**Remember:** If you transfer ownership of the policy to the beneficiary prior to your death, you may be able to remove it from your estate and thus avoid the necessity of paying estate taxes on it.

PART 6

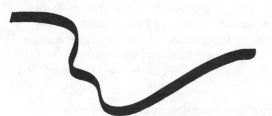

Estate Planning Basics Designed to Limit Probate Fees and Estate Taxes

A. Overview

As we mentioned in Part 1, because of its simplicity most people can safely use WillMaker to make their own will without the assistance of an attorney (except for a final review, if desired). However, let us again emphasize that making a will is not the only thing a wise person will do in preparation for that inevitable day. Although everyone should have a will, it is generally desirable to limit or reduce the amount of your property which is to be passed by it. Why is this? Because, as we have mentioned several times, leaving a large amount of property by will (or by intestate succession) normally results in your estate being subjected to probate (a formal court procedure through which your estate is distributed). This, is turn, often means long delays, as well as significant probate fees.

Practically speaking, the probate process means it will take six months to a year or more for your heirs to receive your property. Also, lawyers will be paid handsomely to accomplish tasks that are not usually necessary. In most states, however, a certain amount of property, usually in the $30,000 - $60,000 range,[1] can be left by will (or by intestate succession) either free of probate or subject only to a simple, informal do-it-yourself probate process. In addition, many states simplify or eliminate probate for property left by one spouse to the other. This generally means that if you have a small estate, you need not worry much about the probate avoidance techniques discussed in Section B of this part. Also, because there are no federal estate taxes on estates valued at less than $600,000, you can also skip Sections C and D and go on to Part 7.

As far as federal estate taxes and state inheritance taxes are concerned, choosing to transfer your property outside of a will can result in tax savings if you are willing to give up ownership or control of your property prior to your death. We discuss this in Section C of this part.

Your next question is probably something like this: "If a will puts property into the probate system and may result in higher estate taxes, why have one at all?" There are a number of reasons. Important among them are:

• If your estate, combined with that of your spouse, is of medium size (up to $600,000), federal tax planning is not necessary because your estate will be obligated for little or no tax and state death taxes are seldom high enough to warrant special tax reduction planning measures. See Section C below for more on this;

• If your estate is modest (in the $30,000 - $60,000 range, depending on state law—sorry we can't be more specific), the elimination of probate or simplified probate procedures substantially reduce the need to pass property outside of your will. As mentioned, some states also do away with the need for probate for property left by one spouse to the other;

• Even if you have provided for your property by some means other than a will, you may end up owning valuable property shortly before death. So, for this reason alone, a will is extremely valuable to back up other estate planning devices;

---

[1]In a few states, this amount is slightly higher.

• Making a will is easy and quick. Other estate planning techniques which are discussed in more detail later in this chapter are more involved. Thus, many people decide that a will is adequate in the short run;

• A will allows you to name a guardian for your minor children; and

• A will allows you to name a personal representative (executor) to handle your affairs after you die.

To sum up, avoiding probate, saving money on taxes, and making a will are the three basic aspects of "estate planning." If you have a medium-sized estate, you will want to at least seriously consider probate avoidance techniques as well as making a will. If your estate is small, however, just making a will is usually sufficient. If your estate is over $600,000, or, if you are married and the combined estate of you and your spouse is over $600,000, you will also want to think about several ways to reduce federal estate taxes.

In the next several pages we will summarize the common techniques used for probate avoidance and estate tax reduction. Please realize, however, that of necessity we only provide an overview. A good source of more sophisticated information on this area is *Plan Your Estate: Wills, Probate Avoidance, Trusts & Taxes*, by Denis Clifford (Nolo Press), a thorough book that everyone with even a moderate-sized estate should read.

B. Probate Avoidance

1. Introduction

The purpose of probate avoidance is quite obviously to minimize the amount of property which must pass through a court supervised probate proceeding after your death. This means passing all or most of your property by one or more legal devices other than by a will. As you should know by now, property disposed of by the will is subject to "probate" unless its total value is small, and therefore exempt from probate by the law of your state. In addition, some states, such as California, allow one spouse to leave property to the other free of probate, no matter what the amount. So, if you plan to leave all, or most, of your property to your spouse, you should check if probate will be required in your state. If not, you don't need to worry about probate avoidance techniques.

Much of the expense of probate results from the fact that the fees of the attorney who takes your estate through the probate court will be a fixed percentage of the probate estate's value. In some states, further, the fees are computed from the estate's total market value. Thus, if the market value of your estate (which is subject to probate) is $900,000, the attorney's fees in some states will be based on the $900,000 figure. This is true even if your equity (the amount you actually own) in the property is much less, say $500,000. Although the percentages vary from state to state, probate fees can devour a modest but significant chunk of your estate, to the detriment of your heirs. A fee of about

$11,000 is typical to probate a $500,000 estate in many states.[2] A fee of this magnitude is an outrageous amount to pay for simply transferring property to close family members and friends, especially in situations where no one is disputing the will. Also, once an estate goes into probate, it can be extremely slow to come out, with common delays of a year or more before your heirs get all of the money or property you leave them. Many probate avoidance techniques are simple. Let's take a closer look at some of these.

Note: Probate avoidance techniques pay big dividends in the form of saving on probate fees, but they obviously only do this at your death. Unfortunately, some of them involve at least some trouble to set up and maintain (e.g., living trusts), while others actually involve your giving up control over some or all of your property (e.g., gifts and joint tenancy). Accordingly, many younger people rely primarily on a will to dispose of their property should they die unexpectedly and wait to make a probate-avoiding estate plan until they are older and more settled. As most people (especially those who are young or middle-aged) have considerable notice between the onset of a life-threatening illness and death, this is often the most sensible approach. See *Plan Your Estate* by Denis Clifford for detailed instructions about how to set up all of the common probate avoidance techniques.

2. Living or Intervivos Trust

This is an arrangement under which title to property is transferred by its living owner (called a "trustor") to a person or institution (called a "trustee") to hold for a third person (called a "beneficiary") until one or more specified events happen. In a revocable living or inter vivos trust, the trustor (the owner of the property) and the trustee are the same

---

[2]Most states base probate fees based on a percentage of the market value of the assets in the estate with the percentage declining as the estate gets bigger. Something on the order of 4% of the first $15,000, 3% of the next $85,000, 2% of the next $900,000, and 1% of all assets above $1,000,000 is fairly typical.

person. This allows the owner of property to put it in a trust completely controlled by herself. The trust can be revoked by the trustee at any time for any (or no) reason. Thus, the owner continues to enjoy the full use of the trust property during her life and can even end the trust, sell the property, and spend the money at the races if he or she chooses. At the owner's death, the living trust device allows the property to be passed to the named beneficiary(ies) under the terms of the trust instrument (the written document establishing the trust) and thus outside of probate.

Example: James wants to leave his valuable painting collection to his son, but wants total control over it until he dies. He doesn't want the value of his collection, $500,000, included in his probate estate. To do this, he establishes a revocable (i.e., he can change his mind) living trust for the paintings, naming himself as trustee while he lives, with his son the beneficiary, to take ownership of the paintings at his death. When James dies, his son receives the paintings outside of probate. However, should James want to sell the paintings and end the trust before he dies, he can do so.

Now, assume James also wants to save on federal estate taxes and wants to know if a revocable living trust will accomplish this goal. No. Living trusts will not reduce death taxes at all. By and large, all property over $600,000 is taxed by the federal government at your death, whether or not it goes through probate. There are several ways that people with larger estates can save on taxes, but they generally involve fully surrendering control of the property prior to death (see Section C, below).

3. Joint Tenancy

Joint tenancy is ownership of property by two or more people under terms that pass title of an owner who dies to the surviving owner or owners, outside of the probate process.[3] While joint tenancy is an excellent probate avoidance technique when you are relatively certain about who you want your property to go to and don't reasonably anticipate a change of heart, it is not as flexible a device as the revocable trust discussed above, since by placing your property in a joint tenancy, you are giving the other joint tenant equal ownership.[4]

Okay, now that you know what joint tenancy is, how do you tell if you own property in joint tenancy? Well, if it is real estate you are concerned with, look at the deed. If it says: "To John Jones and his wife Sarah, in joint tenancy," or "As joint tenants," it's clear. If the deed says, "To John and Arthur Jones as tenants-in-common," then it's just as clear that you are not joint tenants. Tenancy-in-common is another traditional form of co-ownership which does not have rights of sur-vivorship. A tenant-in-common can, and should, use a will or other estate planning device, such as a living trust, to dispose of his share of such property, since it won't pass automatically upon his death.

What if your deed says, "To John and Arthur Jones"? This is one of the most frequently asked questions. The answer is that most states presume a tenancy-in-common on the reasoning that if the co-owners wanted to create a right of survivorship, they surely would have said so in the deed. (Welcome to the world of judicial reasoning!) However, if the persons named on the deed are married, community property states do not engage in this "tenancy-in-common" presumption. Rather, the property will be treated as community property. What this means, and how you can tell whether you are in a community property state, was covered earlier, in Part 5(B).

---

[3]In Florida, there must be a written indication that joint tenants intend the joint tenancy to confer a right of survivorship. Otherwise, it is presumed that none exists.

[4]In some community property states, such as California, married couples may prefer to hold their property "as community property." This is because both the decedent's and the survivor's share of the community property is automatically eligible for a stepped up tax basis. By contrast, only the decedent's one-half of property placed in joint tenancy is automatically eligible for a stepped up tax basis. The other half keeps its original tax basis unless it can be proved that it is community property. See Clifford, Plan Your Estate, for more details.

Note on Tenancy-by-the-Entirety: In some common law property states, title to property owned by married couples is taken in "tenancy-by-the-entirety." Like joint tenancy, this form of ownership carries with it an automatic right of survivorship.

Can personal property (all property that isn't real estate) be held in joint tenancy? Yes, as long as there is a written contract to that effect. Joint tenancy bank accounts, for example, require a written form which is signed by the joint tenants and which specifies the account as a joint tenancy with right of survivorship. If you don't know whether your joint account fits this description, ask the bank.

4. Totten or Informal Trusts

Banks allow people to establish a very simple type of living trust. Anyone with a bank account (e.g., checking, savings, certificate, or bank money market) can simply add a designation that the money be held in trust for a named beneficiary. Depending on local custom, these accounts are called "totten," "savings bank" or "informal" trusts accounts. Again, the original owner of the money going into the account (the trustor) retains complete use of the money until her death, at which point any money left in the account belongs to the named beneficiary. If all the money has been withdrawn prior to death, the beneficiary gets nothing. If you want to establish this type of trust, simply visit your bank and add a "trust" or "pay on death" designation to your accounts.

5. Gifts

Property you give away when you are living is not part of your probate estate at your death. For property to be considered a gift, you must surrender ownership and control over it during your life.

6. Life Insurance

Assuming that you designate a specific beneficiary in your life insurance policy, as is usually done, the proceeds of the policy pass under the terms of the policy and avoid probate. However, if for some reason a person designates his estate as the beneficiary of the policy, which is rarely done, the proceeds would then be part of his probate estate.

7. Retirement Accounts (IRAs and Keoghs)

The funds in individual retirement accounts (either IRAs or Keoghs) pass according to the instrument setting up the account and are not part of the probate estate. In a marriage context, the funds normally belong to the surviving spouse.

8. How Much Is Your Probate Estate Worth?

At this point, you may wish to compute the value of your property that will pass through probate, assuming you make a will to cover all the property not already taken care of by one or another of the probate avoidance devices. Here is how to do it.

First, turn back to the chart at the end of Part 5, Section F, where you computed your net estate. Simply recalculate your total estate by using the market value for all the items you still owe money on. In other words, value your house, car, land in the country, and boat as if you owned them free and clear. This number, which may be larger than the amount you arrived at for your net estate, will be your "probate estate" (in many states, the amount used for computing probate fees), unless you have adopted one or more probate avoidance devices. If you have done so, subtract the market value of all items that will pass outside of probate from this first figure to determine what your probate estate will be.

Many people will find themselves subtracting one or more of the following items:

• The pay-off value of a life insurance policy, unless the estate is designated as the beneficiary (very rarely done);

• The value of any real or personal property held in joint tenancy;

• The value of any property covered by a living trust; and

• The value of any property in a "Totten" (savings bank or informal) trust.

The result of this calculation is your actual probate estate.

Example: Walter Jackson's estate consists of:

1. $10,000 in savings;
2. A house worth $150,000, with a $75,000 mortgage;
3. A car worth $8,000, on which he owes $4,000;
4. A stamp collection worth $25,000.

Applying the approach used in Part 5(F), we can quickly determine that Walter's net estate is $114,000. To compute his probate estate, however, we have to use the full market value of his property, not the amount he owns. Figured this way, Walter's probate estate would be $193,000, unless he adopts one or more probate avoidance techniques. If Walter put his house in joint tenancy or a living trust, for example, it would pass outside of probate and his actual probate estate would be $43,000. In many states, this amount would be exempt from probate altogether.

C. Tax Reduction

1. Introduction

At death, all property owned by you is subject to a federal estate tax (and state inheritance or estate taxes, if your state has these so-called death taxes), unless it is exempt from taxation. This is true not only for property passed by your will, but also for property passed at death outside of probate, such as property in joint tenancy or in a living trust or savings bank trust. Only if you have actually given the property away prior to death will the taxing authorities consider it as being not taxable as part of your estate.[5]

One primary goal of estate planning is to either reduce the amount of property which you leave at death, by giving it away before you die, or to leave property in a way that results in the minimum possible taxation. There are a number of methods for accomplishing this. We discuss here several which are applicable to moderate-sized estates. As we have stressed earlier, if your estate is in the $1,000,000 class, you will be wise to invest a few of those dollars in a consultation with a tax attorney or accountant, or both.

Before we review common estate tax-saving techniques, let's consider whether such planning is necessary for your estate. Fortunately, there is no federal estate tax for an estate with a net worth of $600,000 or less. If your anticipated estate is less than these amounts, and you have not given away large amounts of property while living, you do not need to worry about how to reduce federal taxes. If, on the other hand, either your estate alone, or the combined value of your own and your spouse's estate is expected to be larger than these amounts, then creative thought as to how to reduce your taxes is warranted.

What about state inheritance taxes? A number of states don't have any. And many that do exempt the same or even larger amounts of property than does the federal government. Inquire of your state's taxing authorities for the rules that affect you or obtain a copy of *Plan Your Estate.*

---

[5]However, you will owe a gift tax. Gift taxes are basically the same as estate taxes except you may give away $10,000 per person per year free of any tax.

If you do anticipate estate tax liability (whether federal or state), however, you should be aware, at the very least, of the common ways to reduce or eliminate it.[6] Let's take a closer look at some of these.

2. Gifts

IT'S NICE WE COULD HELP THE KIDS.

YES, ESPECIALLY WITH THE IRS PAYING FOR A LOT OF IT.

One way to reduce your estate and save on estate taxes is to transfer your property while you are still alive. You may give $10,000 to any person free of gift taxes each year. Your spouse may do the same. Thus, if a couple has three children, they could each give $10,000 to each child each year, thus transferring $20,000 free of federal gift tax per child and removing this amount from their estate. In ten years, a total of $600,000 could be transferred in this way tax free. Indeed, this would probably result in your saving a much larger sum because of the interest and dividends this money would earn which would, absent a gift, have ended up in your estate. With a gift, the interest and dividends will instead be earned by the people to whom you give the money and whom, presumably, are in a much lower income tax bracket.[7]

If you are planning to give a substantial gift to a minor, you should consider using the Uniform Gifts (Transfers) to Minors Act

---

[6]WillMaker allows you to specify how your estate's tax liability should be paid. See Part 8, Section B.

[7]Income over $1,000 received by children prior to their 14th birthday is taxed in their parents' bracket. After age 14, the children qualify for their own bracket, which will normally be lower than that of their parents. This means, if you plan to make gifts to your young children or grandchildren, you want to do it in a way that most income is received after age 14. EE U.S. savings bonds, which are tax-deferred until the bonds are turned in, provide one way to do this; zero-coupon tax-exempt municipal bonds are another. Ask your investment advisor for more details.

depending on your state. Under either of these laws you use simple formula language and name a trusted person as custodian of the property to manage it with no cumbersome court supervision until the minor is of an age to take over.

3. Testamentary Trusts

There are a number of ways that irrevocable trusts can be used to save taxes. These do not include revocable living trusts, under which you do not give up control of the property in the trust. To save taxes, a trust must involve a complete surrender of ownership and control over the property placed in it. Two of the simpler ways to accomplish this involve:

a. Having each member of a married couple set up a trust with their children or other loved ones as the ultimate beneficiaries and the surviving spouse receiving the trust income during her life. This device, often called a "spousal trust" or "life estate," is an alternative to each spouse leaving money or property to the other outright and paying a hefty estate tax on the combined property when the second spouse dies. For more on this, see the marital exemption section below.

Example: Marilyn James is married to Martin Smith. Marilyn has two grown children from a previous marriage. Marilyn's major asset is the house she owns, which she and Martin have lived in since their marriage. In Marilyn's will, she uses a spousal trust to leave the house to Martin. This means that Martin has the right to use of the house during his lifetime, but upon his death, his life estate terminates and the house goes to Marilyn's children.

b. Establishing a trust for the benefit of grandchildren (with the income to go to your children during their lives) instead of leaving the money directly to the children and having them pass the money along when they die. Under a special Internal Revenue Code provision, your estate pays an estate tax when you die, but no additional tax is owed when the children die and the grandchildren get the money. However, only $1,000,000 (this will not be an undue hardship for most people) can be passed in this way.[8] Obviously, establishing this sort of trust only makes sense if you have a considerable amount of money you

---

[8]Two million dollars can be passed by this method prior to 1990.

don't need and your children also have enough that they can get along without it.

Tax Planning Note: There are all sorts of trusts and all sorts of ways clever accountants and lawyers have found to reduce the tax bite on very large estates. If you have a large enough estate to worry about taxes, you also have enough money to hire one of these experts to advise you.

D. The Marital Deduction

All property transferred from one spouse to another at death is exempt from federal (and usually state) estate tax. This is true even if you leave far more than the $600,000 amount which is normally exempt. Even so, it may not be wise to transfer a large estate to an elderly surviving spouse. Why? Because if the survivor has property of her own, and that property, combined with what you leave, is worth more than $600,000, a large and unnecessary estate tax will have to be paid when the second spouse dies.[9] The larger the estate, the steeper the graduated tax rate. In this situation, there will be far less total tax liability if the first spouse left all the property, or a portion of it, directly to the children, or established a trust with the surviving spouse getting the income, but the principal going to the children or other object of her affection.

Example: Suppose Calvin and Phyllis, husband and wife, each in their 70's, each has an estate worth $450,000. Calvin dies in 1989, leaving all his property to Phyllis. Because of the marital deduction, no estate tax is assessed. Phyllis dies in 1990. Her total estate is the entire $900,000 (plus any appreciation), which she leaves to the children. In 1990, since $600,000 can be left to anyone free of estate tax, $300,000 of the money left to the children is subject to tax. Unfortunately, however, the rate at which it is taxed under federal estate tax law is the rate for $900,000 (39%).

---

[9]Estate taxes begin at the relatively high rate of 37% of all property that is not exempt. $600,000 of property is exempt from all federal tax.

MR. AND MRS. BUN'S BOUNTY

Now, suppose Calvin had not left his property to Phyllis, but directly to his children. In this situation there would be no tax liability since when Calvin died his $450,000 could be transferred to anyone free of estate tax. Likewise, when Phyllis died in 1990, her $450,000 estate could be transferred to the children, or anyone else, free of estate tax. Or both Phyllis and Calvin could establish trusts (often called A & B trusts by estate planners) with the income of each trust going to the surviving spouse, but the $450,000 principal of both going directly to the children free of estate tax at the death of the second spouse.

Caution: Estate planning approaches which result in money going directly to children or grandchildren normally only make sense if both spouses are elderly and are so affluent that neither is likely to need more money or property after the other dies. If, in the above example, Phyllis and Calvin had been in their 40s or 50s, they would probably have been better off to leave their money (or most of it) directly to the other, as the survivor would have a long life expectancy and might well need the money.

E. Estate Planning Summary

For people with relatively modest amounts of property, a will adequately solves all their estate planning problems because their estate will neither be subjected to federal estate tax nor significant probate fees. For somewhat larger estates, consideration should be given to passing property outside of probate to minimize probate fees and delays. People with large estates will find that estate planning involves both making a will and reducing the amount of taxable property passed by it. The more an estate is worth, the more important estate planning becomes. As noted above, even though you will probably want to limit the property you pass by your will, you still need one.

PART 7

Special Considerations for Children

Most parents who make wills do so because they want to make sure their children will be well taken care of should they die before the children are grown. There are two main decisions to be made: first, who will take responsibility for the physical care of the children, and second, who will manage their financial affairs. WillMaker gives you several ways to provide for the custodial and financial well-being of your children.

A. Provide for the Care of Your Minor Children After Your Death

Among the most pressing concerns of parents with children is who will care for the children if the parents die. Here is the general rule: If there are two parents willing and able to care for the children, and one dies, the other parent will generally take over physical custody and control and may (but is not required to, in most states) carry out the wishes of the deceased parent in respect to any property left to the children.

But what if both parents are killed simultaneously, or you are a single parent and the other parent is dead, missing, or (you believe) unable to care properly for the children? Who will care for the children after your death?

WillMaker recognizes these concerns and is designed to meet them in most instances. Using WillMaker, you can name a guardian for your minor children. This person will be appointed by the court to act as a surrogate parent for your minor children if:

1) the court finds him fit to assume such responsibilities, and

2) no surviving natural or adoptive parent is able to properly care for the children. Unlike natural and/or adoptive parents, a stepparent is not necessarily presumed to be the best guardian for the children. Accordingly, if your spouse is a stepparent to your children and you desire him to be the guardian, and the natural parent is objectively unfit, you should definitely say so in your will.[1]

Example 1: Ariadne names her sister, Penny, to serve as guardian in the event that her husband, Ralph, dies at the same time she does or is otherwise unavailable to care for the children. As it turns out, Ralph and Ariadne die in a plane crash. Ralph's mother wants custody of the children, but the court appoints Penny, since no evidence that indicates she is not a fit guardian has been introduced. If Ralph's will had named his mother, however, then the court would have to choose between Penny and Ralph's mother. The lesson of this is clearly that Ralph and Ariadne should communicate and name the same person, if possible.

Example 2: Susan and Fred, an unmarried couple, have two minor children. Although Susan loves Fred, she doesn't think he is capable of raising the children on his own. She uses WillMaker to name her

---

[1]You should also consider attaching to your will a statement as to why you selected the person. It's particularly wise to do this if you believe that any other person (someone you don't want to have custody of your children) is likely to step forward and try to claim the right to care for them. We provide you with a sample letter in Part 10, Section C.

mother, Elinor, as guardian. If Susan later dies, Fred, as the children's natural parent, will be given first priority over Elinor (despite Susan's will) if the court finds he is willing and able to care for the children. If, however, the court finds that Fred should not be guardian,[2] Elinor would get the nod, assuming she was fit. However, if Fred were not the father, but only the stepfather and had not adopted the kids, Elinor would probably be named as the guardian if Susan had named her in the will.

Example 3: Now let's change a few facts and assume that Susan and Fred live together with Susan's minor children from an earlier marriage or relationship. The natural father is out of the picture, but Susan fears that her mother, Elinor, will try to get custody of the kids if something happens to her, partially because Elinor doesn't approve of anyone who would "live in sin." Susan wants Fred to have custody because he knows the children well and loves them. She should use WillMaker to name Fred as personal guardian and should attach a separate letter to her will making the reasons for this choice clear. If something happens to Susan, and Elinor goes to court to get custody, the fact that Sue named Fred will give him a big advantage. If he is in fact a good parent, he is likely to get custody in most states. (See Chapter 10, Section C for a sample letter.)

A guardian normally functions as a surrogate parent, caring for both the child's person and for property which comes into the child's possession. However, WillMaker also permits you the option of separating these personal care and financial management functions by establishing a trust to handle the property you leave to one or more of your children. We discuss this in detail below in Section B's analysis of how you can use WillMaker to pass property to your children.

To qualify as a guardian, your choice must be an adult (18 in most states) and must be able to demonstrate an ability to carry out the responsibilities associated with this position. The more mature and responsible your choice is, the more likely it is your choice will be confirmed by the court without difficulty.

Separate Guardians Note: WillMaker only allows you to nominate one person as guardian for all your minor children. If you

---

[2]In most states, a natural parent is entitled to custody unless the court finds the children would actually be adversely affected by being in the custody of that parent.

wish to nominate different guardians for different children, you can do so by:

• using Nolo's *Simple Will Book*, by Denis Clifford, instead of WillMaker to draft your will; or

• modifying the WillMaker guardian clause (with the help of an attorney) to accomplish your desires (this will mean retyping the will printed out by WillMaker).

Caution: Parents should agree on who they wish to select as guardian and alternate guardian in their respective wills. Otherwise, if they select different guardians and they die simultaneously, the court will need to determine which guardian is most fit. If agreement is impossible, you might consider choosing one person as guardian for now and then naming the other person as guardian when you update your wills. Remember, this is only a real concern if both parents die in close sequence, which is uncommon. If one spouse dies first (which is far more likely) the other will absent very unusual circumstances assume custody and will be free to make a new will naming a different personal guardian if she wishes.

B. Leaving Property to Your Children

Decisions about how best to leave property to your children can be the most complex ones you will make when using WillMaker. Among the many questions which will inevitably arise are:

• If you are married, do you simply want your spouse to receive all of your property and do the best she can for the children?

• Assuming you answered this question "yes," that is, you want your spouse to receive the property, you must next decide what you wish to happen if your spouse dies simultaneously with you, or fails to survive you by 45 days.

• Assuming you answer the first question "no" (in other words, you want to leave a substantial amount of property directly to your kids), the next question is who should care for this property should you die while the children are minors. Your spouse? Some other person? An institution, such as a bank?

• Assuming you leave property directly to your children and name your spouse or another individual to manage it when you die, you must next decide who you want to take over if this person doesn't survive you by 45 days.

• And finally, you must state what you want to have happen when your children reach the age of 18. Do you want the property you left them handed over in one lump sum, or do you want to delay its final distribution to them until they are somewhat older by use of a trust?

WillMaker offers several options to deal with each of these questions. These are discussed in detail below. However, please be warned that this material can be as confusing as it is important, so please read it carefully, and then reread it, before making your choice.

1. Guardianship Over Property

When thinking about your children, it is important to remember that legally they have two aspects--their person and their estate. Under the law, minors not only need a guardian over their person, but also must have an adult handle any significant amount of property owned by them. When you select a guardian under WillMaker (as discussed in Section A above), you are first and foremost selecting a person to care for your children in a personal sense. However, if you do nothing else, WillMaker also makes this person responsible for your children's property. This means that your choice for guardian will care for the property you leave your children (as well as any other property owned by them) until they turn 18, at which time the property will be turned over to them outright.

This arrangement may be perfectly satisfactory for situations where:

• your choice for personal guardian is also able to competently handle property;

• the amount of property which a child is likely to receive from you is not particularly large (say less than $25,000 in value); and

• you have no objection to the child receiving the property when he or she turns 18.

On the other hand, if you don't want your personal guardian handling your children's property (the person may be loving but an airhead when it comes to money), or you plan on leaving a child a large sum and you don't want the property distributed until an age past 18, you will want to establish a children's trust. WillMaker permits you to do this. Remember, however, that even if you do decide to create a trust (covered in the next section), you will still need to appoint a guardian to personally care for your minor children and to handle any property which they already own or which comes to them from other sources. That is, as we point out in the next section, the WillMaker trust will only include property which you leave to your children, not other property which they have accumulated from other sources.[3]

2. The WillMaker Trust

WillMaker allows you to leave property to one or more of your children in trust, to be handled by a trustee until the child reaches any age from 18 to 30 specified by you. The WillMaker trust, as we point out in the previous section, cannot be used for the children of others. Sorry. Before we get into the details of the WillMaker trust, let's take a minute to define what a trust is.

---

[3]In fact, property left to your children by grandparents or others should normally be left in trust, or to a specified property custodian under the Uniform Transfers to Minors Act, and not directly to the children.

A trust is an arrangement under which a person called a "trustee" is charged with the responsibility of handling money or property which is actually owned by someone else, called a "beneficiary." Under the laws of all states, trustees are required to act:

• In accordance with the written instructions provided by the person setting up the trust (called the "trustor"); and

• Strictly in the beneficiary's best interests.

Here, now, is how the WillMaker trust works:

Using WillMaker you may establish separate trusts for one or more of your children. If you do this, you select a trustee to manage the property and income it produces until the child reaches an age between 18 and 30[4] specified by you.

• You select the age, between each child's 18th and 30 birthday, at which each of your children is to receive the remainder of the property you placed in trust at your death. For instance, if you have three children,and set up trusts for all of them, you may choose to have two of the trusts terminate when the particular child reaches age 25 and the third trust end when the third child reaches 18. You might want to do this, for example, if you observed "spendthrift" tendencies in the two children, but not in the third, or the property being left the children differs in kind or amount. No trust established in this will comes into being unless at the time you die, the child is younger than the age specified for distribution.

• If you decide to establish a trust for a particular child, all property left in your will to that child will pass into the trust. You cannot include some property and exclude other property[5].

---

[4]The WillMaker trust is designed primarily for the purpose of delaying the receipt of benefits by children until a reasonable time after they turn 18. If you desire the trust to last beyond age 30, perhaps because your child is mentally disabled and will need a trust to last for his life, you should consult a lawyer. Long term trusts need to be individually crafted to take into account the many contingencies which can occur over a lifetime. Also, because disabled persons often receive government benefits, it is important to design the trust so that it cannot be used by the agency as a reason to reduce or eliminate the benefits.

[5]Sometimes this can cause an apparent problem if you wish to have a child receive certain personal items or family heirlooms at age 18, but have the bulk of the property stay in trust until a later age. In fact, this usually isn't a real problem because the language of the WillMaker trust gives the trustee power to distribute property at her discretion, and it is common for tangible articles and

• Under each trust established by WillMaker, the trustee has discretion to:

(1) Invest the property and add the income to the trust, and

(2) Distribute portions of the property and accumulated income directly to the child (or on the child's behalf) as appears necessary for the child's health, support, maintenance, and education.[6] The powers given a trustee by the WillMaker trust are fully set out in Chapter 13.

When any child reaches the age specified by you in the trust document to take property absolutely, the trustee dissolves the trust and distributes whatever is left of the property and income to that child.

• You may name a trustee and an alternate trustee to handle the trusts you establish for your children. You may not name separate trustees for different children.[7]

3. Choosing a Trustee

Choosing someone to manage your children's finances is almost as important a decision as choosing someone to take custody of them after your death. You should nominate someone who is familiar with managing the kind of assets you leave to your children, who shares your attitudes and values about what the money should be spent for, and who your family trusts. Your first choice should normally be the child's other parent, if that person meets these basic qualifications. If not, your second choice should be your choice for guardian (assuming you believe that person to be capable of handling the trustee's duties). Otherwise, you should try to select a family member or close friend with good business sense. Your choice should also be a resident of the state where

---

and family heirlooms to be distributed before the date at which the child is otherwise to receive the bulk of the property.

[6]The WillMaker trust gives the trustee complete discretion as to what percentage of the trust is spent on these general categories. If you wish to apprise the trustee of more specific intentions (e.g., 50% for education and 50% for maintenance), you may inform your trustee of this outside of your will in a non-binding letter. See Part 10, Section C.

[7]Of course, if you need separate trustees, a lawyer could help you, or you could use Nolo's *Simple Will Book* (Clifford).

the trust will be administered (normally the state of your residence) since this is required by many states. If you strongly desire to choose an out of state person as your trustee, select an in-state person as your alternate. Then, if your first choice is prevented from serving by the law of your state, the alternate trustee will be able to step in and do the job.

You needn't worry about finding a financial wizard. A trustee has the power to hire (with trust money) financial professionals to prepare tax returns and give investment advice. The trustee just needs to be able to administer the trust assets conscientiously and make the basic decisions about how to take care of the trust assets wisely. In deciding who to choose, think about what kind of assets will be included in the trust. If you're leaving a sizeable amount of stocks, don't choose as trustee an elderly uncle who has bad memories of the 1929 crash and thinks the only safe investment is gold. Similarly, if you believe in keeping your money in U.S. Government Treasury Notes you probably would not want to select a person who loves to speculate in pork belly futures.

It is rarely a good idea to pick a bank or other institution as trustee. Most banks won't accept a trust with less than $200,000 of liquid assets.[8] When they do agree to take a trust, they charge a number of management and administrative fees that we believe are excessive. All trustees are entitled to reasonable compensation (paid from trust assets) for their services, but family members or close friends, often waive payments or accept far less than banks. If you can't find an individual you trust to handle your assets and they are not large enough to be managed by a financial institution, you may be better off not creating a trust.

Whomever you choose, it is wise to get his consent first. This will also give you a chance to discuss, in general terms, how you would like the trust to be managed. If you choose a bank, check into its rules and fees carefully.

---

[8]It's common for banks to manage the assets of all trusts worth less than $1,000,000 as part of one large fund, while charging fees as if they were individually managed. Any trustee who invests trust money in a conservatively-run mutual fund can do as well at a fraction of the cost.

Example: Ralph and Ariadne agree that Ariadne's sister, Penny, should be guardian of their kids should they both die, but that the $100,000 worth of stock the three kids will inherit might better be handled by someone with more business experience. Accordingly, in both of their wills they name Penny as guardian of the children, but also create a trust for the property they are leaving to their children. They name each other as trustees, and Ralph's mother Phyllis (who has some investment and business experience) as the alternate trustee, after securing her consent. Ralph and Ariadne also decide that one of their children (who is somewhat immature) should receive his share of the estate (at least the portion not already disbursed for his benefit by the trustee) upon turning 25, while the other two children should get their shares when they turn 21.

As mentioned, under the terms of the WillMaker trust, each child's property is held in a separate trust for that child. This means your trustee can use some or all of a particular child's property to care for that particular child, as it appears necessary. However, one child's property may not be used for the benefit of another. Similarly, the income earned by one child's property held in trust is accumulated for the benefit of that child and may not be distributed to or spent on another child.

Example: Ralph and Ariadne die in a plane crash. A trust is set up for each of their children as per the instructions in their wills. One of the three children attends an expensive college, and Phyllis distributes his entire inheritance to him over the first three years of his college career. Even though the son may have to get a loan or a job, or even drop out of college, Phyllis has no power, as trustee, to use the property belonging to the two other children to finance his fourth year in college.

4. Relationship Between Trustee and Guardian

As we stressed earlier, even if you decide to establish a trust for property you leave your children, you will still want to name a guardian to care for the persons of your minor children and any property which they have accumulated from other sources. This, of course, raises the question of whether you should choose the same person for guardian and trustee or different persons. It is generally preferable to name the other parent as trustee, if you think that person will make a conscientious asset manager. Otherwise, it is best to name your choice for guardian, assuming that this person meets the criteria mentioned in Section 3 above. By placing the financial and personal decisions about your minor children in the hands of one person, you will reduce the risk of a conflict over when and how much money should be expended on a child, and for what purpose. For instance, if the surviving parent or guardian wants to free up some funds for a special secondary school education, and the trustee believes that public school is adequate, the resulting conflict may ultimately prove detrimental to the child.

If, however, the other parent or your choice for guardian clearly does not meet the criteria for selecting a trustee, as discussed above, it may be better to select different people for these two tasks. Remember, however, that even if you name a different person as trustee, the other parent or your choice for guardian will still be responsible for handling any property not placed in the trust until they turn 18.[9]

---

[9]As we've mentioned, a child may accumulate property from many sources, including grandparents and other sources. Often, this property is under the control of a trustee or custodian appointed by the donor. However, if it's not, the personal guardian handles it until the child turns 18.

5. Overview Of Options For Passing Property To Children Under WillMaker

Will Update Note: To best assure that your true intentions are carried out, you should update your will whenever any major changes occur, including the death of any major beneficiary. Unfortunately not everyone does this. Thus, when we point out in the examples below how the trust will work in the event a beneficiary fails to survive you by 45 days, we do this to cover the situation of the death of a beneficiary when your will was not updated before your death. See Part 12 for a discussion on when and how to update your will.

Now that you understand what the WillMaker trust can accomplish, and the function of the guardian in respect to property you leave your children if there is no trust (and in respect to property left them by others), let's explore some of the options that WillMaker gives you when passing property to each of your children. Not all options apply to every situation.

For instance, if you are married (or have a spousal-type situation) and have minor children, you start with the following two primary options if you want to leave your property to your spouse but have it go to your kids if your spouse does not survive you (If you are not married, skip to Option 3):

Option 1: Leave the property to your spouse (or equivalent), name one or more of your children as alternate beneficiaries, and appoint a guardian who (in addition to taking care of the children) will also handle any property inherited by such children (as alternate beneficiaries) in the event your spouse fails to survive you by 45 days. As discussed above, the guardian will handle the property until the children reach the age of majority (usually 18) and then distribute what remains to them.

Example: John and Hazel are married with two minor children, Petey and Maryanne. If Hazel survives him, John wants her to have his property. If she doesn't survive him, John wants his stocks to pass to Petey and his interest in the family home to pass to Maryanne. John makes a specific bequest of the stocks to Hazel and names Petey as an alternate beneficiary. He makes a specific bequest of his interest in the home to Hazel and names Maryanne as an alternate beneficiary. He leaves his residuary estate to Hazel and names Petey and Maryanne as alternates to take equally. Finally, John names Hazel's sister Christine as guardian for the two children. If Hazel fails to survive John by 45 days, Petey and Maryanne take the property as alternate beneficiaries. If they are minors when they take the property, the property of each is handled by Christine as guardian until that child turns 18. If they are over 18 when their parents die simultaneously, or within 45 days of each other, the property passes to them directly in most states.

Option 2: Leave the property to your spouse (or equivalent), name one or more of your children as alternates, and establish a trust for the children. This means that in the event your spouse fails to survive you by 45 days,[10] the property passes to one or more of your children at any age from 18 to 30 specified by you for the termination of the trust. The trustee can be the same person as you named to be guardian, or a different person. It is normally appropriate to name the same person as guardian and trustee if your purpose in establishing the trust is primarily to delay distribution of the property outright until the child is older than 18, and you are satisfied that the person you named as guardian has the financial savvy to manage the property. It is appropriate to name different people as trustee and guardian when you believe the person named as guardian does not have good financial management skills.

Example: Fred and Virginia are married with three children, Peter, Paul and Mary. Peter and Paul are minors. Mary is an adult. Other than his share of the family home, Fred's separate property consists primarily of 1000 shares of stock worth $150 a share, for a total of $150,000. Fred wants to leave the stock to Virginia and have it go to the children if Virginia should fail to survive him by 45 days. However, Fred doesn't want the children to get control of the stock until they turn 25. Fred can accomplish his desires by leaving the stock to Virginia, naming the three children to receive the property equally as alternate beneficiaries, and using the WillMaker trust option to specify that property passing to each child shall be placed in trust until that child turns 25. If Virginia predeceases Fred and one or more of the children haven't yet reached 25, the property will pass into separate trusts for such children and be managed on their behalf until each turns 25. Fred has named his mother Sallie as guardian. This means if Peter and Paul

---

[10]Of course, as we emphasize throughout this manual, if your spouse (or any major beneficiary) predeceases you, you should make a new will rather than rely on the old one. The more up-to-date your will is, the better the chance your intentions will be fulfilled.

are minors when Fred dies, Sallie will care for them, assuming she is confirmed (formally appointed) by a court. However, the stock will be handled by the trustee named by Fred. Of course, if Fred names Sallie as trustee, then she will handle both jobs.

Whether or not you are married, if you have minor children and you want to leave property directly to them (and not to your spouse first), you should adopt Option 3 or 4.

Option 3: Leave property directly to your children and have your choice for guardian manage it until they turn 18 (as discussed, this usually only makes sense for small amounts of property); or

Option 4: Leave large amounts of property in trust for one or more of your children to be held until the child reaches the age between 18 and 30 that you specify, and appoint a guardian to care for the children themselves. Because you are leaving property directly to your children, the trustee should preferably be the other parent (if he or she is an adult and suitable) or, if not, the same person you select for guardian.

Example: Paul and Norma live together. They have two minor children, Justine and Clea. Paul uses the WillMaker specific bequest screens to leave objects of property to each child as beneficiary. He names Norma's sister Karla as guardian and Norma's brother Peter as alternate guardian should Karla predecease him. Paul is willing to have Norma handle the property until the children turn 18, if she survives him. However, if Norma predeceases him and Karla becomes guardian, he doesn't want Karla to handle the property. He therefore uses the WillMaker trust option to specify that the children receive the property in trust until they turn 21. Paul designates Norma as trustee and Peter as alternate trustee (after obtaining his permission) in case Norma dies before the youngest child reaches 21. The result is that if Paul and Norma both die while one or more children are minors, Karla will be the children's guardian until they are 18, and Peter will handle their property in trust until they turn 21.

Whether or not you are married if none of your children are minors but at least one has not yet reached age 30, you may still select any of the four options outlined above except Option 3 since the children are already adults. WillMaker does not ask you to choose a guardian.

Option 5: Leave property to your children outright, as you would to any other adult.

Example: Joe, a single parent, has two children, Louis and Jack. Louis is 19 and Jack is 21. Joe uses the WillMaker specific bequest screen to leave specific property items to each child.

Life Insurance Note: Often the major source of property left to children comes from a life insurance policy listing the children as named beneficiaries. If you desire the insurance for a particular child to pass into a trust you have created with WillMaker so the age they receive it can be delayed past their 18th birthday, you will need to list the trust you have established by using WillMaker as the life insurance beneficiary. Your insurance agent can help you accomplish this.

Option 6: Leave property to your children in a trust to be distributed at the age between 18 and 30 selected by you.

Example: Same as Option 5, except that Joe uses the WillMaker trust option to specify that the property left to each be held in trust for that child until he turns 25. Since both children are over 18, Joe has no need to appoint a guardian.

6. When Not to Use the WillMaker Trust Option

In certain situations the WillMaker trust is inappropriate. These are:

• If the value of the property left to a child is small (certainly less than $25,000). In this situation, the annual cost of administering the trust (such as filing state and federal income tax returns) will eat up an unacceptably large percentage of the property.

• If you want all the property you leave to your children to be placed in one trust with your trustee having discretion to make uneven distributions to the children, depending on their needs and circumstances. WillMaker simply does not offer this type of "family pot trust" (it does, however, allow you to leave uneven amounts of property to different children). We believe any advantages of a pot trust are outweighed by a number of disadvantages, such as:

(1) putting the trustee in an awkward position of having to choose between the needs and wants of different children; and

(2) having to delay final distribution of the trust principal to all children until the youngest child reaches the specified age.

See a lawyer if you are interested in a "pot" trust.

• In the unlikely event you are leaving a lot of income-producing property to a child and desire to postpone the date he takes this income until well after age 21. Tax returns for income earned by a trust but not distributed annually to a beneficiary who is over 21 can get quite messy. In this situation you should obtain the assistance of a lawyer to help you draft a will that more specifically addresses the question of trust income. Realistically, however, very few people have so much property that they don't want the trustee to distribute all the interest in the year earned. More likely, the trustee will have to pay out all income to cover school and living expenses and invade at least some principal. The WillMaker trust allows you to do this to meet the educational and other needs of a child in her 20's.

• If you desire your trust to function as a tax-planning device. The purpose of the WillMaker trust is to provide a means for property left to your children to be handled by someone else until the children reach the age you specify. This trust has no tax-planning advantages. If your projected estate is very large (certainly if it is over $1,000,000) you should consult with an estate planning expert about other types of trusts that minimize taxes. However, as noted in Part 6 of the manual, on smaller estates (including all of those under $600,000) there are normally no significant savings to be obtained by tax planning.

C. Pretermitted Heirs

There are special rules regarding children (and children of a deceased child) who are not mentioned or provided for in a parent's will. Most states have rules protecting children, and in some cases grandchildren, from being accidentally disinherited. It's not that you can't exclude a child or grandchild from your will if you wish. You can. It's simply that laws are on the books in most states to make sure you really intended to do it. Although the specifics vary somewhat from state to state, the general rule can be stated as follows: If your will fails to either mention or provide for one or more children, or the children of a child who has died before you (called a "predeceased child"), such children and/or grandchildren may inherit anyway. In addition, the laws of most states protect children who are born after the making of the will but prior to your death (called "afterborn children") by also giving them an automatic share of your estate. In legalese, this entire group is called "pretermitted heirs."

Heirs who qualify as being accidentally overlooked, or afterborn, inherit the share of the estate which they would have received had you died intestate— that is, without a will. It may be fine for pretermitted heirs to receive a share of your probate estate if you really did forget to include them, but it can play havoc with your intentions if you didn't mention them precisely because you did not wish them to inherit anything.

For example, assume you leave your house and most of your property to your spouse, with selected items going to your three children. If one of your children dies, leaving children of his or her own, and these children (your grandchildren) are not specifically mentioned and/or provided for in the will, they may each be legally entitled to inherit a portion of your estate. This would result in your spouse and your remaining two children receiving proportionately less than you originally intended.

Fortunately, this pretermitted heir problem is easy to protect against. WillMaker asks you to name all your living children, whether natural, adopted or born out of wedlock (see Section D below if this applies to you), and all living children of any child who has previously died. Each of these named children, or grandchildren if a child is deceased, will then be automatically listed in your will as receiving

$1.00 *in addition to* any other property you specifically leave to them (e.g., real estate, personal property, cash). By naming all children and all children of any deceased child, and providing each with a minimal inheritance of $1.00, you protect your estate against the "pretermitted heir" problem, even if you leave the particular child or grandchild nothing else.[11] On the other hand, as mentioned, if you use WillMaker to leave all or any of your children (or grandchildren of a deceased child) property in addition to the automatic $1.00 gift, they simply get what you leave them, plus a $1.00 bonus.[12]

This protective device will work extremely well *as long as you update your will* in the following two situations:

1. If one of your children dies before you and leaves children of his or her own, you should redo your will, at least to the extent that you list these grandchildren, so that they will receive $1.00 (of course you can leave them more if you wish). If you fail to do this, these grandchildren may qualify as pretermitted heirs, be able to challenge your will, and take a share of your estate.

2. If a child is born to or legally adopted by you after you make your will, you should change your will to provide for the new child. If you don't, that child may qualify as a "pretermitted heir" and sue to receive a share of what you leave. See Part 12 on how and why to keep your will up to date.

Example 1: Todd is married and has one child, Millie, when he makes his will. His will leaves one-half of the estate to his spouse and one-half to Millie. Several years later, Todd fathers two additional children, but forgets to make a new will or amend the old one (execute a formal change known as a "codicil") to mention them as well. In most states, the two additional children (called "afterborn" children) would qualify as being accidentally overlooked (pretermitted heirs), since they were not mentioned in the will. This means that at Todd's death, the two afterborn children will be entitled to the share of Todd's probate estate they would have received had Todd left no will.

---

[11] Although leaving a child something is not necessary in all states to avoid the pretermitted heir problem, it won't hurt, and will make it very clear that you didn't accidentally overlook a child.

[12] In some states, failure to leave a spouse any property may qualify that spouse as "pretermitted." As we discussed in Part 5, it is not a good idea to disinherit a spouse, at least not without expert advice.

Example 2: Now, let's change a few facts and assume that Todd wrote his will after all three children were born, but only left property to two of them, intentionally failing to mention the third because of family differences. Again, in most states, the unmentioned child would inherit the same amount he or she would have been entitled to if there were no will.

Example 3: Now assume that Todd uses WillMaker and lists Millie's name but does not designate her to receive any of his personal or real property. By listing Millie's name, Todd automatically tells WillMaker to give her $1.00 in his will. This takes care of any pretermitted heir problem that might exist in respect to Millie. Millie gets the dollar, but no more.

D. Adopted and Illegitimate Children

For centuries, courts have been confronted with the issue of whether a gift to "my children" includes adopted children and/or children born out of wedlock. In general, judges will attempt to determine what was intended by the person making the will. Unfortunately, this is often not clear. Most states automatically qualify persons adopted while they were minors when a bequest is made to "children." This means that if you have legally adopted a child and leave a gift to "my children" in your will, an adopted child will take her share. When using WillMaker, you are asked to name your children. Make sure you name your adopted child, and there will be no problem.

What about your children who have been adopted by others? As a general matter, once children have been legally adopted by others, they no longer have an automatic right to inherit through their former parents. However, unless you know the specific rule in your state, and are absolutely sure that the adoption was ordered by a court, it is a good idea to name such children as yours in your will. If you do this, WillMaker will automatically leave each of these children $1.00, which will prevent them from claiming more. Of course, you can leave them more if you wish.

The rule in respect to a "child" adopted after he or she is already an adult or to children born out of wedlock cannot be clearly generalized for all fifty states. Basically, states recognize an out-of-wedlock child as a "child" of his mother unless the child was formally released for adoption. However, an out-of-wedlock child is not a "child" of the father unless the father has legally acknowledged the child as his. Just what constitutes legal acknowledgement differs from state to state.[13]

Fortunately, if you are the parent of a child born out of wedlock, WillMaker allows you to make sure such child receives exactly what you desire, no more and no less. When WillMaker asks you to name each of your children, name them all, whether they were born when you were married to your current spouse, adopted by you, born when you were married to a previous spouse, born when you were not married, or born to you but adopted by someone else. Then, leave them what you wish. As discussed above, to solve the problem of an "overlooked" child automatically inheriting more than you wished, WillMaker has you leave every child you name $1.00. If this is all you want to give a particular child, fine. You have fulfilled all the legal requirements necessary to avoid the "pretermitted heir" problem discussed in Section B, above. If you wish to give any child more than the $1.00 amount, simply proceed to do this as you would for any other person.

---

[13]This is discussed in detail in Warner & Ihara, *The Living Together Kit* (Nolo Press). Generally speaking, if a father signs a paternity statement, or later marries the mother, the child is acknowledged for purposes of inheritance and enjoys the same legal standing as a child born to parents who are married.

E. Stepparents

If you are a stepparent you may be a little confused about how the material in this chapter applies to you and your stepchildren. Fortunately (or perhaps unfortunately), the rules are simple. Unless you have formally adopted your stepchildren, you have no legally recognizable relationship with them. This means, for instance, that you will not automatically be selected to take care of the children should they be minors when your spouse dies. Rather, the court will have to decide that it's in the best interest of the children for you to continue your parenting activity. A favorable decision in this regard can be helped along by a recommendation in your spouse's will that you be the guardian. On the other hand, if there is a natural parent of the child who is willing and able to assume a parenting role, that person will usually be given preference.

Stepchildren are treated differently than natural or adopted children by WillMaker when it comes to leaving your property. For instance, WillMaker does not ask you to name your stepchildren when you are listing your children. This means that your stepchildren are not automatically left a dollar (since there is no reason to). And, because stepchildren are not included in the children list, you may not use the WillMaker trust option for them. Simply stated, if you use WillMaker, you must think of your stepchildren as somebody else's children, not yours, when you leave them any property.

If you want to leave property to a stepchild in a trust, you will need to visit a lawyer for a custom drafted will.

PART 8

Planning for the Unexpected

By its very nature, a will is not a perfect instrument for determining what happens to a person's estate after he dies. Time always elapses between the date the will is made and the date it is put into effect. During this period it is not uncommon for other events to intervene; the property in a person's estate may change and beneficiaries named in the will may die. In addition it is not always easy to accurately anticipate exactly how much money will be needed to pay funeral and probate expenses, and if the estate is sufficiently large, death taxes.

Obviously the less time that passes between the time you make your will and the time you die, the less likely it is that major events will cause serious gaps to develop between what your will says and what actually happens. In other words it's essential that you keep your will up to date. Still, even if you make a new will the day you die, the fact that other events such as probate (if necessary), funeral expenses (unless they are prepaid) and taxes (if applicable) must be dealt with in the future means that some contingency planning should be done.

If not sufficiently planned for, expenses which must be paid after death can frustrate the basic desires expressed by your will. Consider the following examples:

• **Debts:** Suppose you leave $150,000 in stock to your three children, but die owing debts of $145,000, and the expenses of your estate are $5,000, , do your children lose their inheritance? The answer is yes if the stock is your only property. If, however, you leave other property that is designated for the payment of debts and expenses, your children can keep their inheritance.

• **Expenses of Probate:** If you greatly underestimate the value of property that you pass under your will, and your estate is saddled with large probate fees and expenses as a result[1], where will the probate fees come from? Unless you specify otherwise, they will be paid in accordance with priorities established by the law of your state. This may result in a bequest to a favored beneficiary being reduced more than you would wish.

• **Estate Taxes:** If your estate increases in value to the point that you owe estate taxes, out of which property will these taxes be paid? Unless you specify otherwise in your will, the taxes will normally be paid out of the estate's liquid assets on a pro-rata basis. This could cause a real problem if, for example, you left a bequest of $50,000 to a favored nephew and your tax liability gobbled up all or most of it.

• **Changes in Your Property:** If you leave your brother a specific car (e.g., a 1985 Buick) , and obtain a new car (e.g., a 1989 Chrysler) after you make your will but before you die, who will get the new car? Normally, the new car will pass as part of your residuary estate and not go to your brother.

• **Shortages in Your Estate:** What happens if you leave $50,000 each to your spouse and two kids (for a total of $150,000), but there is only $100,000 in your estate? Unless you specify otherwise, your personal representative will cut back all bequests on a pro-rata basis.

• **Death of A Beneficiary:** If you name a beneficiary to receive specific property, and that beneficiary fails to survive you by 45 days, who will get the property? Unless you have named an alternate beneficiary to receive the property in that circumstance, the property will pass through your residuary estate, which may not be what you intend.

---

[1]There is often a direct correlation between probate fees and the size of the estate. As we point out in Part 6, Section B, the attorney who handles the probate is commonly allowed as a fee percentage of the gross value of the estate. When you add to this fee the expenses associated with filing, serving notices, obtaining appraisals, and other probate-related costs, the overall expenses of probate can be as high as 10% of the estate.

In this Part of the manual we discuss how you can use WillMaker to deal with these and related situations. Of course, if you are planning on leaving all of your property to your spouse, or equally to two people without specifying which property goes to which person, there is no real need to plan how your debts expenses and taxes should be paid. This is because your spouse or the two beneficiaries can come to an agreement with your personal representative as to how the required cash should be raised. It's only when your property is being distributed among a number of beneficiaries (which is common) that planning for debt and tax payment is truly necessary.

First, in Section A we discuss how to deal with debts you owe when you die and expenses of probate which are incurred after your death. Then, in Section B we discuss how to plan for the payment of estate taxes.

A. Dealing With Debts and Expenses of Probate

Your personal representative is required by law to pay all debts that are clearly due and owing when you die, as well as all expenses that are incurred in the course of winding up (administering) your estate. Ideally, you won't owe any significant debts when you die. Obviously, however, in this credit happy world, this may not necessarily be the case. And even if you die relatively debt free, if your estate passes through probate , it will inevitably produce some expenses of administration (probate fees, payments to creditors while property is locked up in probate, court costs, etc.). Funeral expenses and any expenses of a last illness should also be considered. Many people prepay the former, and have insurance which covers the latter, but if any of these expenses are not taken care of in other ways, your estate will be obligated to pay.

As a general rule of thumb, if your debts and expenses are likely to be small, and your estate is relatively large, no planning is required. When you die, your personal representative will pay off whatever small bills you leave (and your estate accumulates), using assets left in your estate following rules set out in the law of your state. Your personal representative will be able to make the necessary payments without seriously interfering with any particular bequest. The need to plan more carefully tends to arise when the amount that must be paid for debts and/or expenses is large enough to cut significantly into bequests left to individuals and charitable institutions. The danger, of course, is that unless you plan carefully the people whose bequests are used to pay debts and expenses may be the very people who you would have preferred to fully inherit, and vice versa.

If you believe your debts and expenses will be significant, the problem of getting them paid can be easily addressed (and the danger that the money will be taken from the wrong people avoided).You can do this by specifying in your will how you want your debts and expenses paid. Using WillMaker, you have the opportunity to tailor a plan to fit your precise needs. Of course if your debts are large and your assets small, no amount of tailoring is going to get the debts paid at the same time that your inheritors get all or most of your property. One way to deal with this problem is to purchase an insurance policy in an amount large enough to pay your anticipated debts and expense and have it made payable to your estate. You can then state in your will that these proceeds should be used to pay your debts and expenses (with the rest going to your residuary beneficiary or a beneficiary specified in a specific bequest).[2]

Real Property Note: Immediately below we discuss the several choices WillMaker offers you to provide for payment of your debts and expenses of probate. It's important to realize, however, that WillMaker does not give you any choice for the payment of debts relating to real property. If you owe money (normally in the form of a mortgage or deed of trust) or back taxes or assessments on real property, the will produced by WillMaker automatically passes this indebtedness to the same beneficiary you leave the real property to. For instance, assume Sally Rider leaves her house to her son Rory. At the time of Sally's

---

[2]If large sums are involved you will want to talk to an estate planner or accountant before adopting this sort of plan. Having insurance money paid to your estate subjects it to probate. One alternative would be to have estate assets pay the debts with the insurance proceeds made payable directly to your loved ones.

death there is a $50,000 mortgage on the house, and $2,000 of back property taxes owing. Rory not only receives the house, but also the responsibility for both the mortgage and the back taxes. WillMaker does this because in the overwhelming number of situations it's what people want. But suppose you are worried that the beneficiary of your real property will not be able to pay the debts that come with it. If possible, leave him sufficient additional resources to pay off or reduce the debts.

WillMaker offers three basic options for payment of debts (except, as indicated, for real property debts) and expenses of probate . Using WillMaker you can:

Option #1: Specify a particular asset or assets to be used or sold to pay debts and expenses.

Option #2: Specify that payment of debts and taxes be made out of your residuary estate.

Option #3: Specify that the laws of your state control payment of your debts and expenses.

Let's briefly discuss each of these options.

Option #1: Specify an Asset or Assets Which Must Be Used to Pay Your Debts and Expenses Before Other Property Can Be Touched

One good approach to taking care of debts and expenses owed by your estate is to designate one or more specific resources that your personal representative must use for their payment. For instance, if you designate a savings or money market account as the resource to be used for payment of debts and expenses, and the amount in the account is satisfactory to meet these obligations, the problem is easily solved and the other bequests you make in your will won't be affected by your estate's indebtedness.

Of course, if the resource you specify for payment of your debts and expenses is insufficient for this purpose, your estate will still be faced with the problem of which property should be used to make up the difference. For this reason, it is a good idea to list several resources which should be used for payment, in the order you list them, making sure that together they are worth more than what is likely to be required.

Example 1: Frieda, a widow, makes a will which contains the following bequests:

• My house at 1111 Soto St. Albany N.Y. to my sister Hillary

• My coin collection (appraised at $30,000) to be divided equally among my three children.

• My threee antique chandeliers to my brother Herbert;

• The rest of my property to my companion Denise [Although not spelled out in the will, this consists of a savings account [3]($26,000), a car ($5,000), a camera ($1,000) and stock ($5,000)]

Using WillMaker, Frieda specifies that her savings account and stock be used in the order listed to pay her debts and expenses.

When Frieda dies she owes $8,000 worth of debts; the expenses of her estate total $2,000. Following Frieda's instructions, Frieda's personal representative would close the the savings account, use $10,000 of it to pay the debts and expenses, and turn the rest over to Denise along with the stock and camera.

Example 2: Now suppose Frieda has only $6000 in the savings account. When Frieda dies, her personal representative (following the same instructions) would close the bank account ($6,000) and sell enough stock to make up the difference ($4000). The remaining $1000 of stock, camera and the car would pass to Denise.

Let's now consider a third example, this time illustrating how badly things might turn out if you don't plan adequately for payment of your debts and expenses.

Example 3: Ruth has $40,000 in a money market account and several valuable musical instruments also worth $40,000. She makes a will leaving the money market account to her daughter and the instruments to her musician son, but doesn't specify how her debts and expenses should be paid. Due to a propensity for gambling in the stock market and an economic downturn which occurs shortly before her death, Ruth dies indebted to her stock broker in the amount of $35,000. After Ruth's death, her personal representative, who must follow state law in the absence of any instructions from Ruth,, pays the $35,000 out

---

[3]If Frieda had engaged in probate avoidance, she would have placed a lot of her property in a living trust or joint tenancy. For instance, instead of leaving the savings account in her residuary estate, Frieda could have created a simple bank account trust naming Denise as beneficiary. See Part 6, Section B for an overview of various probate avoidance devices.

of the money market account, leaving the daughter with $5,000. The son receives the $40,000 worth of musical instruments.

If you do use option 1 and choose to select specific assets to be used to pay your debts and expenses, here are several rules of thumb for which assets to select:

• **Select liquid assets over non-liquid assets.** Liquid assets are those that are easily converted into cash. For instance, bank and deposit accounts, money market accounts, stocks and bonds are examples of assets that can normally be converted to cash easily and at full value . Conversely, tangible assets such as motor vehicles, planes, jewelry, stamp and coin collections, electronic items and musical instruments must be sold to raise the necessary cash. Forced sales (often called fire sales) seldom bring in anywhere near the full value of the items sold; rather it is common to only receive 30%-50% of the item's full value. In short, if your personal representative must sell tangible assets to pay your debts and expenses (as we see in the example of Harry), the overall value of your estate will be reduced both by the costs of sale and the fact that full value will (most likely) not be received.

In addition, designating a tangible item to pay debts and expenses may also cause severe human problems if you also leave that asset to a designated beneficiary. This is because if most of us leave a specific item to a specific person, we really intend that person to get it. And often the person in question really has her heart set on inheriting the item. In other words, it usually hurts a lot more when a family heirloom must be sold to pay debts than it does for the money to be taken from a bank account or other liquid asset.

Example: Harry writes mystery books for a living. He has never produced a blockbuster but he owns fifteen copyrights which produce royalties in the neighborhood of $40,000 a year. During his life Harry has travelled widely and spent his money collecting interesting artifacts from around the world. Harry makes a will leaving his copyrights to his spouse and dividing the artifacts among his children, according to their expressed preferences. Unfortunately, Harry doesn't specify how his debts and expenses should be paid. When Harry dies, he owes $50,000. Following the law of the state where Harry resides when he dies (which requires debts to be paid pro rata from all property in an estate), Harry's personal representative sells the artifacts for $40,000 (which is about 35% of their true value), and the copyrights for $60,000. He then takes $25,000 from each beneficiary to pay the $50,000 in debts, and distributes the rest of the cash to them. Neither Harry's children nor his spouse inherit what Harry intended them to inherit. And, a large portion of the estate has been lost in the forced sale of the artifacts. If Harry had anticipated this indebtedness and provided for a way to pay it, the artifacts would still be in the family. One way he might have done this was to purchase an insurance policy large enough to cover his anticipated debts.

• **Consider effect of using property that has been named in a specific bequest.** As you know, WillMaker allows you to make up to 16 separate specific bequests as well as a more general residuary bequest (the rest of your property). It's important to review your specific bequests when designating specific items to use to pay debts and expenses. If the property you select for payment of your debts and expenses has also been designated as a specific bequest, the beneficiary who was named in the specific bequest may feel slighted (in the same way that selecting tangible assets to pay debts can be painful for the beneficiary who was to have received them). For this reason, it's usually advisable to designate property that has not been left as a specific bequest (i.e., property that will pass through your residuary estate) for the payment of debts and expenses.

Under this approach, the property not left to a specific beneficiary can be used for payment of debts and expenses if needed, and pass to the residuary beneficiary if it is not. As it is commonplace for wills to designate the residuary (or specific assets which make up part of the residuary estate) to pay debts and expenses, the likelihood of your beneficiary not understanding will be less. This is especially true, of course, if either:

• your residuary is large enough that the beneficiary still gets plenty and/or

• your residuary beneficiary is the same as one or more of the beneficiaries to whom you have already left specific bequests.

Of course, there are exceptions to this general recommendation that specific bequests not also be designated to pay debts and expenses. For instance if you believe that you are unlikely to owe much when you die, and that the expenses of probate will be low, it makes perfect sense for you to designate a substantial liquid asset left as a specific bequest to also pay debts and expenses. For instance, you may wish to leave your child a money market account worth $50,000 but also want this account to be responsible for payment of whatever small incidental debts and expenses must be paid after your death, due to the fact that this is your most liquid asset. If you do this, your debts and expenses have first call on the money with the lion's share going to your child.[4]

Note: If you wish to explain why you are designating a certain asset for payment of debts and expenses, you can do so in a letter that you attach to your will (see Part 10, Section C).

• **If you select property for payment of debts and expenses that has also been listed as a specific bequest, make sure your descriptions of the property are the same.** If for any reason you do decide to designate the same property both as a specific bequest and as a source for payment of your debts and expenses, it is important that your description of the property be exactly the same in both instances.

Example: Paul makes a specific bequest to his nephew Steve of "my savings account # 47112 in Bank of America Hollywood Branch". If Paul also chooses to have this account used for payment of debts and expenses, he should describe it exactly the same (i.e., "my savings account # 47112 in Bank of America Hollywood Branch").

Why the requirement that the descriptions be the same? Suppose Paul described the account to be used for payment of his debts and expenses as "my savings account." If the personal representative tried to use the Bank of America savings account for this purpose, Steve might justifiably argue that he is entitled to the whole Bank of America account, since it was specifically named in the bequest, and that Paul must have been referring to some other account for payment of his debts and expenses.

---

[4]Again, as we point out , you will want to also consider probate avoidance devices when passing large sums of money or other valuable property.

Option #2: Specify Your Residuary Estate as Being Responsible for Payment of Your Debts and Expenses

Using this WillMaker option, you direct your personal representative to pay all your debts and expenses out of your residuary estate, leaving it up to her which assets are to be used, and in which order. This option makes particularly good sense if you are passing the bulk of your estate through specific bequests, and are using your residuary as a basic catch-all for property that comes into your estate after you make your will but before you die. However, if your residuary bequest is an important part of your will (e.g., you make lots of small bequests of specific property items but leave the bulk of your estate to your spouse through the residuary clause), you may wish instead to use the "specific asset" option discussed in Section 1 just above that would permit you to designate a specific asset for payment of your debts and expenses and allow your spouse to receive the full amount in your residuary estate.

Option #3: Authorize Your Personal Representative to Handle the Debts and Expenses as Provided for Under the Law of Your State

This option simply directs your personal representative to pay your debts and expenses as provided for by the laws of your state.

As mentioned, all states permit you to specify in your will how you want your debts and expenses to be paid. If, however, you don't do this, each state has guidelines for how your personal representative is to approach this issue. For instance, some states provide that debts and expenses be paid first out of property in your estate that doesn't pass under your will for some reason (e.g., your residuary beneficiary and alternate both fail to survive you) and next from the residuary of your estate. Other states provide that your debts and expenses be paid first out of liquid assets and then from tangible personal property.

Telling you specifically what your state provides is beyond the scope of this manual. Generally, your personal representative will have discretion to pay debts and expenses in as equitable a manner as possible. The traditional way to meet debts and expenses is to turn to the residue first, and to use liquid assets, non-liquid personal property assets and real property, in that order. If the residue is insufficient, then other assets must be used. It may make sense for you to simply adopt your state's approach, whatever it is, rather than choose one of the other two options offered by WillMaker. This will be the case, for example, if your debts and expenses will be negligible (or represent a tiny fraction of a relatively large estate). Then too, you may know how your state deals with debts and expenses and affirmatively want your personal representative to use that method.

We have covered a lot of ground here. One final example may help you better understand what choices are available for payment of your debts and expenses, and when a particular choice is most appropriate for your situation.

Lisa owns a community property interest in a house ($125,000) , a partnership interest in a Nevada gold mine ($75,000), assorted stocks and bonds ($100,000), an expensive fur coat ($20,000), family jewelry ($15,000), a Ferrari ($60,000) and two original French Impressionist art works (approximately $100,000 apiece). Using WillMaker, Lisa makes the following specific bequests: the interest in her home to her husband Jim, the value of partnership interest to her best friend Pamela, the stocks and bonds equally to her two sons Bob and Steve, the fur coat and jewelry to her sister Viola, the Ferrari to her brother Max and the art works to her favorite art museum. She names her husband as residuary beneficiary. She chooses option 3 (payment according to the law of her state) for payment of her debts and expenses.

By the time Lisa dies, the gold mine partnership interest has turned from a $75,000 asset to a $150,000 liability. Pamela gets nothing under Lisa's will. Following the law of Lisa's state, Lisa's personal representative now must pay the $75,000 debt. She looks first to the residuary for payment. There is nothing in the residuary. Next, she turns to liquid assets. She converts the stocks and bonds to cash. This produces $30,000. She then sells both paintings, adds $120,000 to the $30,000 to pay the partnership liability, and distributes the remaining

$80,000 to the museum, as well as the other items to their intended beneficiaries. The museum is unhappy because they wanted the paintings, not the money (and didn't have the funds to bid for the paintings at the probate sale). Lisa, also, would never have intended this result, but by failing to provide her personal representative with instructions, the paintings were "lost".

What if Lisa had designated her residuary estate as the source of payment of her debts and taxes? Since there was nothing in the residuary, the result would have been the same. However, had Lisa funded her residuary with a life insurance policy or some of the assets left to specific beneficiaries, she could have specified her residuary estate as the source of payment and avoided the loss of the paintings. Similarly, Lisa could have decided to designate specific assets to pay the debts and taxes in a specific order (e.g., the stocks and bonds and fur coat, or the fur coat and Ferrari, or some other combination of assets). In making this decision, Lisa would have favored liquid assets over non-liquid assets and, if possible, designate assets that, if used for payment of debts and expenses, would not cause great stress in the intended beneficiary.

B. Estate Taxes

Before you concentrate on how you want your estate and inheritance taxes to be paid, consider whether you need to be concerned about taxes at all. We cover this point in Part 6 of the manual in some detail, and you may want to briefly review that material before proceeding here.

Basically, Part 6 explains that if the net worth of your estate is less than $600,000 when you die (or property of any amount that is left to your spouse), there will most likely be no federal estate tax. And while some states impose separate inheritance taxes on estates[5] of lesser value, the taxes almost never take a deep enough bite to cause much concern in estate planning unless your estate is truly huge. If the value of your estate is definitely below federal estate tax range, and you have no reasonable expectation that your estate will grow to that level between the time you make your will and the time you die, you can skip our discussion of your options for payment of taxes and proceed to Section C.

How To Compute Your Tax Liability

How do you know what your estate tax liability is likely to be? Obviously before you can do any sensible planning, you must arrive at a pretty good estimate. Here is a chart taken from Denis Clifford's *Plan Your Estate: Wills, Probate Avoidance, Trusts & Taxes* (that book contains far more information about tax planning than we have space for here). It provides a quick overview of the amount of taxes that will be generated from a particular size estate. To determine the portion of your estate subject to estate tax, see Part 6C. Again, if you and your spouse have an estate worth $600,000 or more (certainly if it's worth $1,000,000 or more) we strongly recommend that you get more information about tax planning options and the use of trusts to reduce estate taxes, before adopting a tax payment plan.

---

[5]Inheritance taxes are technically imposed on the beneficiaries of the estate rather than on the estate itself. However, your personal representative has an obligation to pay the taxes and will therefore deduct the taxes from each bequest unless you specify differently in your will, as you can do when using WillMaker.

When computing the value of your estate for federal estate tax purposes, you may subtract projected costs of your funeral, probate expenses (figure 5% of your probate estate—see Part 6B) and last illness (which for most of you will be unknown at present).

How to Read the Chart

1. Locate the numbers in column A and column B between which the anticipated value of your estate falls.	Estate = $700,000 Column A = $500,000 Column B = $750,000	

2. Subtract the number in column A from the anticipated value of your estate.

$700,000
- $500,000
$200,000

3. Multiply the difference by the percentage in Column D.

$200,000
x .37
$ 74,000

4. Add the product of Step 3 to the tax in Column C.

$74,000
+ $155,800
$229,800

5. Subtract the federal estate tax credit ($192,800) from the total in Step 4. The difference is your federal estate tax liability. The federal estate tax credit is the tax on $600,000. This means you can pass $6,000 free of tax. However, if you pass more than $600,000, the entire amount is taxed, not just the amount over $600,000.

Estate Tax Liability:

$229,800
- $192,800
$ 37,000

UNIFIED FEDERAL ESTATE TAX RATE SCHEDULE			
Column A	**Column B**	**Column C**	**Column D**
net taxable estate over	net taxable estate over	tax on amount in Column A	rate of tax on excess over amount in Column A
			(percent)
0	$10,000	0	18
$10,000	$10,000	$1,800	20
20,000	40,000	3,800	22
40,000	60,000	8,200	24
60,000	80,000	13,000	26
80,000	100,000	18,200	28
100,000	150,000	23,800	30
150,000	250,000	38,800	32
250,000	500,000	70,800	34
500,000	750,000	155,800	37
750,000	1,000,000	248,300	39
1,000,000	1,250,000	345,800	41
1,250,000	1,500,000	448,300	43
1,500,000	2,000,000	555,800	45
2,000,000	2,500,000	780,800	49
2,500,000	infinity	1,025,800	50

If, on the other hand, there is a reasonable possibility that the federal tax man will be coming after your estate, we suggest that you plan how your taxes are to be paid. As with debts and expenses, it is possible for you to specify how your personal representative is to pay your estate and inheritance taxes. And, if you don't make this specification, the state will do it for you.

Caution: As you might imagine, many creative ways to plan (and hopefully minimize) for paying estate and inheritance taxes have been developed by experts in the field. If your estate is large enough to warrant concern about possible estate and inheritance taxes, it is large enough for you to afford a consultation with an accountant, estate planning specialist, or lawyer specializing in estates and trusts. Once you adopt a plan, you will probably find that you can use WillMaker to implement it. However, you may find that one of several types of trusts designed to reduce estate tax liability is indicated. If so, you will need to see a lawyer. Obviously if you are a younger, healthy person and your estate is only slightly larger than $600,000, you may want to adopt one of the sensible WillMaker tax payment options now and worry about more sophisticated tax planning later.

WillMaker offers the following four options for payment of your estate and inheritance taxes.

Option #1: Specify an asset or assets to be used or sold to pay your estate and inheritance taxes.

Option #2: Specify that payment of your estate and inheritance taxes be made from all inheritors of your taxable property on a pro-rata basis.

Option #3: Specify that payment of your estate and inheritance taxes be made out of your residuary estate.

Option #4: Specify that the laws of your state control payment of your estate and inheritance taxes

In a moment we'll address these options one at a time. First, however, a word about the marital exemption. In Part 6 we explain that a spouse can pass property to the other spouse free of tax, and that the ability to do this is a significant factor in estate planning, especially for younger couples. However, older couples may not want to take advantage of this exemption and leave assets directly to the surviving spouse if this means the survivor will have an estate of more than $600,000. Again, the reason for this is that there will be substantial estate taxes when the second spouse dies; taxes that could have been avoided if the first spouse to die had left property directly to children or had used a spousal trust. If, however, you are relying on the marital exemption in your estate plan, make sure you select an option that does not use this property to pay your taxes. Otherwise, the property may be gobbled up by the taxes and your estate will not be able to profit from the exemption as planned. Okay, now for the tax payment options.

Option #1: Specify an Asset or Assets Which Must Be Used to Pay Your Estate and Inheritance Taxes Before Other Property Can Be Touched

As with payment of debts and expenses, it may also be a good approach to have your taxes paid by your personal representative from one or more specific property items that you designate in your will. Again, if you designate a savings, brokerage or money market account as the first resource to be used for payment of taxes, and the amount in the account is adequate to meet these obligations, the other bequests you make in your will won't be affected by your estate's indebtedness.

Of course, if the resource you specify for payment of your estate and inheritance taxes is insufficient for this purpose, you will still be faced with the same problem we discussed above when considering debts and expenses—which property will be used to make up the difference. So, again, it is a good idea to list several resources which should be used for payment, of estate and inheritance taxes in the order listed.

There is a potential down side under some circumstances, to choosing a particular asset to be used to pay your taxes. Taxes are assessed against your entire taxable estate, which includes property that you own at your death (including property placed in joint tenancy, living trusts, bank account trusts and many types of insurance policies). Thus, if you pass a significant amount of property outside of your will, and don't impose a proportionate tax liability on those beneficiaries, the beneficiaries of property you pass in your will bear the entire tax burden and may feel slighted. Therefore, if you plan to pass a significant amount of your property outside of your will and this is a concern, you may prefer to choose option 2, which allows taxes to be paid by all inheritors of your property (whether left under a will or in some other way) on a pro rata basis.

If you do choose to select specific assets to be used to pay your taxes, follow our rules of thumb (described in more detail in Section A.1 above). Briefly restated here, these rules are:

• Select liquid assets such as bank accounts over non-liquid assets such as tangible objects of property.

• Consider the possibly negative effect of designating property that has been named in a specific bequest to pay taxes.

• If you do select property that has been listed as a specific bequest to also pay taxes, make sure your descriptions of the property are the same.

Warning: Be sure to select assets for the payment of taxes that are sufficient. If estate or inheritance taxes are owed at your death and you have not done this, taxing authorities are entitled to collect a pro-rata share of estate and inheritance taxes from any beneficiary of any property whether it was left in your estate or through a probate avoidance technique such as joint tenancy or a living trust. This potential liability of virtually all your beneficiaries is eliminated only when the taxes are paid.

Option #2: Specify That Estate and Inheritance Taxes Be Paid By All Inheritors of Your Taxable Property Based on a Proportionate Share of What They Receive

Again, as stated above and discussed in Part 6, for the purpose of computing estate and inheritance tax liability, your estate consists of all property you legally own at your death whether it passes under the terms of your will or outside of your will, under a joint tenancy, living trust, savings bank trust or life insurance policy. Because your estate's tax liability will be computed on the basis of all this property, you may wish to have the beneficiaries of this property all share in responsiblity for paying the taxes, on a proportionate basis.

Example: Julie Jones, a widow, owns a house ($500,000), stocks ($200,000), jewelry ($150,000), and investments as a limited partner in a number of rental properties ($300,000). Julie puts the house in a living trust for her eldest son Warren, the stocks in a living trust for another son Alain, and uses her will to leave the jewelry to a daughter (Penelope) and the investments to her two surviving brothers (Sean and Ivan). She specifies that all beneficiaries of property in her taxable estate shall share in payment of any estate and inheritance taxes, on a pro rata basis. When Julie dies, the net worth of her estate, which consists of all the property mentioned, is $1,150,000. Because this taxable estate is over $600,000 there is a federal estate tax liability. Each of Julie's beneficiaries will be responsible for paying a portion of this liability. This portion will be measured by the proportion that beneficiary's inheritance bears in relation to the estate as a whole. Thus, under this approach, Warren will be responsible for approximately 43% of the tax, Penelope for 13%, and so on. For Warren this would mean a tax liability of $175,139 (Penelope would owe $52,949).

While this option may be the most equitable way to have your taxes paid, it may not be the best approach in your specific circumstances. For instance, suppose Warren (in the example) is chronically ill and does not have a good income or resources to pay his large share of the estate taxes. While it may be possible for Warren to borrow against the house, he will then have a payment which he won't be able to make, with the ultimate result that he will have to sell the house, not at all what Julie intended. In other words, if you definitely don't want to saddle one or more of your beneficiaries with any tax liability, this option will not be the best approach. Of course, if you are leaving beneficiaries such as Warren sufficient additional resources to take care of their potential liabilities, this won't be as much of a concern.

Option #3: Specify Your Residuary Estate as Being Responsible for Payment of Your Estate and Inheritance Taxes

In this option, you direct your personal representative to pay your estate and inheritance taxes out of your residuary estate, leaving it up to her which assets are to be used, and in which order. Is this a wise choice? It can be if the money and property in the residuary is specifically placed there for this purpose. Sometimes, however, it can be a bad mistake. It's particularly likely to be a mistake when these two factors are present:

• your taxable estate is fairly large with a number of assets being passed outside of probate; and

• you intend the residuary to be used for other purposes (e.g., to leave property to your children or to pass large sums to your spouse under the marital exemption[6]).

The problem of course is that if a valuable asset (say a house passed in a living trust) increases in value significantly, estate tax liability will also go up quickly. And if all taxes are to be paid by the residuary estate, there may be no money left for your residuary beneficiaries. Obviously you don't want a situation to develop after your death where taxes wipe out the residuary beneficiary's share while allowing the recipients of other property to get off tax free.

When is it wise to designate the residuary estate to pay taxes? If your estate plan has adequately and specifically addressed the needs of all individuals and institutions that you care about (either outside of or under your will), and the value of property in your residuary estate will be sufficient to meet your projected tax liability, using your residuary estate for this purpose makes sense. As with other decisions on dealing with estate and inheritance taxes, we strongly recommend that you educate yourself as to what your estate planning options are and then consult with an accountant, estate planning expert or probate and trusts attorney before making a final decision.

Option #4: Authorize Your Personal Representative to Handle the Estate and Inheritance Taxes in Accordance With the Priorities Established By the Law of Your State

This option simply directs your personal representative to pay your estate and inheritance taxes as provided for in the laws of your state. As with your debts and expenses, if you don't provide for how your taxes are to be paid, your state law contains rules for how your personal representative is to approach this issue. For instance, some states leave the method of payment up to your personal representative while others provide that all beneficiaries of taxable property are liable on a pro-rata basis. We can't tell you in this manual specifically what your state provides. However, after a consultation with a tax expert you may conclude that it makes sense for you to simply adopt your state's

---

[6]Remember, the marital exemption is far more useful if the surviving spouse has a long life expectancy. See Part 6, Section D.

approach, whatever it is, rather than choose one of the other options offered by WillMaker.

Note: If you decide not to select an option for payment of your estate taxes, WillMaker will select this one.

C. Specific Property No Longer Owned at Death

If your will leaves a specific item (a particular Tiffany lamp, for example) to someone, but you no longer own the item when you die, the person named in the will to receive it is out of luck. He obviously cannot have the actual item, and he is not entitled to receive another item or money in lieu of it.[7] Lawyers call such a failure of a bequest "ademption." People who don't inherit the property in question are often heard to use an earthier term.

D. Shortfalls in the Estate

A similar problem occurs when there isn't enough money to go around. For example, if you leave $50,000 each to your wife and two kids, but there is only $100,000 in your estate, what happens?

The situation necessitates what in law is called an "abatement," or reduction of gifts made in the will. Absent a specific directive in the will, the laws of each state provide the rules for how the personal representative of an estate must conduct abatement proceedings. They normally require a pro-rata reduction of bequests, without the sale of property if possible. If property must be sold, unspecified property (for example, "the rest of my property") is generally the first to go, followed by specific gifts of personal property and then specific gifts of real estate. To say this this another way, if there is a shortage, the persons

---

[7]In some circumstances, if a specific item has "merely changed form," the original beneficiary may still have a claim. Examples of this are:
- a promissory note has been paid and the cash is still available; and
- a house which has been sold in exchange for a promissory note and deed of trust.

who receive the "rest of your property" will normally lose out to those to whom you made specific bequests like "my 1970 VW van" or "my house at 1111 Soto St., Albany, N.Y." or "$10,000."

The subject of what happens if you leave more property in your will than is actually available is far too complex to cover here in any meaningful detail. However, the overall point is relatively simple. Don't give away more than you own, after what you owe and what your estate will need to pay in tax is subtracted. Make a new will whenever your property situation changes significantly. If you are concerned about how your property will be distributed in the event your estate comes up short and an abatement (reduction of gifts) is required, consult an attorney.

E. Death of Beneficiaries

What happens if a person named in your will to receive a bequest fails to survive you? Who gets the property? WillMaker lets you choose among several ways to dispose of the property if your first choice as beneficiary does not survive you. The choices vary depending on whether your first choice as beneficiary is your spouse, an *individual* person or entity, or is a *group* of persons or entities.

Update Note: As you read this chapter, keep in mind that the best route is to update your will whenever a named beneficiary predeceases you. The primary purpose of the many options that WillMaker offers is to fill in the gaps in case you either forget to update or are unable to do so. If you keep your will rigorously up-to-date, most of the material in this chapter as to what happens if a primary beneficiary predeceases you will never apply to your estate. We have devoted Part 12 to updating your will.

1. Simultaneous Death of Spouse

Every will produced by WillMaker for a married person contains the following clause:

"If my spouse and I should die simultaneously, or under circumstances as to render it difficult or impossible to determine who predeceased the other, I shall be conclusively presumed to have survived my spouse for purposes of this will."

The objective of this clause is to provide for what happens if a husband and wife die in the same accident and it can't be determined who died first. Under these circumstances, the clause creates the presumption that the will maker survives his or her spouse. If both husband and wife use WillMaker, the husband is presumed to survive the wife for purposes of his estate, and the wife is presumed to survive the husband for purposes of her estate. This results in the husband's estate passing to his heirs instead of to his wife's, and the wife's estate passing to her heirs instead of to her husband's. Although at first glance this clause appears to be mutually contradictory if contained in the wills of both spouses, it isn't; it simply distributes each spouse's property down their own lines of descent.

Example: Jeanine and Fred have both been married before. They each have a child from their previous marriages but none of their own. Each uses WillMaker to leave their property to each other in their residuary clauses. They name no alternate beneficiaries. Jeanine and Fred die in a plane crash. Under the "simultaneous death" clause, Jeanine's bequest to Fred will instead go to Jeanine's child. Similarly, Fred's bequest to Jeanine will instead pass to his child.

As it turns out, this clause will almost never operate under WillMaker. Why not? Because under a will produced by WillMaker, any beneficiary (including your spouse) must survive you by 45 days to receive property left to them by your will. Thus, in the event of a simultaneous death situation, the property you left to your spouse would pass to your alternate beneficiaries (as we outline later in this part of the manual). If, however, in the extremely unlikely event you name no alternates for property you leave to your spouse *and* fail to designate a residuary beneficiary, this clause would become effective in case of a simultaneous death, and each spouse's property would pass to their heirs under intestate succession principles.

2. Specific Bequests to an Individual Beneficiary

After you have made a specific bequest of property to an individual beneficiary, you are offered a choice as to what happens in the event the beneficiary fails to survive you by 45 days. The first choice that WillMaker gives you is to have the property pass to the beneficiary's children in equal shares. The second choice is for the bequest to pass directly to an alternate beneficiary (or beneficiaries) whom you can name in a later screen. If you do choose to name one or more alternate beneficiaries, these beneficiaries would also take in the event you opt for the first choice but the primary beneficiary leaves no surviving children. In the unlikely event that there are no surviving alternate beneficiaries or children (in the event you opted for choice #1), the property will be left to your residuary beneficiary. All of this can be a little confusing, so let's take a closer look at how it works.

Institution Note: When you designate a primary beneficiary, WillMaker cannot tell whether it is a live person or an institution. Accordingly, it offers you choices for naming alternate beneficiaries that are not appropriate if your primary beneficiary is an institution (since institutions don't "die"). Please forgive this bit of computer stupidity. If you do select an institution as your primary beneficiary, select Option #2 (to your alternate) and then press Return when asked to select an alternate. This will bypass the alternate selection and permit you to proceed with the rest of the program.

Option #1: Property First to Children and Then to Alternate

Example: Janie makes out a will leaving most of her estate to her husband and certain specific family heirlooms to their child Ellen. She uses choice #1 to designate Ellen's children to take the heirlooms if Ellen doesn't survive her, and names her husband as the alternate beneficiary. Ellen fails to survive Janie by 45 days, but leaves three children of her own.

The grandchildren thus inherit the heirlooms in equal shares. If none of the grandchildren had survived Janie by 45 days, her husband, as alternate beneficiary, would have gotten the heirlooms. If no alternate had been named or the alternate (Janie's husband) failed to survive Janie, the heirlooms would have gone into Janie's residuary estate. The following chart shows how this works:

To beneficiary's children

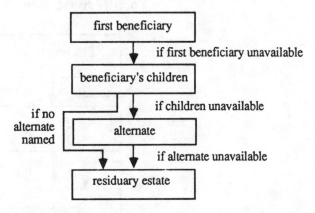

Option #2: Property Direct to Alternate

As mentioned, if you do not use choice #1 to have your beneficiary's children inherit the property in the event the beneficiary predeceases you, but instead make choice #2, you merely shorten the chain of potential beneficiaries. The basic scheme is the same, but the property will go directly to the alternate beneficiary you choose if the first beneficiary is unavailable. If the alternate also does not survive you, the property will become part of the residuary estate.

Example: Sal makes out a will leaving her antique piano to her brother Tim and the rest of her estate (residuary estate) to her friend Justine. Sal does not want Tim's children to receive the piano in the event Tim fails to survive her, so she does not choose that WillMaker option (#1), but instead makes choice #2 and names her sister Val as alternate beneficiary.

If Tim fails to survive Sal by 45 days, the piano will go to Val. Tim's children will not get it. If Val also fails to survive Sal, the piano will go to Justine, Sal's residuary beneficiary.

To alternate beneficiary

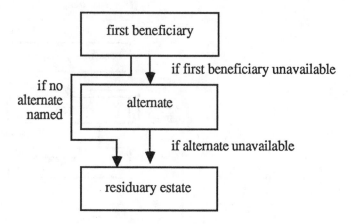

3. Specific Bequests to Multiple Beneficiaries

Choosing alternate beneficiaries becomes slightly more complicated when the original bequest is made to two or more beneficiaries. What happens when one of a group of beneficiaries dies? WillMaker gives you two options:

Option #1: Property First to Children

Under the first option, the property goes first to the surviving children, if any exist, of the deceased beneficiary, in equal shares. If there are no surviving children, the property goes to any surviving beneficiaries in equal shares. If there are no other surviving beneficiaries, the property goes next to an alternate if one has been named. If none has been named, the property passes into the residuary estate.

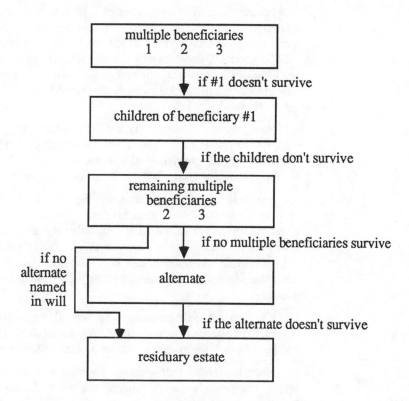

Example: Pat leaves her vacation cabin in the mountains to her children Mike and Jim and her sister Mary Lou. Neither Jim nor Mary Lou survives Pat by 45 days. In her will, Pat chose to specify that the children of named beneficiaries would receive the shares of predeceased named beneficiaries. Thus Jim's two children take his share, and Mary Lou's son takes Mary Lou's share.

If neither the named beneficiaries nor any of their children had survived Pat, the alternate(s) would have taken the bequest. If no alternate had been named, the cabin would have become part of Pat's residuary estate.

Example: Myrna leaves the contents of her savings account to her children Abby, Ben and Charlotte. Myrna uses WillMaker to specify that should any of them not survive her by 45 days, that child's share will go to his or her surviving children (Myrna's grandchildren) and that, if there are no surviving children, to the remaining named beneficiaries (e.g., if Ben predeceases Myrna, to Abby and Charlotte). At Myrna's death, the savings account contains $30,000. First, assume that Ben predeceased Myrna and left no children. His share would be split between Abby and Charlotte, who will each get $15,000. Abby and Charlotte have two children each, who will receive nothing; the only grandchildren entitled to Ben's share are his children, and none survived him.

Now assume that both Abby and Ben predeceased Myrna. In that case, Abby's one-third share would be split equally by her children. Charlotte, the only surviving child, would receive $20,000 (her share and Ben's share, since she is the sole surviving named beneficiary).

Next assume that Abby, Ben Charlotte and one of Charlotte's children predeceased Myrna. In this case, because all three primary beneficiaries have predeceased Myrna, only the surviving grandchildren inherit. Abby's kids would split her original $10,000 share, Charlotte's kids would take her entire share, and Ben's share would pass into Myrna's residuary estate unless she had named an alternate.

Finally, if all of the children and grandchildren had predeceased Myrna, the named alternate(s) would take the $30,000. If no alternate had been named, the money would go into the residuary estate.

Note: Remember that when you choose the multiple beneficiaries option, you can only specify children, not grandchildren, of a named beneficiary to take their parent's share of a bequest. If your will becomes so out of date that not only a beneficiary, but all the beneficiary's children predecease you, any grandchildren of the beneficiary are out of luck. They will not inherit anything; the beneficiary's share will go to surviving named beneficiaries, the alternate, or the residuary estate. See Section 3 below for a method to ensure that grandchildren take before the other surviving beneficiaries.

Option #2: Property Direct to Remaining Beneficiaries

The other way of dealing with multiple beneficiaries using WillMaker simply bypasses children of beneficiaries who don't survive you by 45 days. Under this approach a predeceased beneficiary's share is divided among the other multiple beneficiaries. If none of the original multiple beneficiaries survives, the bequest passes to the alternate beneficiary named in the will. In the unlikely event that none of the named beneficiaries or the alternate survives you, the property becomes part of the residuary estate.

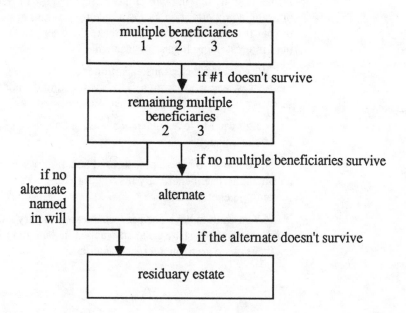

Example: Brandy uses WillMaker to provide in her will that her house will be divided equally between her brother Zeke and her daughter Maria. Her will also specifies that if one of the beneficiaries dies within 45 days after Brandy's death, his or her share will go to the other beneficiary, not to his or her children. Brandy chooses her hairdresser Sabrina as the alternate beneficiary. Maria dies before Brandy, leaving two children.

Zeke, the surviving beneficiary, gets Maria's share of the property. Maria's children take nothing. If Zeke and Maria had both died before Brandy, Sabrina would inherit the property. If Sabrina had not survived Brandy, the property would go to the residuary estate.

4. Custom-Designing Your Specific Bequests to
    Multiple Beneficiaries

The methods explained in Section 2 above for leaving property to multiple beneficiaries are the easiest, but not the only ways to use

WillMaker to bequeath property to a group of beneficiaries. You can achieve a similar result, and have even more flexibility in the terms of the bequest, by making two or more separate gifts of fractional portions of a single property item. For example if you want to leave your house to your three children, you could make three separate gifts of "a one-third interest in my house" to each child.

Why use three steps instead of one to leave a group bequest? In most cases, you won't want to. However, taking the additional steps can be extremely useful in multiple beneficiary situations if:

   • You want to leave *unequal* shares of one piece of property to beneficiaries; or

   • You want to have a predeceased beneficiary's share go directly to a named alternate beneficiary instead of to his children or to the remaining beneficiaries; or

   • You want to have one predeceased beneficiary's share pass to his children, another's share go to any remaining beneficiaries, and/or another's share go to an alternate beneficiary.

Let's look at some examples of these additional options.

Example: Pat wants to leave her cabin to her two children, Mike and Jim, and her sister Mary Lou. However, she wants each child to receive a 40% share and her sister a 20% share. In the event her children fail to survive her by 45 days, she wants their shares to go first to their children, if they have any, and otherwise to whichever one of them survives the other. However, if her sister predeceases her, Pat wants that 20% share to pass to her brother Roger rather than to either her sister's children or to Mike and Jim.

If Pat left her property to her children and her sister as multiple beneficiaries she could not accomplish her desire. That is because the WillMaker multiple beneficiary option requires you both to leave property to the beneficiaries in equal shares and to allow the remaining named beneficiaries to receive the share of the deceased beneficiary before the property would go to a named alternate. If, however, Pat uses WillMaker to leave the cabin in three separate bequests, she can accomplish her goals with ease. Here is how it would work.

Pat would make individual specific property bequests to Mike and Jim of 40% of her cabin (40% to each), and would choose the WillMaker option that would pass those shares to Mike and Jim's children in the event they fail to survive Pat by 45 days. Pat would then make a separate specific property bequest of 20% of the cabin to her sister, and then choose the WillMaker option that would pass the property to the named alternate in case Mary Lou failed to survive her. Then, Pat would name Roger as the alternate. The following chart demonstrates this method.

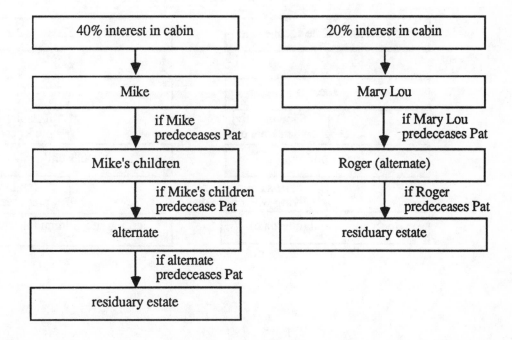

There are many more options available than those demonstrated in this example. For instance, Pat could have provided that Mike's children would inherit his share if he predeceased her while Jim's share would pass directly to Mike (rather than to his own children) in the event he died first. In this way, the same property could have been given to three beneficiaries in unequal shares and with three different provisions for what would happen if the beneficiaries named by Pat failed to survive her. Let's consider one more example.

Example: Kate wants to leave all her real estate in equal shares to her brothers Joe and Paul. If either of them fails to survive her by 45 days, she wants his share to go to his children. If a deceased brother's children also do not survive Kate, she wants that share to be passed on to her deceased brothers' grandchildren instead of to the other surviving brother. Joe has three children, and one grandchild. Paul has one child, who has two children of her own. Kate makes two separate bequests, one to Joe and one to Paul, of half-interests in all her real estate. She can then use WillMaker to choose the children of each to inherit their portion if Joe or Paul predeceases Kate, and then name the grandchildren as alternate beneficiaries. The result is illustrated below.

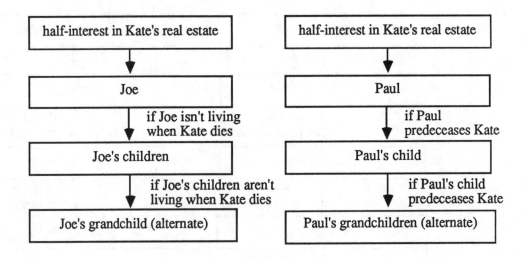

5. Residuary Estate Bequests

As you've seen in the preceding sections, if property is not specifically given away in the will, or if a specific gift fails for any reason, the property ends up as part of the residuary estate. Your residuary estate, as well as specific bequests, can be left to an individual beneficiary or to a group of beneficiaries. It is very important to name a residuary beneficiary or beneficiaries and at least one alternate. If there is no available beneficiary for the residuary property, the leftover property will be distributed according to your state's intestate succession laws, just as if you had died without a will (see Chapter 3). This may lead to results you didn't intend.

WillMaker lets you choose your spouse, children, or any other persons or entities as residuary beneficiary. After you designate the residuary beneficiary, WillMaker asks you to choose what you wish to happen if that beneficiary does not survive you by 45 days. The choices are the same as for beneficiaries named to receive specific bequests (see Sections 1 and 2 above). In the case of an individual residuary beneficiary, the beneficiary's share can pass either to his children or to an alternate beneficiary named in your will. For multiple beneficiaries, the choice is between having a deceased beneficiary's share pass to his children (and then to the surviving beneficiaries) or having it go directly to the surviving beneficiaries (see the Note at the end of this section). Whichever option you choose, remember to name at least one alternate residuary beneficiary.

Example: Janie chooses to leave her residuary estate to her two children, Roy and Ellen. She then specifies that if either child does not survive her, that child's share goes to the child's own children (Janie's grandchildren). Ellen predeceases Janie, but leaves two children of her own. Those children will split Ellen's share. If Ellen had left no children, her share would pass to Roy. If Roy had also predeceased Janie, and neither he nor Ellen had left living children, the residuary estate would go to the alternate beneficiary, or, if the alternate also did not survive Janie, would pass by intestate succession.

Example: Chris wants to divide her entire estate equally among her children, Anne, Bill and Charles. To do this she decides to make no specific bequests, and let all of her property become her residuary estate. Using WillMaker, she types in her children's names as residuary beneficiaries. She does not want the property to go to her grandchildren in the event any of her children fails to survive her, so she specifies that a non-surviving child's share should go to the surviving children.

Bill fails to survive Chris by 45 days and leaves two children. They inherit nothing; Bill's share is divided equally between Anne and Charlie. If no children survived Chris, the alternate(s) would take her entire estate. If she chose no alternates or if they also did not survive her, the entire estate would pass by intestate succession.

Note: Merely naming multiple beneficiaries of your residuary estate results in distribution to those beneficiaries in equal shares. If you want to leave unequal shares of the residuary property to the beneficiaries, you can do so.

When WillMaker asks you to name the residuary beneficiaries, type the names and percentages of the property each one is to receive. For example, to give 30% to your son and 70% to your daughter, type in "My son John, 30% and my daughter Marie, 70%."

We doubt that many people will have a genuine need to complicate their wills this way. In any event, you will have far better control over what happens to your property if you make specific bequests of all significant property rather than rely on the residuary clause to dispose of it.

F. Property Held in Joint Tenancy

Earlier in the manual (and in the program itself) we explain that property held in joint tenancy when you die passes directly to the surviving joint tenant(s) outside of your will. This is straightforward, assuming that you die before the other joint tenant(s). What happens to that property, however, if you and the other joint tenant(s) die at the same time or the other joint tenant(s) dies before you?

First, when all joint tenants die simultaneously, the ownership of each joint tenant reverts to her own estate. Under wills produced by WillMaker, this property would pass under the residuary clause. Suppose, however, that instead of a simultaneous death, the other joint tenant(s) die before you. In that event, the entire property would end up in your estate and pass through your residuary estate.

What if you don't want your residuary beneficiaries to receive the joint tenancy property that comes into your estate as a result of a simultaneous death with, or a prior death by, the other joint tenant(s)? In that situation, you may use the specific bequest screens to specify individuals or organizations to receive such "joint tenancy" property. However, if the joint tenant survives you, your inclusion of joint tenancy property in your will creates an apparent conflict between a surviving joint tenant (who will automatically assume ownership of the property) and the named beneficiary in your will, who may very likely feel aggrieved and possibly be inclined to contest the joint tenancy status of the property, when he learns that the property passes under the terms of the joint tenancy, not under the will.

Our suggestion is not to include joint tenancy property in your will, but to promptly update your will if you become the sole owner of joint tenancy property because of the prior death of the other joint tenants. You should also make sure you select a residuary beneficiary (and alternate) who you want to inherit your interest in joint tenancy property in case of the simultaneous death of all joint tenants.

PART 9

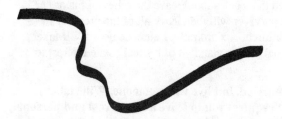

What WILLMAKER Can And Cannot Be Used For

The WillMaker program allows you to write a will that is simple, accurate and legal. Now, let's be more specific as to the type of will you can prepare using WillMaker.

A. What WillMaker Can Do

Here we simply provide a few of the many options you can choose when making your will using WillMaker. As you read what follows, remember we are presenting a great many (often overlapping) scenarios, most of which won't meet your exact needs. Our intention here is to present you with WillMaker's many possibilities.

1. Provides Flexibility for Specific Property Bequests

If you are married, WillMaker allows (but does not require) you to leave all of your real and personal property to your spouse.

Example: Laurence and Betty are married and have three children. Laurence owns one-half of their family home, a car, a boat left to him by his father, some antique coins and a personal computer. Laurence and Betty have agreed that each should leave the other all his or her property and that the survivor will then leave all of the property in equal shares to the children. Accordingly, Laurence uses WillMaker to leave all of his personal property and all of his real estate interest to Betty.

If you are not married, but live with someone, WillMaker allows (but does not require) you to leave all your real and personal property to that person.

Example 1: Assume that everything is the same as set out in the previous example, except that Laurence and Betty are not married. This time Laurence still uses WillMaker to leave all of his personal property and all of his real property to Betty. However, if Laurence were still married to someone else, but living with Betty, in many states he would be forced by law to leave his wife at least part of his estate. See Part 5, Sections C and D.

Example 2: Darryl and Floyd have lived together for several years. Darryl wants to leave Floyd all of his possessions. He can use WillMaker to accomplish this.

• **In either of the above situations, you can use WillMaker to leave a portion of your property to your spouse (or person you live with)** *and* **make specific gifts of personal property, real property, or cash to your children, relatives, friends or charities.**

Example: Laurence leaves his interest in the family home to his spouse, Betty, his coin collection to one of his children, his boat to another child, his computer to a charity, and $500 to his Aunt Agnes.

• **If you are single or divorced, WillMaker allows (but does not require) you to leave your property to friends, family and charity.**

Example: Leonard, a lifelong bachelor, completely disposes of all his personal possessions by describing specific items to be left to particular relatives and friends. He leaves his house to his favorite charity.

• **No matter what your family situation, you can use WillMaker to leave all your real and personal property to your children, or a charitable institution, or any other persons of your choice.**

Example: Although Morton is now married to Becky and has three children from previous marriages, he decides he wants to leave his land, his cars, and his expensive stereo equipment to his best friend, Jim. WillMaker permits him to do this, but if Morton lives in a state following the common law property system, Becky may have a right, under state law, to a share of this property. See Part 5, Sections C and D.

• **No matter what your family situation, you can use WillMaker to leave up to 16 separate, specific bequests (e.g., heirlooms, cash, motor vehicles, tools, furniture, real estate) to one or more beneficiaries of your choice.**

Example 1: Annie and Bill Webber have three children, Ellen, Lance and Chuck. Annie could leave her jewelry, bird and clothes to Ellen, her collection of first editions to Bill, a cash bequest of $5,000 to Lance, her ski cabin to Chuck, a bequest of $500 to the Third World Refugee Committee, and so on.

Example 2: Stephanie uses one of the sixteen bequests to leave her book collection, her copyrights, and her stocks to her three business partners, a second bequest to leave her record collection to her brother

Richard, a third bequest to leave her house to her three children, a fourth bequest to leave her cabin to her sisters Alison and Lori, and so on.

• If you so choose, you can use WillMaker to leave beneficiaries unequal shares of the same personal or real property item.

Example: Leslie decides that because her son Michael has done more work on the farm than her other children, he deserves to receive a greater interest in it. When provided the opportunity to make specific bequests of personal and real property, Leslie designates Michael as a beneficiary of a separate bequest and describes the property being left to him as "a one-half interest in my farm". She then designates her other two children—Jeffrey and Stuart—as multiple beneficiaries of another bequest and describes the property being left to them as "a one-half interest in my farm." This bequest will result in both Jeffrey and Stuart receiving equal shares in the bequest of one half of the farm (i.e. each receives a 25% interest).

2. Provides for Alternate Beneficiaries

• If you choose, you can use WillMaker to select what happens to a bequest in the event one or more of the beneficiaries named to receive it fails to survive you by 45 days. (See Part 8B in addition to the following examples.)

Example 1: Gene wants to leave his house to his daughters Liza and Jenny in equal shares. Jenny has two very young children; Liza has two grown children. Gene wants to structure his gift so that if Jenny does not survive him, her share in the house will go to her husband Greg, and if Liza does not survive him, her share will go to her children. Using WillMaker, Gene makes two separate bequests, one to Jenny and one to Liza, of one-half interests in his house. He designates Liza's children as alternate beneficiaries for her bequest, and designates Jenny's husband as an alternate beneficiary of her share.

Example 2: Here, Gene wants both Liza's and Jenny's children to inherit their parent's share in case either fails to survive him by 45 days. In the event either Liza or Jenny dies without children, Gene wants that child's share to pass to the other. He uses WillMaker to make a single bequest of his house to Liza and Jenny as multiple beneficiaries, and chooses the option that will make a predeceased child's share go to her children (Gene's grandchildren). WillMaker will then automatically provide that if a deceased daughter's children do not survive Gene, the

daughter's share will go to Gene's surviving daughter (either Liza or
Jenny).

3. Provides for Designation of Residuary Beneficiaries

**• You can use WillMaker to designate your spouse, one or more
of your children, or other specific individuals and institutions to
inherit all of your remaining property (whatever is left after you
have made one or more specific bequests of personal property and
real estate). If more than one beneficiary is designated, each will
take an equal share unless you specify differently (see Part 8).**

Example: Annie could make a number of specific gifts to friends
and charities and then leave the rest of her property to Bill, or any other
person or institution of her choice.

Warning: It is very important that you use WillMaker to name a
beneficiary to receive your residuary estate Otherwise, any property
that you have not specifically left to someone, and any property left to
non-surviving beneficiaries (where alternates have not been named or
do not survive either) will be distributed according to the intestate
succession law of your state.

4. Provides a Useful Will as Part of an Overall Estate Plan

**• Before you leave real estate in your will, you should be
thoroughly familiar with the routine probate avoidance techniques
we discuss in Part 6.[1] If you decide to use one or more of these**

---

[1]Probate avoidance devices are especially useful when your property is not likely to change much
before you die and you know who you want to receive it. On the other hand, if you are in good
health and anticipate a number of changes in respect to your real estate or your desires as to who
you will want to inherit it before you die, you may wish to use WillMaker to dispose of the real
estate (despite the possibility of significant probate fees). This is because it is easy to use WillMaker
to update your will as the situation changes and circumstances dictate, and often much more
difficult to change who you want to get property if you use probate avoidance devices such as a
joint tenancy or life insurance. Put differently, when you use probate avoidance techniques, you will

techniques (living trust, savings bank trust, joint tenancy, etc.), it is still appropriate to make a will disposing of the rest of your property.

Example 1: Doug, a 60-year-old unmarried man, has lived with Brenda for 25 years. In addition to various items of personal property, he owns a house and a ski cabin. Doug transfers the house and cabin into a living trust, with Brenda as the beneficiary. He uses WillMaker to make several specific bequests of cash and his personal possessions.

Example 2: Assume now that Doug is a 45-year-old real estate speculator who owns eight different parcels of real estate. Because he doesn't expect to hold on to this property until he dies, Doug will find it easier to leave the parcels to Brenda in his will, despite the possibility of significant probate fees should he die prematurely. This way, property can be sold and new property purchased without the need to do and undo trusts or joint tenancy arrangements. Doug can simply revise his will using WillMaker to add or delete parcels of land as he buys or sells real estate. Later, when Doug is older, he can create an estate plan so that his real property can pass free of probate.

Example 3: Now assume that Doug is 65 years old, married to Brenda, and the father of three children. His sole real estate ownership consists of the family house which he inherited from his parents. Here, Doug might wish to place the house in joint tenancy with, or in a living trust for, Brenda and use WillMaker to dispose of personal property items of lesser value.

---

at the very least have to do and undo some red tape every time you buy and sell property or decide to change beneficiaries. For this reason, younger people in good health might reasonably decide to bypass probate avoidance techniques in favor of a will, at least until a more sophisticated estate plan appears appropriate.

5. Lets You Forgive Debts

• You can use WillMaker to forgive one or more debts owed to you.

Example: In addition to disposing of his property, Marty wants to forgive debts owed him by several former business associates. Using WillMaker, Marty can specify the debts and the person they are owed to and use WillMaker to expressly forgive these debts. If a debt is forgiven, WillMaker also automatically forgives any interest which has accrued on that debt at the time of your death.

6. Allows You to Name a Guardian for Your Minor Children

• You can name a guardian for your minor children in the event there is no surviving natural or adoptive parent able to care for them. The court has the right to review your choice, but will probably accept it unless the person refuses to assume the responsibility, or someone comes forward with evidence which convinces the court that the best interests of your children would be better served by their being in someone else's custody. See Part 7(A).

GUARDIAN FOR YOUR HARES

7. Provides Children's Trust Option

• **WillMaker gives you the option of placing property left to one or more of your children in trust. Under the trust, the trustee whom you name will manage the property for the benefit of the child you name as beneficiary of the trust. The trust terminates at any age (between 18 and 30) you specify. See Part 7(B) for WillMaker trust details.**

Example: Todd has five children. He leaves each child $50,000 worth of stock in a separate trust. He names his brother, Jackson, as trustee. He wants the stock distributed to four of his children when they turn 25 and to the fifth child when he turns 30. He uses WillMaker's trust provision to accomplish these goals. Should Todd die before the children reach the designated ages, Jackson will be named trustee to manage the assets in trust for each of the five children. Under the terms of the WillMaker trust Jackson will have the power to release money for health, education, maintenance and support needs of the children. When each child turns the age indicated by Todd in his will, Jackson will distribute what remains of that child's trust assets.

8. Allows You to Name a Personal Representative (Executor)

• **You can name a personal representative for your estate. This is the individual (often referred to as an executor, executrix or administrator, depending on the context and state) who is responsible for making sure the provisions in your will are properly carried out. She can be any competent person over the age of majority (18 in almost all jurisdictions) and is commonly either a spouse, a close, knowledgeable relative, or a financial institution such as a bank or savings and loan. If you select an individual, she should be a resident of your state, since many states require a bond of out-of-state executors. If you select an institution, be aware that many institutions have internal guidelines determining the kinds and sizes of estates of which they will and will not serve as personal representatives. Also, some individuals would find it a great hardship to serve in this capacity. Accordingly, before you select a personal representative, you should check with the person or institution to make sure s/he or it will assume the responsibility. Also, it is wise to use WillMaker to name an alternate personal representative.**

Example 1: Bill and Annie don't wish to burden their relatives with having to take care of their fairly considerable estate. Each accordingly names the Third National Bank as personal representative after checking that this bank will, in fact, be willing to serve (for a fee, of course) as a personal representative for their estates.

Example 2: Bill and Annie both execute wills naming each other as personal representative in case the other dies first. In the event they die simultaneously, Bill and Annie name Annie's father as an alternate personal representative, after obtaining his permission.

Note: If you own real estate in a different state than the one you reside in, you will need a separate personal representative for that state. See a lawyer.

9. Allows You To Designate How Debts, Expenses and Taxes Are To Be Paid

You can designate how debts owed by you when you die, expenses of probate, and estate and inheritance taxes are to be paid by your personal representative.

Example 1: Payment of debts and expenses: Brent Jones owns a house, savings account, an R.V. and a valuable coin collection. He puts his house in a living trust, naming his brother as beneficiary, and thereby passes it free of probate. He uses WillMaker to make a will leaving his R.V. to his nephew, his coin collection to his niece, and his savings account to his favorite charity, Friends of the River. He also designates the savings account as the source of payment of his debts and expenses of probate. Under this arrangements, the charity will receive whatever is left from the account after debts and expenses of probate have been paid.

Example 2: Brent believes that he may have federal estate tax liability when he dies. He uses WillMaker to specify that his estate tax, if any, should be paid on a pro-rata basis from all the property subject to the tax. This includes both the property passing through probate (R.V., coin collection, savings account) and the property passing outside of probate (the house). If there is estate tax liability, the personal representative will require payment by each of Brent's beneficiaries in the same proportion their bequest bears to the value of Brent's estate as a whole. This approach may not be the best one where the estate consists largely of many tangible assets. Rather, in that instance you may be better off specifying liquid assets to meet the tax liability.

B. What WillMaker Cannot Do

Now let's look at what WillMaker cannot do:

1. Can't Make Conditional Bequests

• You cannot use WillMaker to leave conditional bequests, except to provide that if the beneficiaries named to get the property fail to survive you by 45 days, the property goes to alternate or backup beneficiaries.

Example: Let's assume you wish to leave your dog to Aunt Millie if Aunt Millie continues living in your town (or graduates from a school of veterinary medicine), but to your sister Kate in the event Millie has moved away at the time of your death (or becomes an orthodontist instead of a veterinarian). WillMaker does not let you accomplish this. However, if you wish to leave your dog to Millie if Millie survives you by 45 days and otherwise to your sister Kate, WillMaker works just fine. If you fail to name Kate as an alternative, or Kate also dies within the 45 days, your dog would become part of your residuary estate and go to whoever gets the rest of your property.

2. Can't Make Future Bequests

• Other than the children's trust discussed in Part 7 of this manual, you cannot use WillMaker to make bequests that take effect at a future time beyond your death, either directly or by use of a trust. Bequests become effective when you die.

Example: Emory wants his grandchildren to inherit his house, but also wants his spouse to be able to live in the house until her death. To do this, Emory would have to leave his house in trust to his spouse for her life and then to his grandchildren upon his spouse's death. Because the bequest to the grandchildren would take effect at a time beyond Emory's death, Emory could not use WillMaker to accomplish his desire. Instead, he should visit a lawyer to have the necessary trust prepared.

3. Can't Name Separate Guardians or Trustees

• On occasion it may be desirable to name separate guardians or trustees for different children. However, WillMaker only permits the naming of one guardian and one trustee (and alternates) for all your children. See Separate Guardians Note in Part 7, Section A.

4. No Tax Planning Trusts

• You cannot use WillMaker to create a testamentary trust in your will for tax planning purposes.[2] As we've seen, trusts are legal devices by which property can be left in the care of one person (called the "trustee") for the use of another person (called a "beneficiary"). When they are used in wills to control the ways property left to beneficiaries will be handled, they are called

---

[2]A testamentary trust passes ownership of the property placed in the trust to the beneficiary at death. Control of the property is given to the trustee for the benefit of the beneficiary. This is not the same as either a revocable living (inter vivos) trust or a revocable "Totten" (savings bank) trust under which you can set up a trust during your life and appoint yourself trustee of your own property, with the property to go to the beneficiary outright at your death. Living (inter vivos) trusts, which are primarily valuable to avoid probate, are discussed in more detail in Part 6(B) of this manual.

"testamentary trusts." WillMaker offers the option of a testamentary trust for handling property left to your children so that they don't get it until an age older than 18 that you choose, but does not include trusts commonly used to minimize federal estate taxes. Most people do not need to worry about tax planning because their estates are not large enough.

5. No Requirement for Bond

• **You cannot use WillMaker to require your guardian or personal representative to purchase a bond. A bond is a legally binding guarantee by a bonding company (usually an insurance company) that the person bonded will not wrongfully dispose of funds with which she is entrusted. Because the premium or fee which must be paid for a bond usually comes out of the estate, with the result that there is less money for the beneficiaries, most wills which involve the disposition of small or moderate estates do not require one. Instead, care is taken to appoint persons who are known to be trustworthy. Following this general practice, WillMaker does not provide for a bond.**

6. No Plan for Disposition of Remains

• **You cannot use WillMaker to establish a plan to dispose of your remains. Wills are usually not the best way to explain your funeral desires. Why? Because wills are often located and read long after the fact. It is accordingly wise to leave specific instructions with those who will take responsibility for your funeral arrangements. See Part 10, Section C for suggestions on how to do this. It is also wise to both arrange and pay for funeral and burial (or cremation) details in advance.**

7. No Joint Wills

• **WillMaker requires each person, including married persons, to make a separate will. This is the standard approach to will making. Joint wills are uncommon and not recommended, due to the fact that the one will is far too restrictive on the survivor.**

8. No Spousal Trust

• Some people want to leave their spouse property until the spouse dies and then have it go to the kids. While reasonable, this approach requires the establishment of a trust (called a spousal trust) which sets out the obligations that the surviving spouse has with respect to the property. WillMaker does not provide for spousal trusts. However, you can leave property outright to your spouse and specify your desire outside of your will that this property be passed to your children when your spouse dies.

C. Using WillMaker to Handle Common Situations

You have just read a summary of what WillMaker can and cannot do. How does this apply to you? To help you answer this question, here are some suggestions for how to use WillMaker to leave your property in a number of straightforward situations. One of these scenarios is likely to be similar to yours. For additional options for those of you with children, read the examples in Chapter 7(B). Examples in Chapter 8(B) are also useful for those who are concerned about what happens if one or more of your beneficiaries fail to survive you by 45 days.

Living Together Note: When we designate options below as being suitable for married people, we include non-married people who are living in a marital-type relationship.

1. Married People Without Children—Most Property To Spouse

1. For all gifts to people other than spouse, use specific bequest screens.

2. Use the residuary bequest screen to leave all property to your spouse as the residuary beneficiary.

3. Select another person or an organization to receive the rest of your property in case your spouse fails to survive you by 45 days.

Example: John and Marsha are married but don't have any children. John wants to leave most of his property to Marsha but wants his golf clubs to go to his nephew Carleton and his interest in certain electronics patents to his brother Dave. John uses specific bequest screens to make the gifts to Carleton and Dave and names Marsha as his residuary beneficiary. In case Marsha fails to survive him by 45 days, John names his favorite charity, Physicians for Social Responsibility, as his alternate residuary beneficiary. Marsha makes out a similar will, making John her residuary beneficiary, but leaving several specific items to other persons. She makes her college her alternate residuary beneficiary, in case John doesn't survive her by 45 days.

2. Married People Without Children—All Property to Spouse

1. Do not use the specific bequest screens

2. Use the residuary bequest screen to leave all property to your spouse.

3. Select another person or an organization to receive your residuary estate in case your spouse fails to survive you by 45 days.

Example: Todd and Lucille are married but have no children. They own their home as joint tenants and the rest of their property as husband and wife. Each wants the other to get all of their property at death. Todd skips over the specific bequest screens, names Lucille as his residuary beneficiary, and names his brother as alternate residuary beneficiary in case Lucille fails to survive him by 45 days. Lucille makes a similar will, leaving everything to Todd as residuary beneficiary, and naming her sister Pam as her alternate residuary beneficiary.

3. Married People With Children—Most Property To Spouse As Residuary Beneficiary And To Children Equally As Alternate Residuary Beneficiaries

1. Use specific bequest screens for bequests to people other than your spouse and children.

2. Use residuary bequest screen to leave your residuary estate to your spouse.

3. Name each of your children as alternate residuary beneficiaries if your spouse fails to survive you by 45 days.

Example: Beth and Robert have three children, Peter Paul and Mary. Beth and Robert jointly own a house, a vacation cottage, and two cars. Beth separately owns a boat and Robert separately owns 100 shares of stock in each of five corporations. Beth wants to leave the boat to her partner Mary and uses a specific bequest screen to do this. Beth names Robert as her residuary beneficiary and names the three children as alternate residuary beneficiaries. Robert makes a similar will, using the specific bequest screens to leave some of his stock to his two brothers, naming Beth as his residuary beneficiary, and naming the three children as his alternate residuary beneficiaries.

4. Married People With Children (some property to spouse and other property to children as a group)

1. Use one or more specific bequest screens to describe property being left to spouse and name children or other beneficiaries as alternates.

2. Use one or more more specific bequest screens to leave specific items of property for your children to take equally as multiple beneficiaries.

3. Select your spouse or other person as alternate beneficiary.

4. Select your spouse or children as residuary beneficiaries. Whichever you don't select, name as the alternate residuary beneficiary(ies).

Example: Floyd and Barbara have four children. They own their home and vacation cottage as husband and wife. Floyd separately owns two savings accounts and Barbara separately owns one-half of a partnership business. Floyd uses separate specific bequest screens to leave Barbara his interest in the home and vacation cottage, naming two of his children as alternate beneficiaries to the home and the other two as alternate beneficiaries to the cottage. Floyd then uses one specific bequest screen to leave his savings accounts to all four children as multiple beneficiaries. He names Barbara as alternate beneficiary for this bequest. Floyd then names all four children as residuary beneficiaries and Barbara as alternate residuary beneficiary. Barbara makes out a similar will.

5. Married People With Children—Some Property To Spouse And Other Property To Children Individually

1. Use one or more specific bequest screens to describe property being left to spouse and name children or other beneficiaries as alternates.

2. Use one or more more specific bequest screens to describe property being left to each child.

3. Select your spouse, one or more of your children, or other person(s) as an alternate beneficiary for these specific bequests.

4. Select your spouse or children as residuary beneficiaries and the one(s) you don't select as the alternate residuary beneficiary(ies). If you are worried about both your spouse and your children not surviving you, select someone other than your spouse and children as your residuary beneficiary or alternate residuary beneficiary.

Example: Troy and Suzanne have two children, Joe and Heather. Troy owns a car, a boat, an art collection, a personal computer, and a stamp collection. Suzanne owns 500 shares of Apple stock. They rent their home. Troy uses the specific bequest screens to leave Suzanne his boat and art collection, Joe his car and stamp collection, and Heather his personal computer. He names Suzanne as alternate beneficiary for the car, Troy as alternate beneficiary for the personal computer and boat, and Heather as alternate beneficiary for the art collection. He names Suzanne, Joe and Heather as multiple residuary beneficiaries and his brother Sam as alternate residuary beneficiary in case Suzanne, Joe and Heather all fail to survive him by 45 days. Suzanne makes out a will leaving half of her Apple stock to Troy in one specific bequest screen and the other half to Joe and Heather in another bequest screen, to take equally. Troy, Joe and Heather are named as her alternate residuary beneficiaries and Suzanne's mother Edith is named as alternate residuary beneficiary.

6. Married People With Children—All Property To Spouse With Different Children Taking Different Items of Property As Alternate Beneficiaries

1. Separate property into groups defined by which child or children will take the property as alternate beneficiaries.

2. Use one or more specific bequest screens for each (alternate beneficiary) group, naming your spouse as the main beneficiary of that property.

3. Select the child or children who will receive that property as the alternate beneficiary(ies).

4. Select your spouse or children as residuary beneficiary(ies) and the one you don't select as the alternate residuary beneficiary(ies).

Example: Ralph and Betsy have three children, Amy, Michaela, and Dana. Together they jointly own numerous antiques and family heirlooms which are valuable. Based on the children's expressed preferences, Ralph separates the property into three groups. He then uses specific bequest screens to leave all three groups to Betsy as beneficiary, and names each of the children as an alternate beneficiary for the appropriate property group. Ralph names Betsy as residuary beneficiary and the children as alternate residuary beneficiary(ies). Betsy also writes a will using this same plan.

7. Unmarried Persons With Children—Most Property To Children In Equal Shares

1. Use specific bequest screens for all bequests to persons other than your children.

2. Use residuary bequest screen to leave the rest of your property to your children as multiple beneficiaries.

3. Name your children, child or another person or organization as your residuary beneficiary and alternate residuary beneficiary.

Example: Janice is a single parent of three children. She uses several specific bequest screens to leave certain heirlooms to friends and relatives. She then names her three children as residuary beneficiaries and her sister Kate as alternate residuary beneficiary.

8. Unmarried With Children—Different Items of Property To Different Children

1. Use specific bequest screens for all gifts to children and other beneficiaries.

2. Name your children, a child, or other person or organization as your residuary beneficiary and alternate residuary beneficiary.

Example: Jackie, unmarried, has four children, Ted, Ellen, Keith and Sonya. She owns a house and numerous personal property items. She separates the personal property items into four groups, leaving one group to each child. Then, she names Keith as alternate for the group left to Ted, and Ted as alternate for the group left to Keith, Sonya as the alternate for the group left to Ellen, and Ellen as the alternate for the group left to Sonya. She wants the house to go to Ellen and Sonya but not to Keith or Ted and uses a specific bequest screen to name Ellen and Sonya as beneficiaries of the house. She names her children as her residuary beneficiaries, and the National Organization for Women as her alternate residuary beneficiary.

PART 10

Review And Print Your Will

A. Reviewing Will Preparation

Your next step is to make sure you have taken all the necessary previous steps. Here is a brief checklist. Don't be intimidated by its length. Most of these steps are obvious.

Step 1: Determine what is in your net estate. If you have not already done so, fill out the form contained in Part 5(F). If you are married, make sure you know what property is yours and what belongs to your spouse. Rules vary, depending on the state of your residence and the location of your real property. See Part 5(B).

Step 2: Figure out how much of this property is appropriate to be transferred free of probate by carefully reading Part 6(B).

Step 3: For larger estates, figure out how much of your property ownership can sensibly be transferred in ways that reduce estate taxes. See Part 6 (C). If your estate is very large, see a lawyer and/or accountant specializing in estate tax planning.

Step 4: Use WillMaker to list all your children, whether natural, adopted, or out of wedlock, and the children of any child who has died. As explained in Part 7, WillMaker automatically leaves these children (or grandchildren) $1.00 in addition to whatever other property you leave them, to assure that they are not considered as overlooked or "pretermitted" heirs. Again, if you plan to leave any of these children property, they will receive that property plus $1.00 more.

Step 5: Use WillMaker to designate which specific items of real property, personal property and cash should go to which people under your will.

Step 6: Use WillMaker to specify who should receive the property in the event your named beneficiaries fail to survive you by 45 days.

Step 7: Use WillMaker to designate who is to receive the rest of your property not otherwise validly specified in your will or subjected to probate avoidance technique. This is your residuary estate.

Step 8: If you reside in a common law state, read Part 5(C) of this manual to make sure your spouse is receiving at least his or her minimum statutory share of your estate.

Step 9: If you are using WillMaker to leave a great deal of property to a charitable institution, check to see if the laws of your state restrict your right to make this gift. See Part 5(E).

Step 10: Make sure your anticipated estate which is left after you take advantage of probate avoidance techniques, and which is therefore eligible to be left in your will, roughly matches the property you dispose of in your will.

Step 11: If you have minor children, use WillMaker to select a guardian and an alternate in the event no natural or adoptive parent is able or willing to care for your children after you die. If you desire your minor children's property to be handled by someone other than their guardian, you use WillMaker to set up a trust.

Step 12: Decide whether you wish the property left to one or more of your children to be left in trust. If so, name the trustee and specify the age at which each child is to receive the property.

Step 13: Specify any debts which you wish to forgive.

Step 14: Nominate a personal representative (executor) to handle your estate.

Step 15: Determine how you wish your personal representative to pay your debts, probate expenses and taxes.

Step 16: Finally, depending on the degree of your uncertainty and/or confusion about any of these matters, and the amount of property you have (the value of your estate), you may want to have your will checked by an attorney.

Now that you have prepared your will in electronic form, you will want to print it out (Section B just below) and prepare any supplementary letter which you may desire (Section C). Once your will is printed out, it must be signed and witnessed in a formal manner. We fully explain how to do this in Chapter 11. Do not sign your will until you have read that chapter.

B. Printing Your Will

The first question which arises, of course, is what kind of printer can be used. The answer is that almost any printer that produces clear readable text. This includes such dot matrix printers as the Okidata, Epson, and Apple Imagewriter. Any printer that normally works with your computer can be used with WillMaker.

To avoid problems when printing, you should clear your printer by turning it off and then on again. Also, don't use print spoolers or buffers, as they may adversely affect the way your will prints out.

Next, what kind of paper is required? There are no requirements, but we recommend blank 8-1/2 x 11 inch paper. You can use either continuous form paper or separate sheets. Some people prefer high quality bond for their will as well as a backing sheet to serve as an envelope for their will when it is folded. Both high quality bond and heavy backing sheets can be purchased from most stationary stores or directly from Nolo Press (see back of book for Will Paper Kit details).

Once you have decided on your printer and paper, you will need to make some selections on the WillMaker print screens. Here is how it works for the Apple II and IBM programs. Printing instructions for the Macintosh follow.

1. Printing Your Will (IBM & Apple)

When you are ready to print your will, press "Return." This will take you from the review screen to a menu screen.

Then type "P" and "Return". There will be a brief delay and a message telling you to ready your printer.

a. Continuous Paper or Single Sheets

The next screen asks you whether you are using continuous paper or single sheets. Type "C" and "Return" if you are using continuous paper. Type "S" and "Return" for single sheets. You can also use the single sheet option even though you are using continuous paper. This allows you to check the alignment of the paper in your printer and the desired number of lines per page by printing only one page at a time. When you select the continuous paper option, the entire will prints out at one time.

b. Lines Per Page

You will next be asked if 58 lines per page (60 on the IBM) is okay. When your will prints out, you want a top and bottom margin of approximately one inch. For most printers, 58 lines per page will accomplish this. If you need to change this value for your printer type

"N" and "Return" when you are asked whether 58 lines is okay. You will then be asked to designate your preference.

Note: What if you don't know how many lines your printer prints per page? Although, as mentioned, 58 lines is the proper choice for many printers, it is not right for all. The best approach is to select the 58 line default (i.e., type "Y" and "Return" when asked whether 58 lines is OK), print your will, and see how it looks. Nothing succeeds like trial and error.

c. Centering Will on Page

Next you are asked whether you wish to increase the left margin of your print-out so as to better center your will on the page. There is no legal requirement that the printed portion of your will be centered. Nevertheless, most people will want their will to be visually pleasing. If you discover that WillMaker prints too close to the left side of the page and too far from the right side, there are two ways you can make the appropriate adjustment:

• Move the paper horizontally if your printer allows you to do this;

• Adjust your printer (if you know how); or

• Use the WillMaker option to add spaces to the left margin.

If you do nothing, WillMaker adds five spaces to the left margin. If you wish to increase this number, simply press "N" when asked whether the five space option is OK, and select the number of spaces you desire. You will have to use the trial and error method to discover which number is best for your printer.

d. Printing the Will

Finally, you are asked if you are ready to print. If you type "Y" and "Return," printing will begin. If you type "N", you will be able to go back and reset your print options (e.g., lines per page, spaces in left margin). If you selected the continuous paper option, the program will continue printing your will to its conclusion unless you interrupt it. Consult your computer operator's manual for how to do this. If you selected the single sheet option (i.e., you feed sheets of paper into the printer one at a time), you may stop the printing by choosing one of the following two options at the end of any page:

• Press "Q" to quit the program; or

• Press "R" to return to the main program.

These options are also operative during the print set-up phase, as explained on the screen.

2. Macintosh Printing Instructions

To print your will, select the print option. This will produce a screen allowing you to:

• choose the number of spaces you wish to add to or delete from the left hand margin (determine this by trial and error); and

• select the number of lines per page (the default value (40) works well for most printers).

After selecting these options, click OK. WillMaker assembles your will (you can see this happening on the screen) and then prints it out. You can interrupt the printing by typing the command and period keys. Once your will is printed out, carefully follow our instructions in Part 11 of the manual and the notes that print out with your will.

C. Drafting Letters to Accompany Your Will

1. Expressing Sentiments or Explaining Choices

In addition to the tasks which you can accomplish by using WillMaker, you may also wish to:

• explain why gifts are being given to certain beneficiaries;

• explain disparities in gifts;

• express positive or negative sentiments about a beneficiary; or

• explain why you are nominating a certain person as guardian for your minor children.

Example: John wishes to treat all of his four children equally. He has paid for Sam and David to go to college, but not for Donna and Phillip. Accordingly, he leaves the college-educated siblings $20,000 less than the others. Because he wants everyone to understand his reasons for doing this, he writes a letter explaining them.

The WillMaker program doesn't allow you to do these things for one basic reason: we didn't want to allow users to alter our formula will language and thereby open up the possibility of producing an ineffective or invalid will.

Fortunately, there is a way you can have your final say about any of these things without risking your will's legal integrity. This is to write a letter to accompany your will to express your choices and desires to those who survive you. What you put in the letter won't be binding. Nevertheless, it is wise to be sure that there is nothing in your letter which is inconsistent with the provisions of your will.

Here is a simple introduction to your letter which makes it clear that the letter is an expression of your sentiments and not intended as a will, codicil or interpretation of your will. We concede that it is a bit formal but, as noted above, there is a good reason for this formality; you don't want to take pains to draft your will carefully and then muddy the waters with a letter that nobody knows what to do with.

To My Personal Representative:

This letter is intended solely as an expression of my personal feelings. It is not my will, nor is it intended as an interpretation of my will. My will, which was signed and dated by me on _____, is the sole expression of my intentions concerning all my property, and other matters covered therein. Should anything I say in this letter conflict with, or seem to conflict with, any provision of my will, the will provision shall be followed. I request that my personal representative give a copy of this letter to each person named in my will to inherit property, or act as a guardian or custodian, and to anyone else my personal representative determines should receive a copy.

After this introduction, you are free to express your sentiments, remembering only that your estate can be held liable for any false derogatory statements you make about an individual or organization. Here are some sample statements which you may wish to modify for your own purposes.

Expressing Sentiments:

"The reason I left $10,000 to my veterinarian Dr. Surehands is that she treated my pets competently over the years and was unfailingly kind to them."

Or

"My gift of my fishing boat to my friend Hank Pike is because he always enjoyed fishing with me on the lake."

Explaining Unequal Bequests:

You may also wish to explain your reasons for leaving more property to one person than another.

"I love all my children equally. The reason I gave a smaller percentage of my residuary estate to Tim than to my other children is that Tim received family funds to purchase a house, so it is fair that my other two children receive more of my property now."

Choice for Personal Guardian

"I have nominated my companion, Peter N,. to be the guardian of my daughter Melissa, because I know he would be the best guardian for

her. For the past six years, Peter has functioned as Melissa's parent, living with me and her, helping to provide care for her, and loving her. She loves him and regards him as her father. She hardly knows her actual father, Tom D. She has not seen him for four years. He has rarely contributed to her support or taken any interest in her."

2. Disposal of Bodily Remains

You may also desire to specify what should happen to your bodily remains. This subject is best handled in a letter (as opposed to a will). Although not absolutely binding, it is rare that a deceased person's written statement as to what should be done with his or her remains is not followed. If you have donated organs to a medical institution, arrangements should be made while you are living for the prompt disposition of whatever organs have been donated.

PART 11

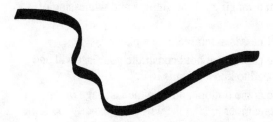

Signing and Witnessing

A. Signing and Witnessing Your Will

A will must be properly executed to be valid. This means that you must sign your will in front of witnesses. And, these witnesses must not only sign the will in your presence, but also in the presence of the other witnesses.

While state laws vary as to how many witnesses you need, three meets the requirements of every state. Even if your state only requires two witnesses, three is better because it provides one more person to establish that your signature is valid during probate, if that becomes necessary.

There are few requirements for witnesses—they need only be:

• Adults (usually over 18) and of sound mind;

• People who will not inherit under the will. That means anyone who is a recipient of any bequest should not be a witness;

• Finally, if possible, the people should be easy to locate in the event of your death. This usually means choosing people who don't move around a lot and who are younger than you are. See Part 12 on updating your will.

Both you and your witnesses must sign the will as we direct below. Here is how to go about arranging for the signing and witnessing of your will:

• Have the three witnesses assemble in one place;

• Tell them that the papers you hold constitute your last will and testament. They don't need to know what is in it;

• Initial[1] each page at the bottom and sign the last page *in the witnesses' presence*. Remember to sign the will using exactly the same form of spelling of your name as you provide in the WillMaker program. This should be the form of the name you use to sign such documents as deeds, checks and loan applications.

• Have the witnesses initial[2] the bottom of each page (on the same line you did) and sign the last page in the place indicated while you are watching. The clause immediately preceding the witnesses' signatures states ("attests") that the events outlined just above have in fact occurred.

Notary Note: If you choose to make your will self-proving as we discuss in Section B below, it may be more convenient for you to have a notary public present when you execute your will.

Important: As mentioned, there is no requirement that the witnesses read your will or that you read it to them. However, they must realize that you intend the document to be your "last will and testament." A little ritual dialogue can be helpful here:

You: "This is my will;"
Witnesses: "He says it is his will;"
You: "I am of sound mind;"

---

[1]The purpose of initialing is to prevent anyone from challenging the will on the basis that subsequent insertions were made by someone else.
[2]The purpose of having your witnesses initial each page is to avoid a challenge to your will on the ground you used your computer to make subsequent changes without going through the proper formalities. If you don't want your witnesses to see what's in your will when they are initialing the pages, simply cover each page with a blank sheet.

Witnesses: "He seems to be of sound mind."

While this may seem somewhat strained or sound a bit like a Gilbert and Sullivan routine, acknowledging to your witnesses that you are making your will is legally required in many states.

Witness Signature Lines:

If the final page of your will contains only spaces for the signatures of your witnesses, and no text of your will, we recommend that you change the number of lines per page by a line or two (on the print set-up screen) to alter the way the will prints out, so that either:

• some text of the will appears on the last page before the witness lines or

• at least one of the witness lines appears on the next-to-last page.

This will help eliminate the suggestion that the witness page was inserted at a later time.

B. Making Your Will Self-Proving

After death, most wills must go through a formal probate process. For a will to be accepted by a probate court, there must be a showing by your executor that the will really is your will. This is called proving your will. In the past, wills were normally proved by having one or two witnesses come into court (or appear by way of written sworn statements called affidavits) to testify that the will was executed by you with all due formality.

More recently, states have passed laws that allow people to make their wills self-proving, that is, admissible in probate without any further showing.[3] This is accomplished when the person making the will, and the witnesses, all appear before a notary public and sign a statement under oath that the will was executed in accordance with the necessary formalities. While it will obviously be somewhat of a nuisance to arrange for you and your witnesses to appear before a

---

[3]The self-proving option is not available in California, Maryland, Michigan, Ohio, Vermont, Wisconsin, or Washington, D.C. This in no way affects the validity of your will in these states. It only means that your personal representative will need to prove your will, a normally straightforward task.

notary public, making your will self-proving will definitely make it easier for your executor, who otherwise will have to locate one or more of your witnesses and have them sign an affidavit or (in some states) appear in court. On the other hand, you should understand that whether a will is or is not self-proving has no effect on its validity. That is, even if you don't make your will self-proving, the will is still perfectly valid. And, one way or another, your personal representative will almost certainly be able to get your will admitted to probate.

How does WillMaker handle this self-proving requirement? Except for New Hampshire residents, when you print your will, WillMaker also produces a self-proving affidavit that is suitable for your state, and accompanying instructions. Once you have appeared before a notary and signed the form, you attach the form to your will. It is important to realize that the self-proving affidavit is not part of your will but rather a separate document. You and your witnesses must still sign the will as we indicated above.

If you decide not to make your will self-proving (many do not), simply file the affidavit and instructions in a safe place in case you change your mind at a later time. You can complete this self-proving affidavit at any time prior to your death.

New Hampshire Note: New Hampshire residents are asked by WillMaker whether they wish to make their will self-proving. If so, the program prints out an affidavit as part of the will. The will should be witnessed and signed in front of a notary public.

C. Don't Alter Your Will

Once you have produced a printed will by using WillMaker, it is extremely important that you not alter it by inserting handwritten or typed additions or changes, either before or after you sign it. Do not even correct misspellings. The laws of most states require that any additions or changes in a will after it is signed, even clerical ones, be done in a formal way. Although it may be legally possible to make handwritten corrections before you sign, the better practice is not to, since it may not be clear to a later reader when the corrections were made.

Assuming your will has been signed and witnessed and you now want to make changes, you must make a new will, or a codicil (formal addition) to the existing one. One of the great advantages of WillMaker is that you can conveniently update or change your will by simply putting the WillMaker floppy disk into your computer and making a new will. So, you have no excuse for attempting possibly illegal shortcuts. See Part 12 below.

Note: WillMaker does not provide for the use of special characters (such as an accent mark or an umlaut). You may be tempted to ink one in where your name, or the name of a beneficiary, carries the mark in question. Don't. The fact that the name appears without the mark may be displeasing to you, but it will have no adverse impact on your will's validity or effectiveness.

D. Copying and Storing Your Will

Once your will is properly signed and witnessed, what do you do with it next? Most people place it in an envelope such as the one that comes in the Will Paper Kit advertised at the back of this book. Simply type your name and the word "will" on the envelope

Your main consideration should be that upon your death the right people know that your will exists and where it is located. Accordingly, it is often a good idea to make one or two unsigned copies (or "will summaries"). Give one to your proposed personal representative and, if it is appropriate, another to your spouse or children. Many people place the original copy of their will in a safety deposit box. Before doing that it is important to know what the bank's policy is about entering the box after your death. If, for instance, the safety deposit box is in your name alone, it will probably mean that the box can only be opened by a person authorized by the court and, then, in the presence of a bank employee. An inventory may even be required. Since many people do not want the bank to inventory the safety deposit box this might not be the best place to store a will. Also, in some states, the box is sealed by tax authorities after a death and entry is delayed. If, on the other hand, your box is held in joint tenancy, access should not be a problem. So, our advice is to check with your bank before using a safety deposit box to store your will. If you decide not to use a safety deposit box, a fireproof metal file cabinet or box kept in your home or office is a good choice.

Some people are tempted to prepare more than one signed and executed original of their will in case one is lost. While in most states the preparation and execution of duplicate originals is legal (each one must be separately signed and witnessed—you can't just prepare one and photocopy it), we do not normally recommend it. This is because if you later want to change your will, it can be difficult to locate all the old ones to destroy them.

What do you do with the WillMaker disk? After all, once you've printed out your will, you still have a copy of it in electronic form. Our suggestion is that you find a safe private place to store it so that you can use it to update your will if that becomes necessary. Also, others should not have access to it without your permission.[4]

Note: As with other unsigned and unwitnessed copies, the copy of your will stored on the WillMaker disk does not constitute a valid will until it is printed out and formally "executed" (signed and witnessed), as indicated earlier in this chapter.

---

[4]Despite good intentions, it is often hard to find a will at death, and even harder to find other types of personal property such as bank books and insurance policies. One good way to save your loved ones the misery of searching for important papers when they are already dealing with the grief of losing you is to make a clear record of all your property, its location and the location of any ownership documents that relate to it, including your will. *Your Family Records: How to Preserve Personal, Financial and Legal History* by Pladsen & Clifford (Nolo Press) offers an excellent way to do this.

PART 12

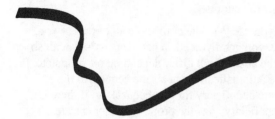

Keeping Your Will Up to Date

A. When Should You Change Your Will?

By now it should be clear to you that what your will contains is heavily dependent on the circumstances. The state of your residence, your marital status, the extent of your estate, whether you have children, and whether a child predeceases you, leaving children of his own are all examples of variables which greatly determine how your will operates after your death. As these or other variables change between the time you make your will and the day you die, you should update your will to reflect such changes. One of the great advantages of WillMaker is that it permits you to easily change your will without having to visit a lawyer and pay a fee each time you do. Such visits are usually necessary with a lawyer-drawn will, since alterations to a will (codicils) must be drafted and signed with the same formality as the original. With WillMaker, however, you can just make a new will that incorporates the changes. As we describe in Section B below, it is easy to print out your new will using WillMaker. Remember, though, that your new will has to be signed and witnessed in the same manner as discussed in Part 11(A).

Here are a number of situations where you will definitely want to update your will:

• If you change your mind about who you want to have your property or the debts you wish to forgive;

• If your marital status changes.

Suppose that after you use WillMaker to leave all or part of your property to your spouse, you get divorced. What happens? As with so many other questions, the answer will differ depending on your state. In many states, the divorce automatically cancels the bequest to the ex-spouse. If so, the alternate beneficiary for that bequest, or, if there is none, your residuary beneficiary, gets the property. In some states, however, your ex-spouse would still inherit as per the will. If you remarry, the issue becomes even more murky. For this reason, we strongly recommend that you make a new will, unless you want your ex-spouse to take what you have left him or her in your will. Also, if you marry subsequent to making a will, make a new one.

• If you have or adopt new children.

Each time a child is born or legally adopted into your family, it is wise to review your will. The new child should be named in the will and provided for according to your wishes.

• If any of your children die before you, leaving children of their own.

If a child dies before you, and leaves children of her own, these children (your grandchildren) may receive an automatic share of your estate (in many states) unless you either provide for them in some way, or they receive property that was left to the deceased child, or you indicate in the will that you desire not to provide for them. In Parts 7 and 8 we explain how WillMaker handles this situation. To make sure that your will effectively carries out your intentions, you should read that material and alter your will accordingly if one of your children dies before you.

• **If any of your beneficiaries die.**

If a beneficiary you have named to receive either a significant specific bequest or your residuary estate dies before you, you should update your will. This would especially be important if you named only one beneficiary for the bequest and failed to name an alternate or the alternate you named is no longer your first choice as the beneficiary for the bequest.

• **If the property in your estate changes significantly.**

If the property you leave in your will either expands or shrinks between the time you make your will and the time you die, you should review your will to make sure it realistically reflects your current situation. This is especially true if there are changes in your ownership of real estate or expensive personal property items.

• **If the person you named as guardian for your minor children is no longer available to serve.**

The person named to serve as a guardian for your minor children may move away, become disabled, or simply turn out to be not the kind of person you would have care for your children. If so, you will want to make a new will naming somebody else who will be more suitable.

• **If a trust for your children becomes appropriate where it wasn't before, or vice versa, or if the person you named as trustee is no longer available to serve.**

• **If the person or institution named as personal representative (executor) is no longer able to serve.**

The personal representative of your estate is the person charged with making sure your wishes are faithfully complied with. You may decide that the person or institution you originally named is no longer suitable.

• **If your witnesses move away or otherwise become unavailable to testify if a dispute over the validity of your signature arises or if it is otherwise necessary to prove your will. This would not be necessary if you have made your will self-proving, as we discussed in Chapter 11(B).**

• **If you are married and move to a different state (especially from a communcommunity property state to a common law state, or vice versa), it is a good idea to review your will in light of the information contained in Chapter 5.**

If your will was valid in the state where you lived when you made it, it will be considered valid in any state to which you move. Simply, you don't need to make a new will just because you move to a different state. On the other hand, if you are married when you make the move, your property ownership situation may be affected by the laws of your new state, especially if you moved from a common law state to a community property state, or vice versa. This is because the law of the state where you live when you die is normally used to interpret your will and determine which property you have to dispose of (except in the case of real estate; in that event, it is the law of the state where the real estate is located that determines its ownership). Especially when a move is between a community property state and a common law state, we recommend that you review Chapter 5 and determine whether you need a new will.

B. How to Change Your Will with WillMaker

The first step in changing your will with WillMaker should be to get the floppy disk with your will on it out of its storage place and boot it. The program will automatically go to a review screen, the same as or similar to the one shown below:

Here is what the review screen for the IBM looks like:

```
|        REVIEW/MODIFY YOUR WILL:          |
|                                          |
     BASICS:   1.Name/Social Sec. #        |
S              2.State
E              3.County                   V
E              4.Married?                 E
               5.Spouse's Name            R
M              6.Facts about Children     I
A              7.Pay Debts and Taxes      F
N                                         Y
U  BEQUESTS:   8.Property
A              9.The Rest (Residuary)     O
L              10.Forgive Debts           N

P  NOMINATE:  11.Guardian                 |
A             12.Trustee                  |
R             13.Personal Representative  |
T                                         |
                                          |
1  Type number of any item you want to    |
0    review or change:__ & "Return"       |
     -------------------------------------66|
     PRESS "RETURN" TO GO TO NEXT SCREEN
       F2=QUIT F3=DEF
```

Here is what the review screen for the Mac looks like:

```
⬛ GOODIES  HELP  WillMaker/Nolo/©1985,86 Legisoft  See Manual § 14
┌─────────────────────────────────────────────────────────────┐
│                    YOUR WILL IS DONE                          │
│          Click any item you want to review or change:         │
│                                                               │
│   Print your will by        BASICS:┌──────────────────┐       │
│   clicking here:☐                  │     Name/SS#     │       │
│                                    ├──────────────────┤       │
│                                    │      State       │       │
│                                    ├──────────────────┤       │
│                                    │      County      │       │
│                                    ├──────────────────┤       │
│                                    │     Married?     │       │
│   Display your will                ├──────────────────┤       │
│   on the screen by                 │   Spouse's Name  │       │
│   clicking here:☐           BEQUESTS:│    Children    │       │
│                                    ┌──────────────────┐       │
│                                    │     Property     │       │
│                                    ├──────────────────┤       │
│                                    │     The Rest     │       │
│                                                               │
│                    NOMINATIONS:┌──────────────────┐           │
│                                │   Forgive Debts  │           │
│                                ├──────────────────┤           │
│                                │     Guardian     │           │
│                                ├──────────────────┤           │
│                                │      Trusts      │           │
│                                ├──────────────────┤           │
│                                │Personal Representative│      │
└─────────────────────────────────────────────────────────────┘
```

For most of the items you will be reviewing, you will be given an opportunity to make the desired changes and then, by pressing return, to return directly to the review screen. For some items, however, you will be warned that a change will require you to continue through the rest of the program rather than returning directly to the review screen. This is required because how you answer certain questions, such as your marital status, your state, and whether you have children, determines the subsequent information presented by WillMaker and the questions it asks you to deal with. For example, if you make a change to indicate that you now have a minor child, you are required to run the rest of the program to deal with such new issues as who will care for the child and her property should something happen to you and the other parent. If you choose not to make a change, you will be returned to the review screen. This process is spelled out in more detail in the User's Manual (see Part 14).

C. What to Do with Your Altered Will

If you make a new will, even if this only involves a few changes, this new will must be signed and witnessed just as your first one was. Your will also needs a new self-proving affidavit if you want your will to be self-proving. Any will produced by WillMaker automatically revokes all prior wills. Just the same, it's wise to physically destroy the original and copies of the superseded will.

D. A Note on Codicils

When minor changes need to be made in a formal will, it is common to do so by drafting a supplementary typewritten document called a codicil. This document, like the original will, must be signed and witnessed in a formal manner. The sole purpose of a codicil is to prevent the entire will from having to be redrafted and retyped when only minor changes are required.

As is probably obvious to you, WillMaker has made the need for a codicil obsolete. Because it is so easy to update your will by using WillMaker, there is no advantage to using a codicil. If you desire to change your will, put your disk in the disk drive and follow our instructions provided in this part and in Part 14. And again, remember that your new will must be witnessed and signed (and made self-proving if you choose) in the same manner as the original one.

PART 13

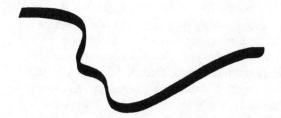

Understanding Your Will's Provisions

In our introduction in Part 1, we stressed that wills are made up of carefully-drafted phrases that can be relied on to give full effect to the testator's intent. The will produced by WillMaker is no different, although we have simplified some language where it is safe to do so.

Because many of you will read your will and want to understand what it says, we provide here annotations for a few of the more important clauses which we feel could stand some additional explanation.

I revoke all wills and codicils that I have previously made.

Comment: In the event you leave more than one will in existence, this clause tells the court you only intended your latest will to be valid.

I have _____ children now living, whose names are:

Comment: By simply listing all your children here, whether natural, adopted, or out-of-wedlock, you will prevent them from being considered as "overlooked" (pretermitted) heirs. (As a further precaution, all children listed here are left $1.00, as explained below.) See Part 7(B).

I make the following bequest of personal property: I give: (property description) to the following person or entity: (Beneficiary).

However, if the beneficiary named above to receive this property fails to survive me by 45 days, his or her share shall go to: (alternate if one has been named, otherwise to residuary estate).

Comment: The first portion of this provision makes a gift (bequest) of the designated personal property items to the indicated beneficiary. Should the beneficiary not survive you by 45 days, however, the second portion of this provision reflects the choice you made to have your gift pass directly to an alternate you have named, rather than to the beneficiary's children. This assumes you have not updated the will to account for the beneficiary's death. Some wills (not made by WillMaker) merely require beneficiaries to survive the person making the will. Others require a survival period of up to 180 days to account for the usual minimum time it takes to get an estate through probate. WillMaker, however, uses a 45 day period because small estates are often exempt from probate, and the formalities necessary to actually transfer property can often be successfully completed within this time period.

I make the following devise of real property: I give: (property description) together with any insurance on that property, and subject to any encumbrances on it at the time of my death, including any mortgage, deed of trust, and real property taxes and assessments, to the following person or entity: (Beneficiary).

However, if the beneficiary named above to receive this property fails to survive me by 45 days, that beneficiary's living children shall take that beneficiary's share, in equal shares. If the beneficiary named above to receive this property fails to survive me by 45 days and leaves no children of his or her own, that beneficiary's share shall go to: (alternate or residuary).

Comment: The first portion of this provision makes a gift (bequest) of real property, along with all obligations attached to the property, to the indicated beneficiary. Should the beneficiary not survive you by 45 days, the second portion of this provision reflects the choice you made to have the gift pass to the surviving children of the beneficiary. If there are no surviving children, the property would pass to the alternate you have named, and otherwise to your residuary estate.

This assumes you have not updated your will to account for the beneficiary's death.

I make the following bequest of personal property: I give: (property description) to the following persons or entities: (person #1) and (person #2).

However, if any beneficiary named above to receive this property fails to survive me by 45 days, his or her share shall go to the remaining surviving beneficiaries named above. If there are no such surviving beneficiaries, this property shall go to: (alternate or residuary estate).

Comment: The first portion of this provision makes a gift (bequest) of the designated personal property items to the indicated beneficiaries. Should one or more beneficiaries not survive you by 45 days, the second portion of this provision reflects your choice to have your gifts pass to the remaining named beneficiaries rather than to the deceased beneficiary's children. This assumes you have not updated your will to account for the first beneficiary's death.

If any beneficiary named above to receive this property fails to survive me by 45 days, that beneficiary's living children shall take that beneficiary's share, in equal shares. If a beneficiary named to receive this property fails to survive me by 45 days and leaves no children of his or her own, that beneficiary's share shall be divided in equal shares among any other surviving beneficiaries named above to receive this property. If there are no such surviving named beneficiaries, the property shall pass to: (alternate or residuary estate).

Comment: This paragraph will appear after any bequest of real or personal property to multiple beneficiaries when you have chosen to have the share of a deceased named beneficiary go to his or her children, if any, before being distributed to the other named beneficiaries. If there are no living children of the named beneficiary, that share will pass to the other named beneficiaries in equal shares. If there are no such remaining named beneficiaries, the share passes to the alternate beneficiary, or if there is no alternate, to the residuary estate. See Part 8, Sec. B for a more detailed discussion.

I give my residuary estate, i.e., the rest of my property not otherwise specifically and validly disposed of by this will or in any other manner, to: (Beneficiary #1) (Beneficiary #2).

Comment: The clause that disposes of your residuary estate is essentially the same as the clauses used for specific bequests. You have the same options for multiple and alternate beneficiaries. However, it is extremely important that you name at least one alternate beneficiary for your residuary estate. If you don't, *and* your named beneficiaries and their children fail to survive you by 45 days *and* you have not updated your will, the property in your residuary estate will pass by intestate succession. While all of these events are extremely unlikely to occur, we strongly recommend that you name at least one alternate for your residuary estate and keep your will up to date.

I hereby leave $1.00 to each of the following 2 persons: (Child #1) (Child #2).

This bequest is in addition to and not instead of any other gift, bequest, or devise that this will makes to such person or persons.

Comment: This provision specifies that you give a $1.00 gift to each person named by you as one of your children, or as a child of a predeceased child, in addition to any other gift you make. The purpose of this technical provision is to make it clear that you have not unintentionally overlooked these people, a consequence that could result in their having an automatic right in some states to inherit a substantial portion of your estate. See Part 7(C) above for more on this important point.

I wish to forgive the following debts, plus accrued interest as of the date of my death.

Comment: Debts owed to you at your death are owed to your estate when you die. This clause negates any debt, plus accrued interest, which you specify.

If any beneficiary under this will, in any manner, directly or indirectly, contests or attacks this will or any or its provisions, any share or interest in my estate given to the contesting beneficiary under this will is revoked and shall be disposed of in the same manner provided herein as if that contesting beneficiary had predeceased me without issue.

Comment: This formidable clause attempts to disinherit anyone who tries to invalidate the will or receive more than what the will provides. In some situations, this type of clause is effective. However, you should know that many courts will find ways to allow heirs to both challenge a will and still inherit in the event their challenge fails.

If my spouse and I should die simultaneously, or under such circumstances as to render it difficult or impossible to determine who predeceased the other, I shall be conclusively presumed to have survived my spouse for purposes of this will.

Comment: See Part 8(E) for an explanation of this particularly confusing clause.

If 45 days after my death there is no living person who is both entitled by law to the custody of my minor child or children and available to assume such custody, I recommend that (name) be appointed guardian of such minor child or children, to serve without bond.

Comment: See Part 7(A)

All bequests and devises made in this will to any child listed immediately below shall be held in a separate trust for that child until that child reaches the age indicated:

_____	_____
[child]	*[age]*
_____	_____
[child]	*[age]*

Comment: These provisions set up a separate trust for each child whom you have indicated you want to receive his or her property in trust. The trust will last until the child turns the age you have indicated.

Any trusts established under this will shall be administered as follows:

1. Beneficiary Provisions

(a) Any trust income which is not distributed to a beneficiary by the trustee shall be accumulated and added to the principal of the trust administered for that beneficiary.

(b) As long as a trust beneficiary is under the age specified above, the trustee may distribute from time to time to or for the benefit of the beneficiary as much, or all, of the principal or net income of the trust, or both, as the trustee deems necessary for the child's health, support, maintenance, and education. "Education" includes, but is not limited to, college, graduate, postgraduate, and vocational studies, and reasonably related living expenses.

(c) In deciding whether to make a distribution to the beneficiary, the trustee may take into account the beneficiary's other income, resources, and sources of support.

Comment: This provision gives the person or institution you name as trustee wide discretion to accumulate income earned from the trust assets, and to distribute the income and/or assets to the child, or on the child's behalf, as the need arises for the child's basic living and educational needs. The trustee also has discretion to refuse a distribution if the child's needs can be adequately met from other sources.

2. Termination of Trust

The trust shall terminate when any of the following events occurs:

(a) the beneficiary reaches the age listed above;

(b) the beneficiary dies before the age specified above; or

(c) the trust assets are exhausted because of distributions under the provisions of this trust.

If the trust terminates for reason (a), the remaining principal and accumulated net income shall be distributed to the beneficiary. If the trust terminates for reason (b), the remaining principal and accumulated net income of the trust shall pass to the beneficiary's heirs.

Comment: This provision allows the trust for a child to be terminated when the child reaches the age set for that event, if the child dies before the indicated age, or if all the income and principal of the trust has been distributed. The provision stipulates what happens to the remaining assets and income if termination occurs because of the first two reasons.

3. Powers of Trustee

In addition to other powers granted the trustee in this will, the trustee shall have the following powers:

(a) all the powers generally conferred on trustees by the laws of the state having jurisdiction over this trust;

(b) in regard to the property and accumulated income in the trust, all the powers conferred on the personal representative by this will;

(c) authority to hire and pay from the trust assets the reasonable fees of investment advisors, accountants, tax advisors, agents, attorneys, and other assistants for the administration of the trust and for the management of any trust asset and for any litigation affecting the trust; and

(d) when distributing assets from the trust the discretion to distribute the assets (i) in kind, including undivided interests in an asset or in any part of it, or (ii) partly in cash and partly in kind, or (iii) entirely in cash.

Comment: This provision gives your trustee all the authority granted trustees by the law of your state, and all the authority your will grants to your personal representative, to independently manage the trust assets and income. In addition, your trustee is given flexibility to distribute trust assets in whatever form he or she deems best. Finally, your trustee is authorized to pay experts out of the trust assets to help him or her fulfill the responsibilities of a trustee. Naming as trustee someone you know and trust, and allowing him to hire expertise as needed, is usually preferable to naming a bank or other institution which will charge you handsomely for its expertise but may not have your confidence. For suggestions on how to choose a trustee, see Part 7, Section B above.

4. Trust Administrative Provisions

(a) It is my intent that this trust be administered independent of court supervision to the maximum extent possible under the laws of the state having jurisdiction over this trust.

Comment: This provision makes clear that you want as little court supervision over the trusts you establish as is possible under the laws of your state. As with the personal representative, WillMaker stresses maximum independence from court supervision. Because costs associated with managing a trust come out of the trust assets it is definitely in the best interest of your children to keep court appearances to an absolute minimum.

(b) The interests of trust beneficiaries shall not be transferable by voluntary or involuntary assignment or by operation of law and shall be free from the claims of creditors and from attachment, execution, bankruptcy, or other legal process to the fullest extent permissible by law.

Comment: This provision assures that the trust property is distributed according to the trustee's discretion rather than involuntarily to pay a beneficiary's debts. However, there may be situations, such as if the beneficiary owes child support or income taxes, where this clause will not protect the trust assets.

(c) Any trustee serving hereunder shall be entitled to reasonable compensation out of the trust assets for ordinary and extraordinary services, and for all services in connection with the complete or partial termination of any trust created by this will.

Comment: This provision authorizes your trustee to be paid a reasonable amount for his or her activities associated with the trust. This may make it easier for you to find someone willing to be named as trustee.

(d) The invalidity of any provision of this trust instrument shall not affect the validity of the remaining provisions.

Comment: This provision is a standard one which upholds the trust as a whole in the event a particular provision is considered invalid under the law of your state. However, this is very unlikely to happen as this is among the simplest types of trusts.

5. Appointment of Trustee

I name the following person or institution to serve as trustee of any trust established under this will:

In the event _____ cannot serve, I name the following person or institution to serve as trustee. No bond shall be required of any trustee.

Comment: This is the provision where you name a trustee and an alternate. See Part 7.B.3 for guidelines on choosing a trustee.

I nominate _____ *as personal representative, to serve without bond. If* _____ *shall for any reason fail to qualify or cease to act as my personal reprsentative, I nominate* _____ *as my personal representative, also to serve without bond. I hereby grant my personal representative the following powers to be exercised as he or she deems to be in the best interests of my estate:*

1. To retain property without liability for loss or depreciation resulting from such retention.

2. To dispose of property by public or private sale, or exchange, or otherwise, and receive and administer the proceeds as a part of my estate.

3. To vote stock, to exercise any option or privilege to convert bonds, notes, stocks or other securities belonging to my estate into other bonds, notes, stocks or other securities, and to exercise all other rights and privileges of a person owning similar property in his own right.

4. To lease any real property that may at any time form part of my estate.

5. To abandon, adjust, arbitrate, compromise, sue on or defend and otherwise deal with and settle claims in favor of or against my estate.

6. To continue or participate in any business which is a part of my estate, and effect incorporation, dissolution or other change in the form of organization of the business.

7. To do all other acts, which in his or her judgment may be necessary or appropriate for the proper and advantageous management, investment and distribution of my estate.

Note: The language in the following seven paragraphs will appear in your will depending on how your will instructs your personal representative to pay your debts, expenses and taxes. At least two of these clauses will appear (one for debts and one for taxes):

Except as otherwise specifically provided in this will, I instruct my personal representative to first pay all my just debts, and all expenses necessarily incurred after my death, from the following asset, or assets in the order listed: _____ .

Except as otherwise specifically provided in this will, I instruct my personal representative to first pay all my just debts, and all expenses necessarily incurred after my death, out of my residuary estate.

Except as otherwise specifically provided in this will, I instruct my personal representative to pay all my just debts, and all expenses necessarily incurred after my death, as provided for by the laws of

_____.

Except as otherwise specifically provided in this will, I instruct my personal representative to first pay all my estate, and inheritance taxes arising from my taxable estate out of the following asset, or assets in the order listed: _____.

Except as otherwise specifically provided in this will, I instruct my personal representative to pay all estate and inheritance taxes arising from my taxable estate out of all the property in my taxable estate, on a pro-rata basis.

Except as otherwise specifically provided in this will, I instruct my personal representative to first pay all estate and inheritance taxes arising from my taxable estate out of my residuary estate.

Except as otherwise specifically provided in this will, I instruct my personal representative to first pay all my estate and inheritance taxes arising out of my taxable estate as provided for by the laws of

_____.

The foregoing powers, authority and discretion granted to my executor are intended to be in addition to the powers, authority and discretion vested in him or her by operation of law by virtue of his or her office, and may be exercised as often as is deemed necessary or advisable, without application to or approval by any court in any jurisdiction.

I direct my personal representative to take all actions legally permissible to have the probate of my will done as simply and as free of court supervision as possible under the laws of the state having jurisdiction over this will, including filing a petition in the appropriate court for the independent administration of my estate.

Comment: The above two clauses give your personal representative (executor) broad discretion to carry out a number of activities without having to first seek court approval, in all states that recognize a personal representative's independent power. This generally cuts down the length of time it takes to get your will through probate. The law of some states may grant a personal representative some or all of these powers without enumeration. However, the fact that WillMaker expressly sets them out in your will won't hurt. Although some of these powers may seem a little broad, we believe they make good sense as long as you choose a personal representative who you have confidence in. After all, your personal representative has a fiduciary duty (duty of trust) to carry out the provisions of your will. See Part 9.A.8 for how to select your personal representative.

I hereby direct that my personal representative administer my estate under the Independent Administration of Estates Act.

Comment: In California wills, WillMaker specifies that the personal representative utilize a statute known as the Independent Administration of Estates Act. The powers granted by this statute for California personal representatives, and those that WillMaker lists for wills in other states, are essentially the same. They both give your personal representative wide discretion to take what actions are necessary to successfully and efficiently handle your estate.

I, (name) , the testator, sign my name to this instrument, consisting of _ pages, including this page signed by me, this ___ day of (month) , 19_, and do hereby declare that I sign and execute this instrument as my last will and that I sign it willingly, that I execute it as my free and voluntary act for the purposes therein expressed, and that I am of the age of majority or otherwise legally empowered to make a will, and under no constraint or undue influence.

*We, the witnesses, sign our names to this instrument, and do
hereby declare that the testator signs and executes this instrument as
his last will and that he signs it willingly, and that each of us, in the
presence and hearing of the testator, and in the presence of each other,
hereby signs this will as witness to the testator's signing, and that to the
best of our knowledge the testator is of the age of majority, or is
otherwise legally empowered to make a will, and under no constraint
or undue influence. We declare, under penalty of perjury, that the
foregoing is true and correct this ___day of (month) ,19__, at _____.*

_____ *residing at* _____

_____ *residing at* _____

_____ *residing at* _____

Comment: This is called the attestation clause. Its language
establishes that the will was executed in the proper manner. In most
states you can take an additional step to ease the acceptance of your
will in the probate proceeding. If you and your witnesses appear before
a notary public and sign a document called a "self-proving" affidavit,
which basically affirms that you and your witnesses did everything we
tell you to do in Part 11, there will be no need for your witnesses to
establish after your death that the will being admitted to probate is in
fact yours. See Part 11(B) for further discussion of this point.

PART 14

WILLMAKER User's Manual

A. Introduction and Overview

1. The WillMaker READ.ME File

Before we get into a description of how WillMaker works, we want to introduce you to the WillMaker READ.ME file. Your WillMaker floppy contains a text file that has information about technical changes that have not yet found their way way into the WillMaker manual and other items that we think you will find of interest. Significant program changes and legal updates will as always be covered in our regular WillMaker update service and the software corner in the Nolo News. Here are brief instructions for gaining access to the READ.ME file, which we hope you will read prior to operating the WillMaker program.

IBM (and clones): Assuming the WillMaker floppy is in drive A, display the READ.ME file on your screen by entering the following string from the DOS A> prompt:

Enter: TYPE READ.ME

The scrolling can be stopped by pressing the Control and S keys simultaneously. It can be restarted by pressing the Control and Q keys.

Macintosh: The READ.ME file is a "text only" file created by Macwrite Version 4.5. You may access this file from your desktop. To get to the desktop from the WillMaker program, select quit from the goodies menu. If you have Macwrite on your desktop, double click the READ.ME Icon. You will be asked the following question: Should a Carriage Return signify a new paragraph or a line break? Respond by clicking the "paragraphs" box. You will then be told, "this document is being converted and will open as Untitled". Click OK. If you have a different word processing program, open that application and then open the READ.ME file from that. The READ.ME file will be converted to a readable form.

Apple II: Exit to ProDos and enter the following string:

RUN INFO

Commodore 64: Exit to DOS, type the following string and press Return:

LOAD "INFO",8

2. About the WillMaker Program

So far, we've covered a variety of legal topics relevant to making a valid and effective will. Here we shift gears a little and concentrate on operating WillMaker as a computer program. Although WillMaker is designed to be "user-friendly," we anticipate that you may have questions about the program that are not completely answered on the computer screens. We hope you will find your answers here.

3. Computers Covered

This manual is designed to be used with:

• the Apple II family of computers (but not on Franklin computers),

• the Apple Macintosh (512E, Plus, SE, II),

• Lisa with MacWorks,

• the IBM PC (as well as the XT, AT and PS/2);

• IBM compatibles; and,

• the Commodore 64 and 128 (with a 64K emulator).

Obviously there is no way to completely generalize across all of these machines. Accordingly, after addressing some general remarks to all users, we break this part of the manual into four separate sections:

• Section B for IBM and IBM-compatible computers;

• Section C for the Apple II+, IIe, IIc, IIgs;

• Section D for Macintosh; and

• Section E for the Commodore 64 and 128 (with 64 emulator).

4. Follow Instructions

Making your will is a serious act and warrants sincere attempts by you to understand our instructions and comply with them to the best of your ability. For instance, when you are asked to enter your name "the way you do when signing formal legal documents," please do so. There's a good reason for the instruction: entering a nickname can lead to problems after your death. The point is, we have done our best to present you with complete information and instructions so that you can make a valid and effective will. It's your job to do your best to understand the information and follow the instructions. Okay, end of sermon.

5. Make a Backup Copy

WillMaker stores one will on a floppy. If additional members of your family desire to use WillMaker simply make a separate copy of the WillMaker floppy for each user before running the program. You will also want to make a backup copy. You can copy WillMaker by using the copy utility that comes with your system. If you have a hard disk, we recommend that you not try to run WillMaker from it. It is fine, however, to backup your floppy by copying all the files onto your hard disk (they may be later copied onto another floppy). There is no reason to actually run WillMaker from the hard disk, and the contents of your will are more confidential when kept in floppy disk form. If you disagree, instructions for copying to a hard disk (for IBM and Macintosh computers) are contained in Sections B and D, respectively.

6. You Must Print Your Will for It to Be Valid

You must print and sign your will for it to be valid. If you don't have a printer, then you might consider running the program on your own computer and then printing it out at a friend's or at an obliging computer store. WillMaker uses only the most basic printing commands and will work with almost any printer that works with your computer.

7. You May Not Open Print Files

Many WillMaker users wish to open up the print files that WillMaker produces in response to their input and alter some aspect of the will's language. We have deliberately chosen not to facilitate this type of alteration and accordingly WillMaker does not produce a text file that you can alter with your word processor. Simply, we spent hundreds of hours making sure that WillMaker produces a will that is both valid and effective. If the text is altered, you might end up with a will that contains ambiguities or self-contradictory provisions. To avoid this type of undesirable result, we have opted for less flexibility but more certainty in WillMaker's output. If you nevertheless want a will different than the one produced by WillMaker we recommend that you first consult with an attorney about your suggested changes and then retype the WillMaker will with your changes included. We, of course, take no responsibility for your final product.

8. Basic Outline of the Program

Here we give you the "big" picture of the program. We get into more details about the program's specific features in the computer-specific sections.

In its most basic manifestation, WillMaker is a series of messages and questions in the form of "screens" that are displayed on your monitor. After you read each screen, you will be asked either to answer a question (usually "Yes" or "No"), *or* to enter some piece of information (such as the name of a person you want to leave property to), *or* to simply press the "Return" key (or click a button, on the Macintosh) to move to the next screen. When you are done with the screens, WillMaker produces a valid and effective will reflecting your personal information and choices. More specifically, WillMaker is organized into the following four parts:

1. An introduction to:

- wills in general;

- the will you can write using WillMaker; and

- instructions for operating the WillMaker program.

2. A series of questions that you answer in order to:

- provide the program with necessary personal information (marital status, etc.);

- express your wishes regarding your property;

- designate a guardian for your minor children;

- nominate your personal representative (executor) and trustee (if you choose to establish a trust for your children); and

- choose how your debts, expenses and taxes are to be paid.

3. An opportunity to review and change your previous entries

4. Specific instructions on readying your printer and printing out your will. Also, in this part of the program you may:

- display your will on the screen before it prints out (in 40-column mode on the Commodore; an 80-column card is needed for the Apple II+ and IIe);

- return to the review process;

- erase your will and start over; or

- temporarily quit the program before you print your will (for example, if you need to get more information to finish the will).

9. Customer Support

Nolo and Legisoft are dedicated to providing reasonable assistance for WillMaker users who have trouble operating the program or who encounter issues that aren't covered in the manual. On the other hand, we expect our users to conscientiously read the manual and apply a little "self help" energy to the problem before seeking our assistance.

If you need help on a technical matter—i.e., you encounter a problem when running the program or the will won't print—call Nolo Press and have the following information ready:

- name;

- address;

- phone number;

- hours you will be at that phone number;

- your version of WillMaker (available on your manual cover);

- type of computer and its memory capacity (RAM); and

- type of printer and printer interface being used (if printing is your problem).

If you have received a specific error message while running WillMaker, please write down the entire message.

If you need assistance on a legal matter, please understand that our editors, although attorneys, do not intend to give you legal advice when answering your question. Instead, they are only intending to clarify the manual and provide you with an appropriate perspective for answering your own questions. If you desire legal advice, backed by a malpractice insurance policy, you should contact a lawyer knowledgeable about your state's laws on wills and probate.

Now that you have some sense of how the WillMaker program works overall and how to contact Nolo Press if it doesn't, it's time to turn to the details.

IBM and Compatible Users—Go to Section B

Apple II Users—Go to Section C

Macintosh Users—Go to Section D

B. IBM User's Manual

1. What You Need To Get Started

WillMaker is written in compiled BASIC for the PC DOS and MS DOS operating systems. When we say "IBM," we mean the IBM PC, XT, AT, PS/2, and most IBM compatibles. Some compatibles require 256K, rather than the 128K required for the IBM.

In addition to an IBM or compatible computer (except as noted) and the WillMaker floppy, you need the following:

a. The PC Disk Operating System (PC DOS version 2.1 or later) or a compatible equivalent;

b. At least one floppy disk drive;

c. A monitor;

d. 128K of Random Access Memory for IBM products (256K RAM for some compatibles).

Items a - c are usually included as part of your computer system. Generally, all IBM PCs have at least 128K of memory, and most compatibles come with the 256K minimum.

Quotation Mark Note: Throughout this section, we refer to specific commands and keys on your keyboard (e.g., Press "Return", Type "Q", Enter "Y"). When we do, we usually enclose the reference in quotation marks. Do not get confused and think you should type the quotation marks as well as what is in them. They are only used to set off the particular command or key. However, every rule has its exceptions. On the rare occasions when we want you to type the quotation marks, we'll tell you.

2. How to Start WillMaker

Once you've made a backup copy of your WillMaker floppy (see Section A(5) above), take the following steps:

For users with one disk drive:

1. Boot your machine with your system disk (DOS disk)

2. After the machine is started, remove your DOS disk and insert a copy of the WillMaker disk into drive A

3. At the A prompt, type "WM"

For those with two disk drives:

1. Boot your machine with your system disk (DOS disk) in drive A

2. Place a copy of the WillMaker disk in drive B

3. At the A prompt, type "B:" then press "Return"

4. At the B prompt, type "WM"

For those with a hard disk and one drive:

1. Boot your machine using your hard disk

2. Place a copy of WillMaker into the A drive

3. At the C prompt (assuming your hard disk is drive C), type "A:" then press "Return"

4. At the A prompt, type "WM"

Alternative for hard disk users:

1. Boot your machine using your hard disk

2. At the C prompt (assuming your hard disk is drive C), create a subdirectory by typing the following:

MD \WM

This will create a subdirectory in your root directory named WM

3. Place a copy of WillMaker into the A drive

4. Type the following:

COPY A:*.* C:\WM

This will copy all the files from the WillMaker disk in drive A to the WM subdirectory on drive C

5. At the C prompt, type "CD /WM" then press "Return"

6. Type "WM"

Note to Users with IBM PCs, PC Juniors and PC Compatibles: If your computer returns an R6005 error at any time, do the following:

1. Insert the DOS disk in drive A

2. Reboot the machine

3. If you have disk drives, insert WillMaker in drive B. If not, skip to step 6.

4. Type "B:" and press "Return"

5. At the B prompt, run WillMaker by typing "WM"

6. If you have only one drive you may have to increase the buffer size. See your DOS manual for instructions on how to do this.

3. Is Something Wrong?

If you have trouble running the program, check the following:

• Did you first boot DOS from a system floppy? The WillMaker floppy is not a system floppy and cannot be booted.

• Are you typing exactly what the manual indicates? Sometimes spaces matter. For example, if WillMaker is in Drive A, you may copy it to a formatted blank floppy in Drive B by entering:

COPY A:*.* B: (Observe spacing)

However, copy A: *.* B: will not work.

If the program crashes while you are using it, check the following:

• Is there a write-protect tab on the floppy? The WillMaker program writes data to the floppy and cannot be run with a write-protect tab. We recommend putting a write-protect tab on your original floppy, copying this master to a blank floppy, and then running from the copy.

• Do you have the required amount of RAM? Remember that while IBM PCs require 128K RAM to run WillMaker, many compatibles require 256K.

• Is your printer connected properly when you try to print? If there seems to be a problem in printing out, turn your printer off and on and then try again. (See Part 10 of the manual for instructions on printing your will.)

Here is the meaning of the following error messages:

Error 7: Out of memory. This means there is not enough RAM available to operate the program. Eliminate unnecessary utilities or application programs while running WillMaker.

Error 24 at Line 0: This indicates a problem with your printer connection. Also, try clearing your printer by shutting it off and on.

Error 71: The disk drive is not ready. Check to see that the drive door is closed.

Error 70: Take off your write-protect tab.

Error 68: The printer is not connected.

Special Note: WillMaker will generally not run properly on a machine that is in Turbo mode. If your computer has two processor speeds, set it to the lower one BEFORE running the program. The instruction manual that came with your computer should explain this simple procedure. Since WillMaker does not have many processor intensive operations, you should not notice the difference in your computer's performance while running WillMaker.

Also, in most cases, WillMaker will not operate properly if you run it from a program shell. If you start the program from somewhere other than DOS, WillMaker will not be able to locate the other program modules it needs while running, and will crash or give you a program error.

4. Some Tips on Running WillMaker

Important Manual Format Note: The rest of this section is being read by IBM, Apple and Commodore users. This presents a problem, since the IBM program uses some special function keys for certain WillMaker features, while the Apple and Commodore program use keyboard letters and symbols. To accommodate all users, we have adopted the following format. When we talk about which key to press when using a feature, we put the function key first and the keyboard letter/symbol second, in parentheses. Here is an example of what this format looks like:

F1(B)

So, IBM users should use the function key, while the Apple and Commodore users should use the letter/symbol in parentheses.

There is one other difference. When B and Q are used, it is necessary to press "Return." It is not necessary to press "Return" for the function key equivalents (F1 and F2). Thus, if you see an instruction such as "Press F1(B) and Return," you IBM users can ignore the return part of the command. Nothing bad will happen if you don't.

Tip 1:   Use the "Return" key only after your entry is completed.

When the program asks you to *enter* something, it means type it and then press the "Return" key. WillMaker asks you for two different types of input. You will be requested either to answer a question (usually "Y" for yes or "N" for no) or to type in some information (such as your name or the description of a bequest). Either way, you should press the "Return" key only after your *entire* entry is complete. This is especially important where the information you want to enter takes up more than one line (for instance, when you are describing bequests). You may be tempted to press the "Return" key at the end of one line in order to move the cursor to the following one. Please don't do this. The cursor moves from one line to another by itself. Pressing the "Return" key terminates the particular entry being worked on and signals the program that you are ready to go on to the next step. If you slipped up on this by pressing "Return" at the end of the line, just type "N" when you are asked to verify your entry.[1] You will get another try.

Tip 2:   Correct information by using the back arrow key.

You can correct information by using your delete or "back arrow" key. Simply press this key until the error has been erased and then retype the correct information. Obviously you must do this before you press "Return" and move to the next screen. Of course, as we mentioned in Tip 1, you can undo a premature pressing of "Return" by simply typing "N" when you are asked to verify your previous entry. Then, you will be given another opportunity to erase and retype.

---

[1] This assumes you choose to leave the verification feature operational. Later we tell you how to turn it off by using the F5 function key, see Section 6(h) below.

Tip 3:   Don't worry about irregular word breaks.

If your entry lasts more than one line, the program may break a word in the middle and continue it on the next line. Don't worry about this. When you print out your will, the word will be in one piece. Similarly, you may be tempted to fill the space at the end of the line with spaces, thus bringing the cursor to the next line before you continue your entry. Please don't do this. With WillMaker the cursor *automatically* goes to the next line when the first is completed.

Tip 4:   Use + character when naming multiple beneficiaries.

If you type in the names of two or more people to receive either a specific property bequest or the rest of your property as beneficiaries, use a + sign to separate the names. This tells the program that you are leaving the bequest to two or more people and it will conform the language of your will accordingly. If you provide an address with the names, use the + sign to separate the last element of the address and the next name.

Example: Raphael J. Rabbit, 4507 Burrow Lane, Fudsville, Mo. 55667+Ruby J. Hare, 4496 Turnip Rd., Carrotown, La. 90874

Tip 5:   Do not interrupt the program or touch the disk drive while the drive is running.

If the red light on the front of your drive is on, or you hear a whirring sound, your drive is running. If you remove a floppy during this time, the file containing your will information may be destroyed and the program itself damaged. Throughout the program, we provide you with an opportunity to quit without losing information or doing damage, by simply entering F2(Q). See Tip 7 just below.

Tip 6:   Save your information.

When operating WillMaker you may wish to save what you've already done and leave the program. You do this by pressing the F2(Q) function key. After all your entries are saved on the floppy, you will then be asked if you really want to quit. If you do, enter "Y". When you next operate WillMaker, you will return to where you were when you quit. If you wish to continue the program, enter "C". We recommend that you frequently save what work you've done by using the "Quit and Continue" option. Then, if a power or system failure occurs, your frustration level will be kept to the absolute minimum. Also, from time to time the WillMaker program saves to disk on its own. Then, if a system failure occurs, you are returned to the place where this automatic saving occurred, unless you used the F2(Q) option at a later point in the program.

Tip 7: Don't worry about truncated screen displays.

When you make lists (e.g., of your children), WillMaker displays each entry you make and gives you the option of either changing it, adding new entries, or going on to the next screen. Due to space limitations, only the first part of a long entry is displayed and an ampersand appears at the end of the abbreviated display to indicate this fact. However, the entire entry has been saved and will be printed out during that phase of the program.

Tip 8: Enter the information.

Here are some pointers on entering names, descriptions of bequests, or other information:

• Type in the information requested just as you would with a typewriter. But, unlike a typewriter, which requires you to manually press the "Return" key at the end of each line, the computer takes care of line returns without your intervention (Tip 3, above). In other words, just keep typing until you're done. Then press "Return".

• Read each screen carefully so you will know what information or decision is being asked for. Each screen is carefully worded so that you can provide the correct response.

• Provide only the information requested. Thus, when you are asked to name your children, don't use that space for other persons. See Section B(8) of this Part for important rules that apply when you specify who is to inherit your property.

• If you are known by two names, provide both of them, separated by an "AKA" (also known as), e.g., Joan Willis AKA Joan Kleinfeldt.

Tip 9:   Use WillMaker manual reference feature to locate additional information.

In the left margin of each main WillMaker screen, you will see a reference to the WillMaker Manual. This reference sends you to the part of the manual that is most relevant to the subject matter treated on the screen. For example, on the screens dealing with trusts, the reference is to Part 7 of the manual, the part dealing with children. If the definitions and discussions accessed through the Help Menu (described in Section 6(d) below) do not fully answer all your questions, go to the manual for additional reading. This reference is also a reminder that the WillMaker program and manual are designed to be used together. Only by understanding the relevant material in the manual will you get the most out of WillMaker.

5. General Operational Features of WillMaker

The two lines in the bottom margin of each screen tell you which program options are available for that screen and what to do when you are through reading the screen or entering information (e.g., type "Y" or "N" and "Return," type requested information and then "Return," press "Return" to go to next screen).

Let's now take a closer look at these bottom-margin instructions and options.

a. Yes and No

WillMaker frequently asks you to answer a specific question (e.g., "Do you have children under 18?") "Yes" or "No". You should type either "Y" or "N" and then press "Return". The "Yes" and "No" question is also used when you check information already entered by you (e.g., "Is this correct?"). This is what you can expect to occur next:

• If when you are asked to verify your answer, you type "Y" and then press the "Return" key, WillMaker saves your answer and moves to the next screen.

• If when you are asked to verify your answer, you type "N", and "Return", you get another chance to answer the question.

• If you forget to press the "Return" key, the computer does nothing.

• If you give any answer other than "Y" or "N" (unless you select one of the special options listed in the bottom margin), the computer will beep and do nothing.

b. Press "Return" and Go to the Next Screen

You must always press the "Return" key to tell the computer when you are ready to go from one purely informational screen to the next screen. In this situation, the screen will say "Press Return And Go To The Next Screen."

c. Type Requested Information And Then Return

WillMaker also makes frequent use of the "Return" key to tell the computer you are finished providing information requested in a particular screen. In this instance, the screen says "Type Requested Information and Then Return." After you have done this (and assuming you have not turned the "verify" feature off), you will again see displayed on the screen the information you have just entered. This time it will be followed by the question, "Is this OK?". If you say "N" (meaning it is not OK), you will then go to a screen with the same information displayed and the cursor flashing at the end of the text. This gives you the chance to correct it by using the "left arrow" key described earlier (see Section 4, Tip 2, above). This same sequence occurs when you back up and when you review your will after you have completed the program.

d. Type F3(?) for Definitions of Legal Terms

By typing F3(?), you may obtain a brief on-screen definition of legal terms used in the screen being viewed. The terms for which definitions are provided are displayed in capital letters.

If you desire a definition of any such term, simply type F3(?). Each defined term will then become highlighted and numbered. For example:

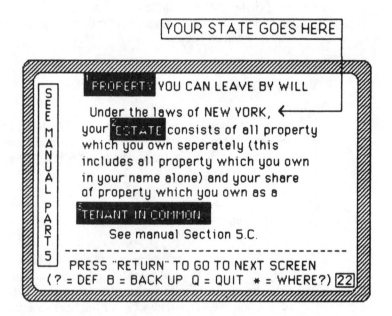

When you type the number of the term you want defined and then (as always) press "Return", the definition (and often a cross-reference to the manual) will appear. When you are done reading it, press the "Return" key. You will be returned to the screen where the defined terms are highlighted and numbered. If you want additional highlighted terms defined, simply select the appropriate number and press "Return".

When you desire to leave the screen with the highlighted and numbered terms and return to the main program, simply press "Return". You will come back to the screen you were on before you typed F3(?) in the first place. You may then continue as if you hadn't asked for a definition. By the way, you can skip one step if you are done reading a definition and do not want to see any other definition on that screen.

Simply press the "escape" (ESC) key and you will return to the normal screen.

e. Type F1(B) for backup

There will be times when you desire to go back to a previous question to check your answer or change information. Although you are provided an opportunity to do this near the end of the program under a master menu of most program sections (we call it the "Review" screen), it is also usually possible to back up a screen at a time while still in the main part of WillMaker. You do this by typing F1(B) and then "Return", assuming the F1(B) option appears at the bottom of the screen. Each screen that you back up to displays your previous answer and then asks you, "Is this OK"? If you type "N" and "Return", you are able to change your answer. If you type "Y" and "Return", your previous answer remains and you go forward. If you again type F1(B) and "Return", instead of "Y" or "N", you back up to the previous screen.

If the F1(B) option does not appear at the bottom of the screen, this means you cannot back up from that screen. To get around this, keep going until you get to a screen with the F1(B) option. When you select the backup option, the program will return you to the screen that began that particular section of the program. Then you can get to the screen you wanted.

All of this probably seems a little cumbersome. Fortunately, if the reason you want to back up is to review a portion of your work (e.g., the bequests you have made, and to whom you have made them), there is a better alternative than backing up. We detail it in Section 7 below.

Apple and Commodore Note: We recognize that the backup option may seem a little confusing at times for Apple and Commodore users. For example, suppose you want to use the "B" option at a time when the screen is asking you for information. If you have not yet entered any information and type "B", the "B" appears on the screen in the space where you would otherwise be entering the information. Don't worry. When you then press "Return", the program interprets the single "B" as a request to back up, rather than as the requested information.

What happens, however, if you want to back up after you have entered some information? In that case, simply press the "left arrow" key repeatedly to erase any information you have already entered. Then type "B" and press "Return." As we mentioned earlier, you first see a "B" where the program was expecting information, and then the previous screen appears.

Note: If you make certain changes after having backed up, you may encounter some new information or questions which have become appropriate because of your changes. For example, if you originally said you had no spouse, but later back up to that section and change your answer to the affirmative, you will encounter some new screens dealing with leaving property to spouses. See Section 9 below.

f. Type F2(Q) for Quit

There may be times when you want to stop in the middle of writing your will and store what you've done without having to start again at the beginning. Or, you may wish to store your information on disk as a hedge against a power or other failure (see Section 5, Tip 7, above). If you type F2(Q) and "Return," WillMaker first stores the information already entered on the disk and then asks you whether you really want to quit for now. If you then type "Y", you get your wish. If you type "C" for "continue", you are returned to where you were. Once you have quit, you will be returned to DOS. When you run the program again, you are returned to the place where you left off. Thus, by using F2(Q) you can quit without wasting the time you already devoted to making out your will.

h. Type F5(^) to Change Verification Feature

The verification feature shows your response to the previous input screen and asks you if it is "OK" or whether you want to change it. You may eventually find the verification feature tiresome, however, and we provide you with the option of turning it off. You do this by pressing F5(^). The right side of the screen will then tell you that "verify" is off. To turn the verify feature on again, press F5(^). It will stay on for all future screens unless you turn it off again.

Even when the verify feature is turned off, you will still be asked to verify your answers when you have returned to and changed an entry from the final review screen, and when backing up.

6. Making Lists Using WillMaker

At different places in the program, WillMaker asks you to list:

• Your children;

• Any children of a deceased child; and

• Specific bequests of property to individuals or institutions.

Each time you add an entry to a list, WillMaker displays the entry in abbreviated form (see Section 5, Tip 9). You are then given a chance to add additional names, change the entry you have made, delete an entry, or proceed to the next part of the program.

Let's take a closer look at these options.

a. "A" for "Add More Names"

If you wish to add another name (or bequest) to the list, type "A" and "Return". You have a maximum of 16 entries in any of these lists.

b. "R" for "Review Any Previous Entries In This List"

If you wish to review (or change) one of your previous entries on the list, type "R" and "Return". If there is only one entry on the list, you go directly to a screen that contains the full entry and are asked if the entry is okay, or whether you want to change it. If there is more than one entry, you are asked to select the number of the one you want to review or change.

This is a way to see the entry in full, and is particularly useful for the list of bequests, where only limited information (the first 16 characters of the name of the beneficiary and of the description of the bequest) appears in the summary list. In fact, alternative beneficiaries do not appear at all. Thus, this option allows you to see what property you have described in any particular bequest, or the full name of the person (or alternate) to whom you have left such property.

Note: As we mentioned in our earlier discussion on backing up, when you want to check and perhaps change an entry in a list, you must use this review utility since you can't back up with F1(B). Thus, if in the middle of leaving specific bequests you decide you want to see what you've already left, simply advance until you reach the screen providing the "R" option and then select the appropriate entry for review.

c. "D" for "delete any previous entries in this list"

The "D" entry works much the same as "R", only the entire entry is eliminated. In the children or grandchildren lists, the space left by deleting is closed up and the list then has one fewer entries. For the bequests, this space is left open; you may fill it up later by using the "R" option on this space. But no harm is done by leaving the space open, since the section of the program that prints your will simply ignores any space that is blank because of deletions or because of an initial failure to enter both a beneficiary and a description of the bequest.

d. "Y" for "yes, everything is OK and I want to move on"

To quit making the list and advance to a new section of the program, type "Y" and "Return". This is what you choose when you are either satisfied with the list as it stands or plan on coming back to it later. If you don't return to make changes, WillMaker will consider the list complete.

Again, to select any of the options just discussed, simply type the appropriate letter ("A", "R", "D" or "Y") and "Return".

7. Leaving Property Under WillMaker

The heart of the WillMaker program is the flexibility it provides users in how they can leave their property when they die. Under WillMaker you can:

• Make up to 16 specific bequests of personal property or real estate;

• Choose among several alternatives to take effect if a beneficiary fails to survive you by 45 days;

• Leave the rest of your property (your residuary estate) to one or more persons or institutions of your choice;

• Choose among several alternatives to take effect if the beneficiary of your residuary estate fails to survive you by 45 days;

• Forgive debts owed to you at death;

• Establish a trust for property left to one or more of your children; and

• Choose which assets should be used by your personal representative to pay your debts, probate expenses and taxes.

These options are fully explained in:

•Part 7 (Special Considerations for Children). Here we wish to discuss several points you should keep firmly in mind when using WillMaker to leave property.

•Part 8 (What Happens If Your Will Is Out of Date When You Die) and

•Part 9 (What WillMaker Can and Cannot Be Used For)

a. No Conditional Bequests

Suppose you make a specific bequest of your 1984 Mercedes 480SL to Mike and then add the condition "but only if he continues to live in Marin County." When your will's provisions are carried out by your personal representative, Mike will receive the Mercedes. However, what type of ownership will Mike have? And, what happens if he moves out of Marin County? Who will enforce this provision? To prevent such ambiguities from arising after you die, you should do the following:

• When you are asked to name the beneficiary or beneficiaries of particular items of property or your residuary estate, simply type out their names (and addresses, if you desire, although we generally recommend against it because addresses tend to change frequently).

• When you are asked to specify the property you wish to leave to beneficiaries you have named earlier, simply describe the property without attaching any conditional statements.

b.   No Mixing of Real and Personal Property In Specific Bequest Screens

After you identify the property you wish to include in specific bequests, you are asked whether the items are real or personal property. The clause in your will that accompanies each item differs somewhat, depending on which category the bequest falls into.

If you have included real property (say your home) and personal property (say a car) in a single bequest, the will language will be wrong, whichever option you choose (personal property or real property). To avoid this problem, use separate screens for real property and personal property bequests.

c.   Using More Than One Bequest Screen for the Same Beneficiary

If you run out of room on a screen while making a bequest of personal or real property, you may, as a practical matter, continue the bequest on the next screen. To do this, take the following steps:

1. Complete your description of the property items being left on your current screen. That is, don't attempt to carry over descriptions of any particular item to the next screen. Also, don't leave incomplete sentences on the screen where you ran out of room. Backspace and erase the incomplete sentence.

2. Complete the following three screens that follow that bequest screen (i.e., what type of property is being left, what happens to the bequest if the beneficiary fails to survive you by 45 days, and the naming of the alternate beneficiary).

3. Choose the "add to list" option when you come to the bequest review screen.

4. When you come to the screen for naming the beneficiary, enter the beneficiary's name exactly as it was entered on the previous bequest screen.

5 Continue specifying the items you wish to go to the beneficiary. If you again run out of room, proceed as we have explained in these instructions.

6. Do not mix personal and real property in your "single" bequest, and don't impose conditions on the gifts.

7. You may use as many of the sixteen bequest screens for a single bequest of personal or real property as you need.

When your will prints out, this "single" bequest will appear as separate bequests. However, these separate bequests will have exactly the same effect as if you had combined them in a "single" bequest.

d. Creating a Children's Trust With WillMaker

If later in the program you decide to create a trust for one or more of your children, here is what happens. You are first presented with a numbered list of your children and asked to select a number of a child for whom you wish to establish a trust. For instance, if you have three children, the list will appear as follows:

```
┌─────────────────────────────────────────────┐
│¦ YOUR CHILDREN :                          ¦   │
│¦ 1.TOM JONES                         ¦XX  ¦   │
│L 2.RUBEN JONES                       ¦XX  ¦   │
│E 3.KAREN JONES                       ¦XX      │
│G                                          V   │
│I                                          E   │
│S TYPE NUM. OF 1ST CHILD YOU WANT TO       R   │
│O SET UP A TRUST FOR (1 AT A TIME).        I   │
│F                                          F   │
│T                                          Y   │
│/                                              │
│N                                          O   │
│O                                          N   │
│L                                              │
│O 1_                                       ¦   │
│                                           ¦   │
│P                                          ¦   │
│R                                          ¦   │
│E                                          ¦   │
│S                                          ¦   │
│S                                          ¦   │
│¦ ------------------------------------50¦      │
│                                               │
│  TYPE "Y" WHEN LIST IS OK                     │
└─────────────────────────────────────────────┘
```

If you select the number 1, for instance, you indicate your desire to establish a trust for your child, Tom. If you wish to establish a trust for either of the other children, you will later be provided an opportunity to do so. First, however, another screen appears asking you to choose the age at which you desire the trust to terminate for child number 1.

```
¦                                          ¦
¦  ENTER AGE AT WHICH YOU WANT             ¦
L                                          
E  TOM JONES                               
G                                          V
I  TO RECEIVE THE PROPERTY IN TRUST        E
S                                          R
O  (PRESS RETURN TO ELIMINATE TRUST)       I
F                                          F
T                                          Y
/
N                                          O
O                                          N
L
O  23                                      ¦
                                           ¦
P                                          ¦
R                                          ¦
E                                          ¦
S                                          ¦
S                                          ¦
¦                                          ¦
```

If you type 23 and press "Return", this number will then appear on the list of children as shown in the following screen:

```
¦  YOUR CHILDREN :    IN TRUST TO AGE:     ¦
¦  1.TOM JONES                      ¦23    ¦
L  2.RUBEN JONES                    ¦XX    ¦
E  3.KAREN JONES                    ¦XX
G                                          V
I                                          E
S  TYPE NUM. OF NEXT CHILD YOU WANT TO     R
O  SET UP A TRUST FOR (1 AT A TIME).       I
F                                          F
T                                          Y
/
N                                          O
O                                          N
L
O  __                                      ¦
                                           ¦
P                                          ¦
R                                          ¦
E                                          ¦
S                                          ¦
S                                          ¦
¦  ------------------------------------50¦
                                           
   TYPE "Y" WHEN LIST IS OK
```

Now you can select the number of another child for whom you desire a trust and then select an age for that child. If you don't want any more trusts, simply press "Y" and you will proceed to the next part of the program.

Supposing you select a child for a trust and then change your mind. In that case, press ""Return"" when asked for the age.

Note: For information on selecting your trustee, See Part 7.B.3

e. Forgiving Debts

As mentioned, WillMaker gives you an opportunity to forgive debts owed to you at your death. You are first asked whether you want to forgive a debt. If you say yes, you are asked to describe the debtor and the debt. You should be reasonably specific when you describe the debt. WillMaker automatically forgives any interest owed on the debt. If you wish to forgive more than one debt, separate your description of the debtors and debts with a plus sign. For instance, if you wish to forgive two debts, it might appear as follows:

```
:             FORGIVE DEBT(S)              :
:                                          :
S   Enter the name(s) of one or more       :
E   persons you would like to release      :
E   from debt at your death, and           :
    DESCRIBE THE DEBT(s).                   :
M                                          :
A   Example: Hector Smith, $5,000          :
N   loaned on 3/27/85                      :
U                                          :
A                                          :
L                                          :
                                           :
P   Hector Smith, $5000, loan on 3/27/85 + :
A   Bessie Smith, $2500, loaned in April   :
R   of 1935._____
T   _____
    _____
1   _____
4   _____
:                                          :
:   ----------------------------------44:
:   TYPE REQUESTED INFO.& THEN "RETURN"   :
:   (F1=BACK  F2=QUIT  F3=DEF  F4=WHERE?)  :
```

8. Reviewing Your Will

After the question and answer portion of WillMaker is completed, you are presented with a screen that lists each portion of the program and asks you whether you care to go back and review any of your answers. If you do, you are told to type the number next to the portion to be reviewed.

Here is the screen (taken from the IBM program):

```
|        REVIEW/MODIFY YOUR WILL:              |
|                                             |
|     BASICS:   1.Name/Social Sec. #          |
S              2.State
E              3.County                       V
E              4.Married?                      E
               5.Spouse's Name                R
M              6.Facts about Children          I
A              7.Pay Debts and Taxes          F
N                                             Y
U  BEQUESTS:   8.Property
A              9.The Rest (Residuary)         O
L              10.Forgive Debts               N

P  NOMINATE:   11.Guardian                    |
A              12.Trustee                     |
R              13.Personal Representative     |
T                                             |
                                             |
1  Type number of any item you want to       |
0    review or change:__ & "Return"          |
   ------------------------------------66|
     PRESS "RETURN" TO GO TO NEXT SCREEN
         F2=QUIT F3=DEF
```

For some of these items, when you type the number, you are returned to the part indicated and are then provided an opportunity to review your answers, make desired changes, and come directly back to the review screen. For the following items, however, the review process works a little differently:

• Your state;

• Your marital status;

• Basic facts about your children; and

• Whether you desire to name a guardian for your minor children.

If you decide to make any changes in these items once you have reviewed your previous answer, a message is displayed warning you that you must come back through the rest of the program, reviewing your answers to later items and maybe being asked some new questions. If you decide to not make a change, you will be returned to the review screen.

Why does the program work this way in respect to these particular items? Simply put, changes in these items logically require you to reconsider previous answers and to consider new questions. For example, suppose you have your first child, and therefore decide to make a new will incorporating this fact. You will need to go back and change your answers to the questions about whether you have children and whether any such children are below 18 years of age. Because you did not have children before, WillMaker did not ask you to name them, did not request that you name a guardian, and did not offer you the option of creating a trust. Now, however, your answer requires that you name the child and that you reflect on the potential need for a guardian and a trust. Accordingly, WillMaker brings you up through the program so that these new items can now be presented for your consideration.

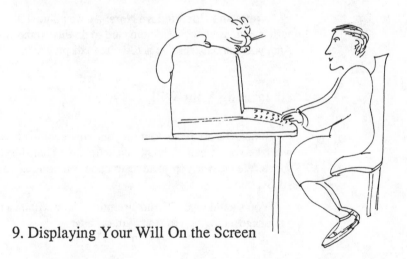

9. Displaying Your Will On the Screen

Either before or after you review specific items you may wish to see what your will looks like as it has been written up to that point. You can do this by taking the following steps:

• From the review screen, press "Return";

• Select the "S" option on the following screen:

```
:              CONGRATULATIONS                :
:                                             :
S             Your will is done!              :
E                                             :
E                                             V
    In order to:           Type:             E
M   -----------            -----             R
A  Print your will          "P"              I
N                              \             F
U  Quit                     "Q" \            Y
A                                  \
L  Review your will         "R"              O
                                   & "Return" N
P  Erase your will          "E"   /
A   and start over               /           :
R                               /            :
T  Display your will        "S"              :
      on screen                              :
1                                            :
4                                            :
:                                            :
:  -------------------_------------------56:
:                                             :
```

Apple and Commodore Note: As we pointed out in Section A earlier, you need an 80-column card to do this on the Apple II+ and IIe. And, you can only receive a 40-column display on the Commodore.

10. Printing Your Will

When you are ready to print your will, simply pressing "Return" will take you from the review screen to the screen shown in Section 9 above. We provide complete instructions on printing your will in Part 10, Section B.

You should type "P" and "Return". There will be a brief delay and a message telling you to ready your printer.

11. The WillMaker Program Screen by Screen

Now that we have covered the nuts and bolts of operating the WillMaker program, you may wish to look at the actual major screens that WillMaker uses. If so, turn to Section F. If you proceed directly to the program and become confused about a particular screen while using

WillMaker, you can locate it in that section by finding the number at the lower right corner of the program screen.

Note: Each screen of the WillMaker program is numbered. Since not every screen is reproduced, however, the screens you find in that section will often jump numbers (e.g., you will go from screen 20 to screen 24).

C. Apple II+, IIe, IIc, IIGS

1. Getting Started with WillMaker

To operate the WillMaker program you need:

• An Apple II+, IIe, IIc or IIGS

• At least 64K of RAM; and

• A monitor.

An 80 column card is needed (for the II+ and IIe) to view a completed will on the monitor. However, you can write and print a will without one.

After making a backup copy of your WillMaker floppy, take the following steps to get WillMaker up and running:

• Turn on the monitor;

• Insert the WillMaker floppy in the disk drive; and

• Turn on the computer.

The program will then begin operating (i.e., "boot up"). If the computer is already on and you are running either of the Apple operating systems (i.e., DOS or ProDOS)[2], as indicated by the appearance of the "]" symbol on the screen, you can avoid turning the

---

[2]DOS and ProDOS are trademarks of Apple Computer, Inc. WillMaker is a ProDOS program under license from Apple. You do not need to obtain ProDOS for your computer, however, as it is included on the WillMaker disk.

computer off and on again by typing "IN#6", followed by pressing the "Return" key. This and other ways to boot the disk are described in your Apple User's Manual.

You will first see an identification of the program for a brief time as the program is put into memory (i.e., "loads"). Then the program will offer you an introductory screen, which asks you to remove the floppy, turn it over, and reinsert it.

2. Is Something Wrong?

If you have trouble running the program, check the following:

• Do you have an older Apple II+ that does not have 64K RAM? If so you cannot run WillMaker without installing a memory card.

If the program crashes while you are using it, check the following:

• Is there a write-protect tab on the floppy? The WillMaker program writes data to the floppy and cannot be run with a write-protect tab. We recommend putting a write-protect tab on your original floppy, copying this master to a blank floppy, and then running from the copy that doesn't have a write-protect tab.

• Do you have a CPM card or other special card in a slot of your computer? Some exotic cards interfere with the printing. Try running without the card in place.

• Is your printer connected properly when you try to print? If there is a problem turn your printer off and on and try again.

Technical Note: Some problems may arise when printing on an Apple Imagewriter printer with an Apple II, especially a IIc. If you have such a system and experience printing problems, check the following points:

• First, if you have a IIc, check that the printer is connected through the printer port with a number "1" stamped next to it. The connector will fit in the modem port (picture of a telephone, and a number "2"), but WillMaker will not print through this port.

• Next, try setting your printer switches as follows:

SW1: all "open" except 5 and 6

SW2: all "open" except 1 and 2

• If the problem still is not cured, try this experiment:

1. Turn your printer on and be sure the "select" light is on;

2. Get the ProDOS BASIC system running (by interrupting WillMaker with "control-reset");

3. Type PR#1 ("Return");

4. Type the following, including the quotation marks:

PRINT "This is a test message." Press "Return".

5. If this produces nothing on your printer, then most likely your printer is connected in a non-standard way, or there is a problem in the connection between your computer and printer. If this test works, but WillMaker doesn't, then your WillMaker floppy is probably damaged.

Here is what the following error messages mean:

Error 8:I/O: Check your disk drive with other software.

Error 4: Remove write-protect tab.

Error 3: No device connected: The printer is not connected. Check the printer connection at both ends of the cable.

3. Additional Information About Running WillMaker on the Apple Computer

We now do something that will strike at least some Apple users as treason, pure and simple. That is, we ask you to turn to Sections B(5) through B(12) for further reading about how the WillMaker program works. Section B, you may recall, is the IBM section. What possible reason would we have for referring an Apple II user to such material? Simply, the Apple and IBM programs work in virtually identical ways, and the information contained in Sections B(5) through B(12) is therefore applicable to Apple as well as IBM computers. These sections discuss:

• Some specific tips on how to use the WillMaker program [B(5)];

• The general operational features of WillMaker [B(6)];

• How to use the WillMaker list facility [B(7)];

• How to leave property using WillMaker [B(8)];

• The ins and outs of keeping your will up to date [B(9)]; and

• How to display your will on the screen before printing it out [B(10)];

• A word about printing your will [B(11)]; and

• A referral to the section containing the WillMaker screens [B(12)].

Note: There are several minor differences between the two programs. The main one is that the IBM program uses special function keys to activate certain WillMaker features, whereas the Apple program uses letters and symbols from the keyboard to accomplish the same result. For instance, if you push the F2 function key on the IBM computer, the program will allow you to quit the program (assuming the "Quit" feature is operational at the time). This same result is accomplished on the Apple by pushing the "Q" key on the keyboard, followed by a "Return".

When the WillMaker features are discussed in Section B, the appropriate key for the Apple program immediately follows the function key reference and is enclosed in parentheses. Thus when we talk about the "Quit" feature, we tell you to press F2(Q). As long as you remember that the letter in parentheses is the Apple key (Q in this example), and that you must press "Return" after the letter in question in order to make the feature work, this IBM/Apple difference should present no difficulty for you at all.

Also, in Section B, we occasionally provide a special Apple user's note when we want you to be aware of something specifically pertaining to the Apple II+, IIe and IIc computers.

Turn now to Section B(5) to finish your reading about the WillMaker Apple program.

D. The Macintosh

As you undoubtedly know, there are many species of Macintosh computers—the Macintosh 128 and 512, the Mac Plus, the Macintosh SE, the Lisa, and the Mac II—as well as the Macintosh XL (it used to be a Lisa). Fortunately, WillMaker works on all of these (except the Mac 128) as long as you follow our instructions carefully. Throughout this portion of the manual we include special notes when you need to do something different for a particular Macintosh type.

1. Copying WillMaker

Before you actually use WillMaker, you should make a backup copy of the program floppy. If you do not have a disk copy program, here is how:

Turn the computer on and put WillMaker in a disk drive. Get to the desktop.

If you have one disk drive, eject the WillMaker disk and put in a blank disk.

If you have a second disk drive put a blank disk in the second drive.

• Initialize the empty disk (this will already have been done if you've previously used it for another purpose). If the disk has other files on it, it is recommended that you first erase them with the "Erase Disk" menu selection. Do this even though the copy procedure promises to replace everything on the new floppy.

• Then name it (e.g., WillMaker copy). Once named, the new floppy's icon will appear below the WillMaker icon in the right hand part of the screen.

• Now use your mouse to point at the WillMaker icon, press the key, drag that icon onto the icon for the empty disk (which now has a name), and release the button.

• You will then be asked whether you want to replace everything on the empty disk. Answer yes. The copying will occur and you will then have a backup disk. Using one disk drive, you will need to change disks several times as the machine copies and writes the various sectors of the program floppy. Remember to use the copy and save the original floppy as a backup

Hard Disk Note: If you want to copy the WillMaker floppy to your hard disk rather than make a separate floppy backup, follow our instructions for doing this in section 3 below.

2. Let's Get Started

First, we recommend that you reset your computer between your use of another application and your use of WillMaker. Unless you install WillMaker on a hard disk, you should also cold boot WillMaker from the floppy for the Mac Plus, the Mac SE and the Mac II, due to potential differences in the fonts installed on your machine and those contained on the WillMaker floppy. If you do want to install WillMaker on a hard disk, see Section 3 just below.

Insert the WillMaker floppy (or probably your copy) in the internal disk drive and turn on the computer. The program should then automatically begin operating (i.e., "boot up") without your having to "click" anything. If, however, you are presented with the disk contents, double click the icon on the screen that says WM. You will then be put into the WillMaker program. The first screen you see will welcome you to WillMaker.

Warning: Do not attempt to open up any of the other programs on the WillMaker disk when operating WillMaker. WillMaker is designed to be run sequentially and any attempt to open and run a program other than the one with the WM icon will result in a program crash.[3] Also, keep the individual program files in a single folder. If you do place the

---

[3]There is one exception. The file labelled FIX allows you to erase all data entered by you and start over. This same option is available to you in the "Goodies" menu when you are operating the main WillMaker program.

program files in separate folders, the program will not run if you have an HFS operating system.

3. Installing WillMaker on a Hard Disk

First, we strongly recommend that you work off a floppy (a separate floppy for each will) so that the data associated with each person's will can remain confidential and be separately stored in a safe place until updating is desired. However, for those users who want to install WillMaker on their Macintosh hard disk, here are instructions on how to do this. To follow these, you will need a good working knowledge of your Macintosh system, especially the font mover. If you are a novice, seriously consider getting some informed help before attempting this installation.

Step #1: Make a backup of your WillMaker floppy

Step #2: Boot the system without using the WillMaker floppy

Step #3: Insert the WillMaker floppy and open the system folder.

Step #4: Use your font mover (such as the DA font mover) to compare the fonts on your WillMaker floppy with those in your system. Copy to your system all fonts on the WillMaker floppy which are not in your system (e.g., Geneva 14).

Step #5: Return to the WillMaker system folder and delete it.

Warning: Remember to follow this step carefully. If you inadvertently copy the WillMaker system files to your hard disk, they may replace the system files already there. This in turn may have operating consequences for your particular computer.

Step #6: Make a new folder named WillMaker. Copy all remaining WillMaker files onto the hard disk in a single folder and **keep the files in that folder** (remember, the WillMaker system files should have been deleted and should not be copied to the hard disk). Then run WillMaker by clicking the WM Icon.

Note: If the file "WX" exists on your floppy (it is sometimes off on a part of the desktop that is not visible when you boot up), be sure to copy it too.

4. What To Do If You Run Into Trouble

If you have trouble running the program, check the following:

• Is your write-protect tab in the closed position? The WillMaker program writes data to the floppy and cannot be run with the write-protect tab closed.

Two Warnings: (1) When operating WillMaker, don't turn off the computer until you have returned to the desk top and the disk drive has stopped completely. There is an error handling procedure which will allow recovery from the file corruption this may cause, but you also will lose all data you have entered since the last time you saved (with either "Quit" or "Save and Resume" from the Goodies menu).

(2) Making a screen dump to the printer may cause a subsequently printed will to be printed with small closely spaced lines, because the mode of the printer has been set to a greater number of lines per inch. Turn the printer off and back on after making a screen dump and do a cold reboot of the program.

Here is what the following error messages mean:

• **Error 7 or 14: "out of memory":** Try booting WillMaker from scratch, i.e., turn the Mac off and then back on with WillMaker in the disk drive;

• **Error 57: "device input/output error":** Check the disk drive with other software. If it works, your WillMaker floppy is probably damaged;

• **Error 61: "disk full":** Remove any extraneous files that you have copied onto the WillMaker floppy by mistake;

• **Error 68: "device unavailable":** The printer is not securely connected. Check the printer connection at both ends of the cable.

• **Error 70:** Open write-protect mechanism;

• **Input past end:** This may arise from a corrupted floppy; the most likely cause is that the power was shut off (or the floppy rejected abnormally) while the disk drive was running. Discard this disk, make another copy from the WillMaker original, and start over.

5. Basic Outline of the Program

In Section A of this part, we provided you with an overall description of the WillMaker program for all computers. Here we give you a similar overview of the program, but intended solely for Mac users. Following this overview is a brief table of contents of the rest of this section.

As we mentioned, in its most basic manifestation, WillMaker is a series of messages and questions in the form of "screens" that are displayed on your monitor. These screens are of three basic types:

• Information Screens: These screens explain certain aspects of operating the WillMaker program, and a number of important legal concepts that you should consider when making your will. They appear throughout the program, but are especially concentrated in an introductory section. At the end of each information screen is a button labelled "continue." Either click on this button or press the return key to advance to the next screen.

• Question Screens: On some screens WillMaker asks you a question such as "Do you have any living children?" You will see two or more buttons on this type screen (e.g., "Yes", "No", "OK," "Change"). Simply click the appropriate one with the mouse.

• Entry Screens: On other screens WillMaker asks you to name a person, describe an item of property, and so on. Type in the name and accompanying information (such as an address). When you are satisfied that the information is correct, click the O.K. button or press "Return." Although you will be given a chance later to review all of your entries, at the end of the program, we suggest that you go slowly to get your answers right the first time through. To help you do this, WillMaker asks you to verify your answer to each question. This feature can be shut off if you find it too time-consuming. For editing instructions, see Section 10, below.

Now that you have some sense of how the WillMaker program works overall, it's time to turn to the details. The rest of this part contains the following information:

• General operational tips (Section 6);

• Goodies Menu—Useful Features (Section 7);

• Help Menu—Legal Definitions and Cautions (Section 8);

• Manual Reference for Each Screen (Section 9);

• Entering and Editing Information (Section 10);

• Making lists of names and property under WillMaker (Section 11);

• Leaving property under WillMaker (Section 12);

• How the WillMaker review (and update) process works (Section 13);

• Displaying Your Will On the Screen (Section 14);

• How to print your will (Section 15);

6. Some General Tips on Running WillMaker

Tip 1:   Using Macintosh Buttons

As a Macintosh user you are probably acquainted with the term button. These are little circles, squares, or rectangles that are used to give you options on a particular screen.

◯ Circles are generally used when you asked to pick one or more of a number of items. When you click the ◯ button of your choice a solid dot ◉ appears in the middle of it. If only one of the buttons can be "pressed", as when indicating your state, (e.g., California) clicking a second button (e.g., New York) will automatically "unpress" the first. This ensures that only one button is "on" at a time. Again, the one which is currently on is always indicated by a solid dot. However, if more than one of the buttons can be pressed (for instance when you are asked if you want to delete one or more children in a list of all of your children) clicking a button which is on will have the result of turning it off.

Rectangular buttons ⬭ on the other hand, refer to an operation or choice that will go into effect immediately after you click the button. Examples are the ⬭Continue⬭ button that sends you to the next screen, the ⬭Yes⬭ and ⬭No⬭ buttons that let you indicate your answer to a yes/no question, and the buttons labeled ⬭Add To List⬭ ⬭Review/Change⬭ ⬭Delete⬭ and ⬭OK⬭ that you click to indicate what to do when you are entering items in a list (e.g., the list of your children's names or the list of property bequests that you want to make). See Section 11 below.

Tip 2:   Click ⬭OK⬭ Or Use your "Return" Key Only
             After Your Entry is Completed

At different points WillMaker asks you to type some information in a rectangular box presented on the screen for this purpose. For example, you will be asked to name your spouse if you are married. You should click the OK button or press the "Return" key only after your *entire* entry is completed. This is important especially where the information you want to enter takes up more than one line (for instance, when you are describing bequests). You may be tempted to press the "Return" key at the end of one line in order to move the cursor to the following one. Please don't do this. Pressing the "Return" key terminates the particular entry being worked on (say a name and accompanying address) and signals the program that you are ready to go on to the next step. If you slipped up on this by pressing "Return" at the end of the line, just click the change button when you are asked to verify your entry. You will be returned for another try. If you have turned off your verify function use the goodies menu (this is described in detail in Section 7, below) to select "back up." You will then be returned to your prematurely terminated entry with the option to change it.

Tip 3:   Use WillMaker Manual Reference Feature To
             Locate Additional Information

In the top margin of each main WillMaker screen you will see a reference to the WillMaker Manual. This reference refers you to the part of the manual that is most relevant to the subject matter treated on the screen. For example, on the screens dealing with children, the reference is to Part 7 of the Manual, the part dealing with children. You will very likely find that the definitions and discussions accessed through the Help Menu (Described in Section 8 below) do not fully answer all your questions. If so, go to the indicated part of the manual for additional reading.

Tip 4:   Use + Character When Naming Multiple Beneficiaries

If you type in the names of two or more people to receive either a specific property bequest or the rest of your property as beneficiaries, you must use a + sign to separate the names. This tells the program that you are leaving the specific bequest (or residuary bequest) to two or more people. You will then be offered specific options as to who should receive the property if a beneficiary predeceases you. Also, the program will conform the language of your will accordingly. See Part 8, Section B of this manual. If you provide an address with the names, use the + sign to separate the last element of the address and the next name.

Example: Raphael J. Rabbit, 4507 Burrow Lane, Fudsville, Mo 55667+Ruby J. Hare, 4496 Turnip Rd., Carrotown, La 90876

Tip 5:   Distinguish the Letter "O" from the Number "0" and the Letter "1" from the Number "1"

Many users (even experienced ones) confuse the letter "O" with the number "0", and the letter "1" with the number "1". The result is that information entered is not what is intended. When using WillMaker, please keep these commonly-blurred distinctions in mind.

Tip 6:   Understanding Truncated Screen Displays

When requesting you to make lists (e.g., list your children), WillMaker displays each list entry you have made and gives you the option of either changing it, adding new entries, or going on to the next screen. Due to space limitations, only the first part of the entry is displayed.

 GOODIES   HELP   /WillMaker/Nolo/©1985 Legisoft/   See Manual § 9

BENEFICIARY/BEQUEST...SHORTENED FOR DISPLAY
John Rabbit Hareb../My Mint U.S. Stam..

Don't think that WillMaker has lost part of your entry. The full entry is stored and will be printed out at the appropriate time.

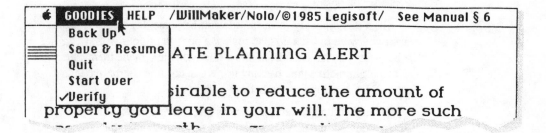

At the top of the WillMaker screen you will see the word "GOODIES". Use the mouse to point on this word, press the button, and hold the button down. You will then see the GOODIES menu, which contains a number of features such as "Back Up," "Save/Resume," "Quit," and "Start Over," which you will find useful while operating WillMaker. These features are almost always operational, but occasionally they are not, simply because they are not appropriate to the context of the particular screen. You can tell when a feature can't be used because the word describing it in the menu will be "dimmed"— that is, written very lightly. To select a given feature, hold the mouse button down until the arrow points to the feature and then release it. Here is a brief description of each feature in the GOODIES menu.

Back Up:

This feature will take you to the previous section of the program. Often, this will be the previous screen but not always. In two instances two or three screens are lumped together into a section. These are specific property bequests and the instructions near the beginning of the program. Although you can use this facility while in the middle of making an entry on the current screen, it is usually more efficient to finish making your entry and click the OK button before asking to back up.

The backup feature is usually but not always operational. For example, once you begin the sequence of naming beneficiaries of specific property bequests and describing the property you wish to leave to them, you cannot back up until you complete the process for that bequest. Then, if you back up, you will be returned to the beginning of that sequence, where you can back up to still earlier screens if you desire.

All of this probably seems a little cumbersome. Fortunately, if the reason you want to back up is to review a portion of your work (e.g., the bequests you have made, and to whom you have made them), there is a better alternative than backing up. We detail this alternative in Section 11 ("Making Lists"), below.

Note: If you make certain changes after having backed up, you may encounter some new information or questions which have now become appropriate because of your changes. For example, if you originally said you had no spouse, but later back up to that section and change your answer to the affirmative, you will then encounter some new screens dealing with leaving property to spouses. See Section 13, below.

Save & Resume:

This option simply writes the information you have already entered onto your WillMaker floppy. It is good practice to perform this operation from time to time while you are using the program in case you are worried about loss of data due to a power failure, a glitch in the Macintosh operating system (called "system error"), or even a problem with WillMaker itself (perish the thought).

Quit:

If you want to leave the program for awhile, simply click on the "quit" feature. This will save all your work to the floppy, just as with Save and Resume, but this time the program will terminate, leaving you free to run another program or turn off the computer. When you reboot the program, you will return to where you left off.

Caution:

Make sure that the screen has returned to the desktop and the disk drive has completely stopped before you turn off the computer. Otherwise you may lose data that has been input but not yet been saved. See Section A above.

Start Over:

You may decide that you want to start the program over from scratch. Clicking this item will let you do this. The current WillMaker screen disappears and you are asked if you want to erase everything and start over, "quit," or cancel the "start over" request and resume the WillMaker program. If you click the "erase all" option, you are then asked if you are sure you want to do this. If you do click "erase all" a second time, all the work you have completed will be erased. As we discuss later in Section 13, below, it is possible to go back and correct any previous information without erasing your entire input.

Verify:

The verification feature shows your response to the previous input screen and asks you if it is OK or whether you want to change it. This is particularly useful when you use the "semi-colon" feature (Tip 4, above) because it allows you to see your entry displayed on the screen just as it will be printed in your will.

You may eventually find the verification feature tiresome, however, and for that reason we provide you with the option of turning it off by clicking this menu entry. When you do, the check mark will disappear for future screens in your current session. This means that the verification feature is inoperative. If you click it again, the check mark will appear and the feature will be on again for all future screens. If you quit while the verify feature is turned off and later return to the program, the verify feature will be turned on again by default.

Now that we have told you how to turn the feature off, here's some heartfelt advice. Leave it on in the interests of accuracy. The few extra minutes it will take you to complete the program will more than be outweighed by the certainty that your will accurately reflects your desires.

8. The Help Menu

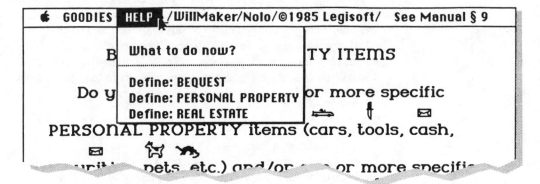

At the top of your screen you will see the word "help". By using the mouse to point on the word and drag downwards, the help menu will be exposed. You can select the desired item by releasing the button when the arrow rests on it. The help menu is divided into two parts by a dotted line. The part above the dotted line contains two items:

Help with the current screen:

These are help screens that generally describe what is happening with the current screen and what you are expected to do.

The portion below the dotted line contains definitions and cautionary advice regarding legal terms that appear in capital letters (e.g., PROPERTY) on the screen. Occasionally, terms are defined that don't appear on the screen but which are conceptually related to the material on the screen. If you desire to use "help" on more than one item, it is necessary to click the "continue" button on the current help screen, return to the original screen and then select another item from the "help" menu.

9. The Manual Reference

In the top-right margin of each screen, you are provided with a reference to the WillMaker manual part that is most relevant to the subject being covered on that screen. (See Tip 3 above.)

Note: If you click on the term "Manual," you will see the current screen number. This can be useful if you desire to communicate with Nolo about any particular screen.

10. Entering And Editing Information

Here are some pointers on entering names, descriptions of bequests, or other information, and editing your input with the Mac.

• Type in the information requested, the same as you would with a typewriter. But, unlike a typewriter, which requires you to manually press the "Return" key at the end of each line, the computer takes care of line returns without your intervention (Tip 1, above). In other words, just keep typing until you're done. Then press "Return."

• Provide only the information requested. Thus, when you are asked to name your children, don't use that space for other persons. When you are asked to name a beneficiary to receive a specific bequest, simply name the beneficiary (and provide an address, if known). Don't add additional phrases (such as, "but only if he continues his marriage with my friend Sue," or "but only if she sells her 1959 Volkswagen").

• If you are known by two names, enter both, separated by an AKA (also known as), e.g., Joan Willis AKA Joan Kleinfeldt.

• Keep your entry within the number of spaces provided for it. Each entry screen displays the number of allowable characters in the lower right hand corner. As you type a character, this number decreases by one, allowing you to keep numerical track of your entry. If you exceed the number of characters, you will receive a beep for each extra character and the extras will not be saved by the computer or printed out in your will. If you don't have enough room on a screen to complete a bequest, see Section 12(d) below for how to use two or more screens for the same overall bequest.

There are three primary methods of editing when you are entering information for the first time.

1) Use the backspace key to erase all text to the left. If you have little text, it is usually quicker to simply erase what you have and start over.

2) Use the mouse to point and click at the exact location where you want to insert text. Then, when you start typing, your new text will be inserted where the arrow is pointing.

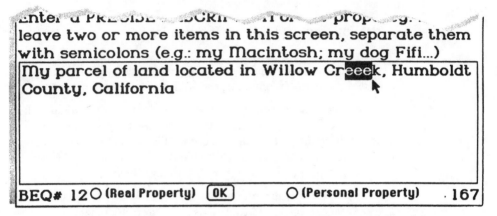

Enter a PRECISE description of the property. To leave two or more items in this screen, separate them with semicolons (e.g.: my Macintosh; my dog Fifi...)

My parcel of land located in Willow Creeek, Humboldt County, California

BEQ# 12 ○ (Real Property) [OK]   ○ (Personal Property)   . 167

3) Select a portion of the text by "clicking and dragging" with the mouse. This involves pointing the arrow at the beginning of the text to be selected, pushing the mouse button, moving the arrow (while keeping the button depressed) across the text to be selected, and then releasing the button when you've come to the end of the text to be selected. The selected portion will be portrayed in reversed video (white on black). You can then delete this selected portion by pressing backspace, or by typing whatever you want to replace the highlighted text. Anything you now type will be inserted.

You cannot use the Macintosh cut and paste features with this program. Sorry.

• Changing text when reviewing it from the verification prompt or review screen:

When you seek to change a previous entry, (e.g., the name "Hortense Jones") either because you are responding to a verification prompt or because you have travelled there from the final review screen, you will be presented with your former entry in reverse video ("Hortense Jones" in reverse). In this situation, you have two options.

1) If you type any character, the entire entry will disappear and be replaced with the character and any succeeding characters you type.

2) You can use the mouse to point and click at the place in the entry where you want to insert or delete text. Then, when you start to

type, the text will be inserted to the right of where you are typing. Use the backspace key to delete characters to the left of the cursor. This presents essentially the same options as does the regular editing feature, except that the text has been preselected.

There is an "undo" feature that operates when you are making these types of changes. Suppose you make the prior entry disappear by beginning to type a new entry. Then you decide you want to modify the previous entry instead. By clicking the "undo" button at the bottom of the screen, the previous entry will reappear.[4]

11. Making Lists of Names and Property Under WillMaker

At different places in the program, WillMaker asks you to list:

• Your children;

• Any children of a deceased child; and

• Specific bequests of property to individuals or institutions.

Anticipating that you will want to be kept abreast of what you have already put in the list, and to have an opportunity to make deletions or corrections, WillMaker provides you with these options. For example, assuming you affirmatively answer WillMaker's question as to whether you have any children, you then see a screen that asks you to enter the name of the first child (the actual order doesn't matter—just that you get them all in). After entering each name, and verifying your entry if you have kept the verify feature on, you will see a summary list of all children entered, including the most recent. If the name is too long for the space on the screen, it is shortened (truncated) for display purposes only. Don't worry, the name is still stored in full in the computer's memory and will be properly printed out when you actually print your will.

Now let's examine the major list-making options offered by WillMaker. First consider the following screen:

---

[4]The "undo" option only works on actions which have been taken since the last time you clicked the mouse.

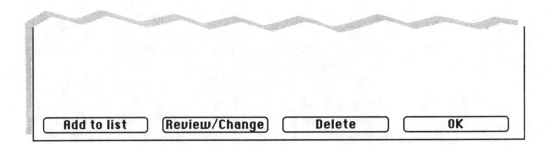

| Add to list | Review/Change | Delete | OK |

1. Click "Add to List" to add more names to the list

If you wish to add another name (or bequest) to the list, click the add button at the bottom of the screen. You have a maximum of 16 entries in any WillMaker list (i.e., 16 bequests, 16 beneficiaries [or groups of beneficiaries], 16 children, and 16 children of a deceased child).

2. Click "Review/Change" to review any previous entries in this list

If you wish to review (or change) one of your previous entries on the list, click the Review/Change button at the bottom of the screen. This is a way to see each entry in full, and is particularly useful for the list of bequests, where only limited information (the first 16 characters of the name of the beneficiary and of the description of the bequest) appears in the summary list. For example, consider the following summary screen. You intended to leave your 1937 Leica camera to your nephew Robert F. Johnson of 1172 Peacock Rd. All you can see on this screen, however, is:

 GOODIES HELP   / WillMaker/Nolo/©1985 Legisoft/   See Manual § 9

BENEFICIARY/BEQUEST...SHORTENED FOR DISPLAY
Robert F. Johnson /My 1932 Leica cam..

| Add to list | Review/Change | Delete | OK |

By clicking on the "review/change" button and then selecting the bequest that was made to Robert, you can go back to see whether you properly described Robert's name and address and the camera you wish to leave to him.

In other words, this option allows you to see what property you have described in any particular bequest or the full name of the person (or alternate) to whom you have left property. If there is only one entry on the list, the program goes directly to a screen that contains the full entry and asks you if the entry is okay, or whether you want to change it. If there is more than one entry, you are asked to select the one you want to review or change by clicking the button located next to it.

Note: As we mentioned in our earlier discussion on backing up, when you want to check and perhaps change an entry in a list, you cannot use the BACKUP feature. However, the review facility described here is just as effective. Thus, if in the middle of leaving specific bequests you decide you want to see what you've already left, simply advance until you reach the screen providing the Review/Change option and then select the appropriate entry for review.

3. Click "Delete" to delete one or more entries in this list

The "Delete" option works much the same as "Review/Change," only the entire entry is eliminated. To take advantage of it, simply click the Delete button at the bottom of the screen.

4. Click "OK" to indicate you are satisfied with the list as it stands, and are ready to go to the next part of the program

To leave the list sequence and advance to a new section of the program, click the OK button at the bottom of the screen. This is what you choose when you are either satisfied with the list as it stands or you plan on coming back to it later. If you don't return to make changes, WillMaker will consider the list complete and print all of the information contained in it.

Again, to select any of the options just discussed, simply click the appropriate button at the bottom of the screen.

12. Leaving Property Under WillMaker

a. Overview

The heart of the WillMaker program is the flexibility it provides users in what happens to their property when they die. Under WillMaker you can:

• Make up to 16 specific bequests (or groups of bequests) of personal property or real estate;

• Choose among several alternatives if the primary beneficiaries for these bequests fail to survive you by 45 days;

• Leave the rest of your property (your Residuary Estate) to one or more persons or institutions of your choice;

• Choose among several alternatives if the primary beneficiaries of your residuary estate fail to survive you by 45 days;

• Forgive debts owed to you at your death;

• Establish a trust for property left to one or more of your children; and

• Choose which assets will be used by your personal representative to pay your debts, probate expenses and taxes.

Each of these options is fully explained in other parts of the manual [Parts 9 (What You Can and Cannot Do With WillMaker), 8 (What to Do If Your Will Is Out of Date When You Die) and 7 (Special Considerations for Children)]. Here we wish to discuss several points you should keep firmly in mind when leaving property under WillMaker.

In respect to the first type of property disposition (specific bequests), the introductory screens tell you not to make conditional bequests and not to mix personal and real property in a single bequest. These rules are very important. This is why.

b. No Conditional Bequests

Suppose you make a specific bequest of your 1984 Mercedes 480SL to Mike and then add the condition "but only if he continues to live in Marin County." When your will's provisions are carried out by your personal representative, Mike will receive the Mercedes. However, what type of ownership will Mike have? And, what happens if he moves out of Marin County? Who will enforce this provision? In other words, the more conditions you attach to bequests, the more these types of questions multiply. To prevent such ambiguities from arising after you die, you should do the following:

• When you are asked to name the beneficiary or beneficiaries of particular items of property, simply type out their names (and addresses if you desire although we generally recommend against it due to the increased need for updating when they change).

• When you are asked to specify the property you wish to leave to beneficiaries you have named earlier, simply describe the property without attaching any conditional statements.

If you follow these two simple rules, you will avoid creating ambiguities that may come back to haunt your intended beneficiaries.

These same principles apply when you type out the names of beneficiaries to receive your residuary estate. That is, when you type the names, don't add conditions.

c. No Mixing of Real and Personal Property

When you are asked to describe the property you wish to include in specific bequests, WillMaker allows you to identify as many items as the space for inputting allows. At the bottom of the screen you are requested to click either the real estate button or the personal property button. The reason for this choice is that the clauses in your will implementing these items differ somewhat, depending on which category the bequest falls into.

If you have included some real property (say your home) and some personal property (say a car) in a single bequest, you will be unable to make a clear-cut selection as to which type of property is involved. Whichever option you choose (personal property or real property), the language in the will will be wrong. To avoid this problem, use separate bequest screens for your real property and your personal property.

d.   Using More Than One Bequest Screen for the Same Beneficiary

If you run out of room on a screen while making a bequest of personal or real property, you may, as a practical matter, continue the bequest on the next screen. To do this, take the following steps:

1. Complete your description of the property items being left on your current screen. That is, don't attempt to carry over descriptions of any particular item to the next screen. Also, don't leave incomplete sentences on the screen where you ran out of room. Backspace and erase the incomplete sentence.

2. Complete the following three screens that follow that bequest screen (i.e., what type of property is being left, what happens to the bequest if the beneficiary fails to survive you by 45 days, and the naming of the alternate beneficiary).

3. Choose the "add to list" option when you come to the bequest review screen.

4. When you come to the screen for naming the beneficiary, enter the beneficiary's name exactly as it was entered on the previous bequest screen.

5 Continue specifying the items you wish to go to the beneficiary. If you again run out of room, proceed as we have explained in these instructions.

6. Do not mix personal and real property in your "single" bequest, and don't impose conditions on the gifts.

7. You may use as many of the sixteen bequest screens for a single bequest of personal or real property as you need.

When your will prints out, this "single" bequest will appear as separate bequests. However, these separate bequests will have exactly the same effect as if you had combined them in a "single" bequest.

e. Creating a Trust with WillMaker

If later in the program you decide to create a trust for one or more of your children, here is what happens. You are first presented with a numbered list of your children and asked to click next to a child for whom you wish to establish a trust. For instance, if you have three children, the list will appear as follows:

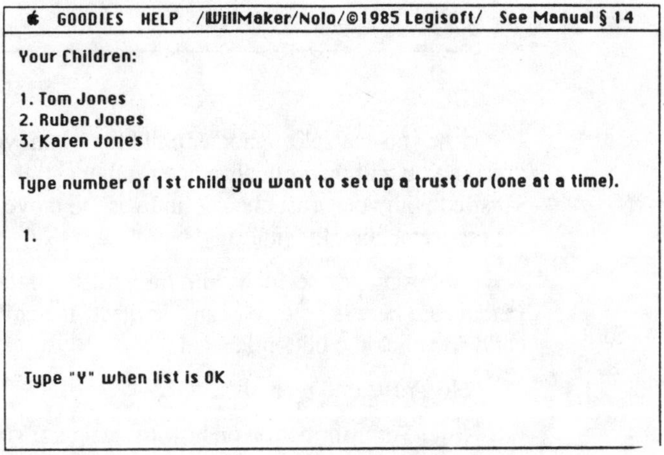

```
 GOODIES   HELP   /WillMaker/Nolo/©1985 Legisoft/   See Manual § 14

Your Children:

1. Tom Jones
2. Ruben Jones
3. Karen Jones

Type number of 1st child you want to set up a trust for (one at a time).

1.




Type "Y" when list is OK
```

If you click next to Tom Jones, for instance, you have indicated your desire to establish a trust for that child. If you wish to establish a trust for either or both of the other children (Phil Jones or Rubin Jones), you will later be provided an opportunity to do so. First, however, another screen appears displaying a button for each of the permitted ages (18 through 30). Click the desired button and then click OK. The chosen age will then appear opposite Tom Jones, as shown in the following screen:

```
 ⬧  GOODIES  HELP  /WillMaker/Nolo/©1985 Legisoft/  See Manual § 14

Your Children:                              In trust to age:

1. Tom Jones                                     23
2. Ruben Jones                                   ХХ
3. Karen Jones                                   ХХ

Type number of 1st child you want to set up a trust for (one at a time).


1.




Type "Y" when list is OK
```

Now you can select another child for whom you desire a trust. If you do, you will then select an age for that child. When you are satisfied with your trust choices and wish to move to the next part of the program, click the indicated button to "OK."

Supposing you select a child for a trust and then change your mind. In that case here is how you can "deselect" the child. Simply select that child and click the button labeled

"No Trust" and then click "OK".

Note: For information on how to select a trustee, see Part 7.B.3 of the Manual

f. Forgiving Debts

As mentioned, WillMaker gives you an opportunity to forgive debts owed to you at your death. You are first asked whether you want to forgive a debt. If you say yes, you are asked to describe the debtor and the debt. You should be reasonably specific when you describe the debt. When you forgive a debt, WillMaker automatically forgives any interest owed on the debt. If you wish to forgive more than one debt, separate your description of the debtor and debt with a plus sign. For instance, if you wish to forgive two debts, it might appear as follows:

```
 GOODIES  HELP   /WillMaker/Nolo/©1985 Legisoft/   See Manual § 14

                        Forgive Debt(s)

    Enter the name(s) of one or more persons you would like to release
    from debt at your death, and DESCRIBE THE DEBT(S).

    Example: Hector Smith, $5,000 loaned on 3/27/85

    Hector Smith, $5000, loan on 3/27/85 + Bessie Smith, $2500, loaned
    in April of 1935.



                 Type requested info. and then "Return"
```

13. Reviewing Your Will

In our discussion in Part 12(B) of this manual on updating your will, we briefly described how you can review and change portions of your will after you have completed the program. Here we cover this subject in more detail.

After the question and answer portion of WillMaker is completed, you are presented with a screen that lists in boldface each portion of the program that is relevant to your situation as indicated by your previous answers. By clicking a button located next to any one of these items you can to go back and review your answer. Here is a sample of that screen:

```
 GOODIES  HELP   /WillMaker/Nolo/©1985 Legisoft/   See Manual § 14
                        Review/Modify Your Will:
          Basics:    1. Name/Social Sec. Number
                     2. State
                     3. County
                     4. Married?
                     5. Spouse's name
                     6. Facts about Children

        Bequests:    7. Property
                     8. The rest (residuary)
                     9. Forgive debts

        Nominate:  10. Guardian
                   11. Trust
                   12. Personal representative
    Type number of any item you want to review or change and "Return"
              Press "Return" to go to next screen
```

For most of these items, you return directly to the review screen after you have made any desired changes. However, for a few items, the review process works a little differently. When you desire to review your entries for

- your state,

- your marital status, or

- basic facts about your children

you will go directly to these items the same as with the other items. But if you decide to make changes, you will be shown the following message:

```
If you make this change you must

then review the rest of your will.

    OK              CANCEL
```

This means that once you make a change in one of these items, you do not return directly to the review screen, but instead must proceed through the rest of the program (reviewing your previous answers and encountering new questions) until you reach the review screen again.

Why does the program work this way in respect to these particular items? Because changes in these items logically require you to reconsider your previous answers and to consider questions you did not answer before. For example, suppose the birth of your first child causes you to decide to make a new will incorporating this fact. To provide for your child properly, you will need to go back and change your answers to the questions about whether you have children and whether any such children are below 18 years of age. Because you indicated that you did not have children when you made your first will, WillMaker did not ask you to name them and did not request that you name a guardian. Now, however, your answer requires that you not only name the child, but that you reflect on the potential need for a guardian. Accordingly, WillMaker brings you up through the program so that these new items can now be presented for your consideration.

14. Displaying Your Will On the Screen

You may have noticed on the review screen set out above that you are also provided the option to display your will on the screen or print your will. Either before or after you review specific items, you may wish to see what your will looks like as it has been written up to that point. By clicking next to the display option you will see your will displayed a screen at a time.

At the end of each screen you may continue by clicking the "Continue" button or pressing return. In addition, there is a Special Menu that lets you "QUIT" (terminate the program) or cancel (return to the review screen). Once you complete this display, you are automatically returned to the review screen where you can review and change specific items, display your will again, or this time choose to print it.

15. Printing Your Will

Now that you have finished reviewing and changing your entries, and reviewing your will on the screen, you will want to print it. By clicking the "Print your Will" button, you will proceed to a screen with four separate options on it. We explain how to print out your will in Part 10, Section B.

E. The WillMaker Program Screen by Screen

Now that we have covered the nuts and bolts of operating the WillMaker program, you may wish to look at the actual major screens that WillMaker uses, along with brief explanatory comments. We show the IBM/Apple screens in this section. While the Macintosh screens differ in appearance, their content is substantially the same. Many of you may wish to skip this section for now and proceed directly to the program. If any of you become somewhat confused about a particular screen while using WillMaker, you can locate the numbered screen in that section by looking at the number at the lower right corner of the program screen.

Note: Each screen of the WillMaker program is numbered. Since we do not reproduce every screen, however, but only the major ones, the screens you find in that section will often jump numbers (e.g., you will go from screen 20 to screen 24).

```
[*******************************************]
[                                           ]
[   ...........................             ]
[   .                             .         ]
[   .      \ / |\|                 .        ]
[   .      \/\/ILL | |AKER          .       ]
[   .                             .         ]
[   ...........................             ]
[                                           ]
[   PUBLISHED BY: NOLO PRESS                ]
[                                           ]
[        950 PARKER STREET                  ]
[                                           ]
[        BERKELEY, CA  94710                ]
[                                           ]
[                                           ]
[   (C) Copyright 1985 by LEGISOFT INC.     ]
[                                           ]
[   > LOADING PROGRAM...PLEASE WAIT <       ]
[                                           ]
[                                           ]
[*******************************************]
```

```
!          Welcome to WILLMAKER           !
!                                         !
S   ...a program to help you write a      !
E   simple but effective will.            !
E                                         !
    USING WILLMAKER YOU CAN:              !
M                                         !
A   > give property to your spouse,       !
N     children, domestic partner, to      !
U     charity, or to anyone else          !
A                                         !
L   > set up a trust for your children    !
                                          !
P                                         !
A       AND YOU CAN NAME:                 !
T                                         !
    > a guardian for minor children       !
9                                         !
    > a personal representative           !
      (executor)                          !
!-----------------------------------------1!
!   PRESS "RETURN" TO GO TO NEXT SCREEN   !
```

```
!     WILLMAKER UPDATE SERVICE            !
!                                         !
    To be notified about new legal and    !
L                                         !
E   software developments related to      !
G                                         !
I   WILLMAKER, please register with       !
S                                         !
O   Nolo Press by mailing in the card     !
F                                         !
T   located at the back of the manual.    !
/                                         !
N                                         !
O       For more information write to:    !
L                                         !
O           NOLO PRESS                    !
                                          !
P           950 PARKER STREET             !
R                                         !
E           BERKELEY, CA  94710           !
S                                         !
S-----------------------------------------2!
!   PRESS "RETURN" TO GO TO NEXT SCREEN   !
!        <F1=BACK UP    F2=QUIT>          !
```

```
!        THE WILLMAKER MANUAL             !
!                                         !
S   The manual for this program has       !
E   important explanatory and cautionary  !
E   information, plus material on:         !
                                          !
M       > Who can make a will             !
A       > What wills do                   !
N       > Estate planning                 !
U       > Legal definitions              !
A       > How to use the program          !
L                                         !
    In the left margin of every screen    !
P   is a reference to the manual.         !
A                                         !
R                                         !
T                                         !
    TO UNDERSTAND YOUR WILL               !
4                                         !
    YOU MUST READ THE MANUAL!             !
!-----------------------------------------3!
!   PRESS "RETURN" TO GO TO NEXT SCREEN   !
!        <F1=BACK UP    F2=QUIT>          !
```

```
!       ESTATE PLANNING ALERT             !
!                                         !
S                                         !
E   To avoid high probate fees and        !
E                                         !
    estate taxes, it is often desirable   !
M                                         !
A   to reduce the amount of property      !
N                                         !
U   you leave in your will.               !
A                                         !
L   There are several estate planning     !
                                          !
P   techniques, discussed in Part 6 of    !
A                                         !
R   the manual, which may be used along   !
T                                         !
6   with your will to accomplish this.    !
                                          !
!                                         !
!-----------------------------------------4!
!   PRESS "RETURN" TO GO TO NEXT SCREEN   !
!        <F1=BACK UP    F2=QUIT>          !
```

```
!       APPLICABILITY OF THE WILL         !
!                                         !
S   This program is appropriate for       !
E                                         !
E   most American citizens and permanent  !
                                          !
M   residents over 18 who want to write   !
A                                         !
N   a basic will.                         !
U                                         !
A   If your estate is large or your       !
L                                         !
    requirements complex, it is wise to   !
P                                         !
A   design a personalized estate plan     !
R                                         !
T   with an expert's help. Even so,       !
                                          !
2   WILLMAKER will serve in the interim.  !
                                          !
!                                         !
!-----------------------------------------5!
!   PRESS "RETURN" TO GO TO NEXT SCREEN   !
!        <F1=BACK UP    F2=QUIT>          !
```

```
┌─────────────────────────────────────┐  ┌─────────────────────────────────────┐
│ ¦          INSTRUCTIONS?          ¦  │  │ ¦       HOW TO ENTER INFORMATION   ¦  │
│ ¦                                 ¦  │  │ ¦                                 ¦  │
│ S                                    │  │ S (1) To answer a yes/no question,   │
│ E                                    │  │ E     type "Y" or "N"...& "Return"   │
│ E   The next several screens contain │  │ E                                    │
│                                      │  │    (2) To enter information such as a│
│ M important instructions on how to use│  │ M     name type it...& "Return"      │
│ A                                    │  │ A                                    │
│ N the WILLMAKER program.             │  │ N (3) When entering information,     │
│ U                                    │  │ U     continue typing until your entry│
│ A                                    │  │ A     is complete. DO NOT press      │
│ L     Do you want to see these?      │  │ L     "Return" at the end of each line│
│                                      │  │       on the screen.                 │
│ P   Type "Y" for Yes or "N" for No:  │  │ P                                    │
│ A                                    │  │ A (4) Do not worry if you see a word br│
│ R                 ...and then "Return"│  │ R     oken at the end of a line.  It │
│ T                                    │  │ T     will be printed correctly.     │
│                                      │  │                                      │
│ 1                                    │  │ 1 ...Reminder: Always press "Return" │
│ 4                                    │  │ 4                after making an entry.│
│                                      │  │                                      │
│ ¦-------------------------------6¦   │  │ ¦-------------------------------7¦   │
│ ¦  TYPE "Y" OR "N"--AND THEN "RETURN"¦│  │ ¦ PRESS "RETURN" TO GO TO NEXT SCREEN¦│
│ ¦      <F1=BACK UP   F2=QUIT>       ¦ │  │ ¦      <F1=BACK UP    F2=QUIT>     ¦ │
└─────────────────────────────────────┘  └─────────────────────────────────────┘

┌─────────────────────────────────────┐  ┌─────────────────────────────────────┐
│ ¦     DEFINITIONS OF LEGAL WORDS   ¦  │  │ ¦         PROGRAM FEATURES         ¦  │
│ ¦                                 ¦  │  │ ¦                                 ¦  │
│ S  You may obtain definitions of legal│  │ S  There are three more ways to depart│
│ E                                    │  │ E  from the normal program sequence: │
│ E terms displayed on the screen like │  │ E                                    │
│                                      │  │   > Press F1 to back up...all entries│
│ M this: BEQUEST or PROPERTY.  To do so,│  │ M       will be remembered.          │
│ A                                    │  │ A                                    │
│ N press the "F3" key (or type "?").  │  │ N > Press F2 to store your work on the│
│ U                                    │  │ U       disk and quit.               │
│ A This will cause all terms for which │  │ A                                    │
│ L                                    │  │ L > Press F4 to see where you are on a│
│   definitions are available to be    │  │        map of the entire program.    │
│ P                                    │  │ P                                    │
│ A highlighted and numbered.          │  │ A   These features are available when│
│ R                                    │  │ R the corresponding symbols (F1, etc.)│
│ T   Next type the number of the term │  │ T appear in the bottom margin.       │
│                                      │  │                                      │
│ 1 you want defined and press "Return."│  │ 1 --> To turn the "verify" feature off│
│ 4                                    │  │ 4 (or back on) press F5.             │
│                                      │  │                                      │
│ ¦-------------------------------8¦   │  │ ¦-------------------------------9¦   │
│ ¦   PRESS "F3" TO TRY DEFINITIONS  ¦  │  │ ¦ PRESS "RETURN" TO GO TO NEXT SCREEN¦│
│ ¦                                 ¦   │  │ ¦      <F1=BACK UP    F2=QUIT>     ¦ │
└─────────────────────────────────────┘  └─────────────────────────────────────┘

┌─────────────────────────────────────┐  ┌─────────────────────────────────────┐
│ ¦       USE OF ; IN ADDRESSES      ¦  │  │ ¦      READY TO MAKE YOUR WILL     ¦  │
│ ¦                                 ¦  │  │ ¦                                 ¦  │
│ S   You need not provide addresses in│  │ S                                    │
│ E your will.  However, for people who│  │ E                                    │
│ E may be hard to locate, it may be a │  │ E  You are now ready to enter the    │
│   good idea.                         │  │                                      │
│ M   If you do, separate each item    │  │ M information needed to make your will.│
│ A with a semicolon, as follows:      │  │ A                                    │
│ N                                    │  │ N                                    │
│ U                                    │  │ U                                    │
│ A JOHN SMITH;123 FIRST ST.;TROY, N.Y.│  │ A                                    │
│ L                                    │  │ L                                    │
│   The name will be printed as:       │  │    Relax, take your time, and enjoy  │
│ P                                    │  │ P                                    │
│ A          JOHN SMITH                │  │ A            the experience...       │
│ R          123 FIRST ST.             │  │ R                                    │
│ T          TROY, N.Y.                │  │ T                                    │
│                                      │  │                                      │
│ 1                                    │  │ 1     Press "Return" to go on.       │
│ 4                                    │  │ 4                                    │
│                                      │  │                                      │
│ ¦------------------------------10¦   │  │ ¦------------------------------11¦   │
│ ¦ PRESS "RETURN" TO GO TO NEXT SCREEN¦│  │ ¦ PRESS "RETURN" TO GO TO NEXT SCREEN¦│
│ ¦      <F1=BACK UP    F2=QUIT>     ¦ │  │ ¦      <F1=BACK UP    F2=QUIT>     ¦ │
└─────────────────────────────────────┘  └─────────────────────────────────────┘
```

Screen 6 — INSTRUCTIONS? (SEE MANUAL PART 14)

The next several screens contain important instructions on how to use the WILLMAKER program.

Do you want to see these?

Type "Y" for Yes or "N" for No:

...and then "Return"

TYPE "Y" OR "N"--AND THEN "RETURN"
<F1=BACK UP   F2=QUIT>

Screen 7 — HOW TO ENTER INFORMATION (SEE MANUAL PART 14)

(1) To answer a yes/no question, type "Y" or "N"...& "Return"

(2) To enter information such as a name type it...& "Return"

(3) When entering information, continue typing until your entry is complete. DO NOT press "Return" at the end of each line on the screen.

(4) Do not worry if you see a word broken at the end of a line. It will be printed correctly.

...Reminder: Always press "Return" after making an entry.

PRESS "RETURN" TO GO TO NEXT SCREEN
<F1=BACK UP   F2=QUIT>

Screen 8 — DEFINITIONS OF LEGAL WORDS (SEE MANUAL PART 14)

You may obtain definitions of legal terms displayed on the screen like this: BEQUEST or PROPERTY. To do so, press the "F3" key (or type "?"). This will cause all terms for which definitions are available to be highlighted and numbered.

Next type the number of the term you want defined and press "Return."

PRESS "F3" TO TRY DEFINITIONS

Screen 9 — PROGRAM FEATURES (SEE MANUAL PART 14)

There are three more ways to depart from the normal program sequence:

> Press F1 to back up...all entries will be remembered.

> Press F2 to store your work on the disk and quit.

> Press F4 to see where you are on a map of the entire program.

These features are available when the corresponding symbols (F1, etc.) appear in the bottom margin.

--> To turn the "verify" feature off (or back on) press F5.

PRESS "RETURN" TO GO TO NEXT SCREEN
<F1=BACK UP   F2=QUIT>

Screen 10 — USE OF ; IN ADDRESSES (SEE MANUAL PART 14)

You need not provide addresses in your will. However, for people who may be hard to locate, it may be a good idea.

If you do, separate each item with a semicolon, as follows:

JOHN SMITH;123 FIRST ST.;TROY, N.Y.

The name will be printed as:

```
          JOHN SMITH
          123 FIRST ST.
          TROY, N.Y.
```

PRESS "RETURN" TO GO TO NEXT SCREEN
<F1=BACK UP   F2=QUIT>

Screen 11 — READY TO MAKE YOUR WILL (SEE MANUAL PART 14)

You are now ready to enter the information needed to make your will.

Relax, take your time, and enjoy the experience...

Press "Return" to go on.

PRESS "RETURN" TO GO TO NEXT SCREEN
<F1=BACK UP   F2=QUIT>

```
! .............YOUR NAME..............!        ! ......YOUR SOCIAL SECURITY NUMBER....!
!                                    !        !                                     !
S    ENTER your name below.  Spell it!        S    Enter your social security number.!
E                                    !        E                                     !
E exactly the way you do when signing V        E Example: 123-45-6789.  This optional V
M                                    E        M                                     E
A formal legal documents. Enter first R        A information may be helpful to your   R
N                                    I        N                                     I
N name first, last name last.        F        A personal representative (executor)  F
U                                    Y        U                                     Y
A                                    !        N in applying for government benefits. !
L                                    O        L                                     O
                                     N        A                                     N
P                                    !        P                                     !
A _____    !        A _____               !
R                                    !        R                                     !
T                                    !        T                                     !
                                     !        2                                     !
2                                    !        !                                     !
                                     !        !                                     !
!                                    !        !                                     !
! ----------------------------12!              ! ------------------------------13!
!  TYPE REQUESTED INFO.& THEN "RETURN" !       !  TYPE REQUESTED INFO.& THEN "RETURN" !
! (F1=BACK  F2=QUIT  F3=DEF  F4=WHERE?)!       ! (F1=BACK  F2=QUIT  F3=DEF  F4=WHERE?)!
```

```
! ..............YOUR STATE............!        ! ............YOUR COUNTY..............!
!                                    !        !                                     !
S   1 Alabama   18 Maine   35 Oklahoma!        S                                     !
E   2 Alaska    19 Maryland 36 Oregon !        E                                     !
E   3 Arizona   20 Mass.   37 Penn.   V        E    Enter the name of the county     V
    4 Arkansas  21 Michigan 38 R.Island E                                           E
M   5 Califor.  22 Minn.   39 S.Carol R        M       in which you live.           R
A   6 Colorado  23 Miss.   40 S.Dakota I        A                                     I
N   7 Conn.     24 Missouri 41 Tenn.  F        N                                     F
U   8 Delaware  25 Montana 42 Texas   Y        U                                     Y
A   9 Florida   26 Nebraska 43 Utah   !        A                                     !
L  10 Georgia   27 Nevada  44 Vermont O        L                                     O
   11 Hawaii    28 New Hamp 45 Virginia N        The County of:                     N
P  12 Idaho     29 New Jer. 46 Wash(St.)!       P                                     !
A  13 Illinois  30 New Mex. 47 W.Virg. !        A _____  !
R  14 Indiana   31 New York 48 Wisconsin!       R                                     !
T  15 Iowa      32 N.Carol  49 Wyoming !        T                                     !
   16 Kansas    33 N.Dakota 50 D.C.    !       5                                     !
5  17 Kentucky  34 Ohio               !        !                                     !
!                                    !        !                                     !
! Type your state's number:__ &"Return"!       ! ------------------------------15!
! ----------------------------14!               !  TYPE REQUESTED INFO.& THEN "RETURN" !
!  PLEASE ANSWER THE ABOVE QUESTION   !        ! (F1=BACK  F2=QUIT  F3=DEF  F4=WHERE?)!
! (F1=BACK  F2=QUIT  F3=DEF  F4=WHERE?)!
```

```
! ..............MARRIED?..............!        ! ..........YOUR SPOUSE'S NAME.........!
!                                    !        !                                     !
S  NOTE: If you are getting a divorce !        S                                     !
E  or are uncertain about your marital!        E                                     !
E  status, see Part 5B of the manual  !        E                                     !
   before answering this question.    !        !                                     !
M                                    !        M                                     !
A                                    !        A Enter the full name of your SPOUSE: !
N        Are you MARRIED?            !        N                                     !
U                                    !        U  (First name first, last name last.)!
A                                    !        A                                     !
L                                    !        L                                     !
                                     !        !                                     !
P     IF YES TYPE "Y" AND "RETURN"   !        P                                     !
A                                    !        A _____  !
R     IF NO  TYPE "N" AND "RETURN"   !        R                                     !
T                                    !        T                                     !
                                     !        !                                     !
5                                    !        5                                     !
!                                    !        !                                     !
!                                    !        !                                     !
! ----------------------------16!               ! ------------------------------17!
!  PLEASE ANSWER THE ABOVE QUESTION   !        !  TYPE REQUESTED INFO.& THEN "RETURN" !
! (F1=BACK  F2=QUIT  F3=DEF  F4=WHERE?)!       ! (F1=BACK  F2=QUIT  F3=DEF  F4=WHERE?)!
```

```
+-------------------------------------+  +-------------------------------------+
!              CHILDREN?              !  !          CHILDREN'S NAMES           !
!                                     !  !                                     !
! S    Do you have any living CHILDREN,! S    Name your living children. Include
! E                                   !  ! E  adopted children, your children from
! E  including legally adopted children,! E  prior marriages, and children born
!                                     !  !    out of wedlock.
! M  children born out of wedlock, or  ! M    It is important to name all your
! A                                   !  ! A  children. However, you need not
! N  your children from prior marriages?! N  leave a child any property, except
! U                                   !  ! U  the $1 that WILLMAKER automatically
! A                                   !  ! A  leaves all your children.
! L    IF YES TYPE "Y" AND "RETURN"   !  ! L
!                                     !  !      Enter the full name of child #1
! P    IF NO  TYPE "N" AND "RETURN"   !  ! P
! A                                   !  ! A  ------------------------------------
! R                                   !  ! R
! T                                   !  ! T
!                                     !  !
! 7                                   !  ! 7
! !                                   !  ! !
! !                                   !  ! !
! ! ------------------ ------------18 !  ! ! ------------------------------19 !
!   PLEASE ANSWER THE ABOVE QUESTION  !  !   TYPE REQUESTED INFO.& THEN "RETURN"
! (F1=BACK  F2=QUIT  F3=DEF  F4=WHERE?)!  !        (F3=DEF   F4=WHERE?)
+-------------------------------------+  +-------------------------------------+

+-------------------------------------+  +-------------------------------------+
!          CHILDREN UNDER 18?         !  !          DECEASED CHILDREN?         !
! !                                   !  ! !
! S                                   !  ! S
! E  Do you have any CHILDREN under 18?! E
! E                                   !  ! E
!    (If so you will have the opportunity!
! M  to name a guardian later in the  !  ! M    Do you have any deceased CHILDREN?
! A  program.)                        !  ! A
! N                                   !  ! N
! U                                   !  ! U
! A                                   !  ! A
! L    IF YES TYPE "Y" AND "RETURN"   !  ! L    IF YES TYPE "Y" AND "RETURN"
!                                     !  !
! P    IF NO  TYPE "N" AND "RETURN"   !  ! P    IF NO  TYPE "N" AND "RETURN"
! A                                   !  ! A
! R                                   !  ! R
! T                                   !  ! T
!                                     !  !
! 7                                   !  ! 7
! !                                   !  ! !
! !                                   !  ! !
! ! ------------------ ------------20 !  ! ! ------------------ ------------21 !
!   PLEASE ANSWER THE ABOVE QUESTION  !  !   PLEASE ANSWER THE ABOVE QUESTION
! (F1=BACK  F2=QUIT  F3=DEF  F4=WHERE?)!  ! (F1=BACK  F2=QUIT  F3=DEF  F4=WHERE?)
+-------------------------------------+  +-------------------------------------+

+-------------------------------------+  +-------------------------------------+
!            GRANDCHILDREN            !  !  NAME CHILDREN OF DECEASED CHILDREN  !
! S  Are any children of your deceased !  ! S
! E  children now living (i.e., your   !  ! E
! E  GRANDCHILDREN)?                   !  ! E  List all children of each of your
!                                     !  !
! M    If so, we will ask you to name  !  ! M  deceased children.
! A  them, but you need not leave them !  ! A
! N  anything more than the $1 which   !  ! N
! U  WILLMAKERautomatically gives them.!  ! U
! A                                   !  ! A      Enter the full name of
! L    IF YES TYPE "Y" AND "RETURN"   !  ! L
!                                     !  !            grandchild #1
! P    IF NO  TYPE "N" AND "RETURN"   !  ! P
! A                                   !  ! A  ------------------------------------
! R                                   !  ! R
! T                                   !  ! T
!                                     !  !
! 7                                   !  ! 7
! !                                   !  ! !
! !                                   !  ! !
! ! ------------------ ------------22 !  ! ! ------------------------------23 !
!   PLEASE ANSWER THE ABOVE QUESTION  !  !   TYPE REQUESTED INFO.& THEN "RETURN"
! (F1=BACK  F2=QUIT  F3=DEF  F4=WHERE?)!  !        (F3=DEF   F4=WHERE?)
+-------------------------------------+  +-------------------------------------+
```

(Left margin of each panel reads vertically: S E E M A N U A L P A R T 7)

```
+--------------------------------------------------+   +--------------------------------------------------+
|       PROPERTY YOU CAN LEAVE BY WILL             |   |       PROPERTY YOU CAN LEAVE BY WILL             |
| S                                                |   | S                                                |
| E          <STATE NAME>                          |   | E                                                |
| E                                                |   | E    Under the laws of <STATE NAME>,             |
| M    is a COMMUNITY PROPERTY STATE.              |   | M  your ESTATE consists of all property          |
| A                                                |   | A                                                |
| N                                                |   | N  which you own separately (this                |
| U    Your ESTATE consists of:                    |   | U                                                |
| A                                                |   | A  includes all property which you own           |
| L                                                |   | L                                                |
|      one-half of all COMMUNITY PROPERTY          |   | P  in your name alone) and your share            |
| P                                                |   | A                                                |
| A                                                |   | R  of property which you own as a                |
| R    plus all of your SEPARATE PROPERTY          |   | T                                                |
| T                                                |   |    TENANT IN COMMON.                             |
|                                                  |   | 5                                                |
| 5    See Section 5.B of the manual.              |   |      See manual Section 5.C.                     |
|                                                  |   |                                                  |
| ------------------------------------------24     |   | ------------------------------------------25     |
|   PRESS "RETURN" TO GO TO NEXT SCREEN            |   |   PRESS "RETURN" TO GO TO NEXT SCREEN            |
|   (F1=BACK  F2=QUIT  F3=DEF  F4=WHERE?)          |   |   (F1=BACK  F2=QUIT  F3=DEF  F4=WHERE?)          |
+--------------------------------------------------+   +--------------------------------------------------+

+--------------------------------------------------+   +--------------------------------------------------+
|       PROPERTY YOU CAN'T LEAVE BY WILL           |   |          BEQUESTS OF PROPERTY                    |
| S    You cannot use a will to leave:             |   | S   Do you want to leave property               |
| E                                                |   | E                                                |
| E                                                |   | E  (either PERSONAL or REAL) to one             |
|    > The proceeds of life insurance              |   |                                                  |
| M      where you name a beneficiary              |   | M  or more persons, charities, or               |
| A                                                |   | A                                                |
| N    > Any assets held in JOINT TENANCY          |   | N  institutions?                                |
| U                                                |   | U                                                |
| A                                                |   | A                                                |
| L    > Any property already disposed of          |   | L      IF YES TYPE "Y" AND "RETURN"             |
|        by a contract or a trust                  |   |                                                  |
| P                                                |   | P      IF NO  TYPE "N" AND "RETURN"             |
| A                                                |   | A                                                |
| R                                                |   | R                                                |
| T                                                |   | T                                                |
|                                                  |   |                                                  |
| 9                                                |   | 9                                                |
|                                                  |   |                                                  |
| ------------------------------------------26     |   | ------------------ ------------------27          |
|   PRESS "RETURN" TO GO TO NEXT SCREEN            |   |   PLEASE ANSWER THE ABOVE QUESTION              |
|   (F1=BACK  F2=QUIT  F3=DEF  F4=WHERE?)          |   |   (F1=BACK  F2=QUIT  F3=DEF  F4=WHERE?)          |
+--------------------------------------------------+   +--------------------------------------------------+

+--------------------------------------------------+   +--------------------------------------------------+
| DON'T MIX REAL AND PERSONAL PROPERTY             |   | WARNING ABOUT CONDITIONS ON BEQUESTS            |
| S                                                |   | S   When you name beneficiaries or              |
| E   The following screens let you                |   | E  specify the property being left              |
| E  make sixteen separate bequests of             |   | E  to them, do not use conditions.              |
|    personal property or real estate to           |   |                                                  |
|    specific beneficiaries.                       |   | M  For example:                                 |
| M                                                |   | A                                                |
| N    It is important not to mix                  |   | N  When naming a beneficiary DON'T say:         |
| U  personal property with real property          |   | U                                                |
| A  in the same bequest.                          |   | A    "John Smith if he lives in Ohio"           |
| L                                                |   | L                                                |
|      If you wish to leave both real              |   |                                                  |
| P  and personal property to the same             |   | P  When describing property DON'T say:          |
| A  beneficiary (or beneficiaries),               |   | A                                                |
| R  make two or more separate bequests.           |   | R  "My 1983 VW unless John owns a car"          |
| T                                                |   | T                                                |
|                                                  |   |                                                  |
| 1                                                |   | 1                                                |
| 4                                                |   | 4                                                |
|                                                  |   |                                                  |
| ------------------------------------------28     |   | ------------------------------------------29     |
|   PRESS "RETURN" TO GO TO NEXT SCREEN            |   |   PRESS "RETURN" TO GO TO NEXT SCREEN            |
|   (F1=BACK  F2=QUIT  F3=DEF  F4=WHERE?)          |   |   (F1=BACK  F2=QUIT  F3=DEF  F4=WHERE?)          |
+--------------------------------------------------+   +--------------------------------------------------+
```

```
+------------------------------------+  +------------------------------------+
|       YOU MAY NAME ALTERNATES      |  |  MAYBE YOU SHOULD SET UP A TRUST   |
|                                    |  |                                    |
| S    Although you may not attach   |  | S  Now you will be asked to name the|
| E                                  |  | E  persons or institutions you wish to|
| E  conditions to BEQUESTS, WILLMAKER|  | E  receive your property.          |
|                                    |  |                                    |
| M  allows you to name an ALTERNATE |  | M  Later in the program you can set|
| A                                  |  | A  up trusts for property you leave to|
| N  BENEFICIARY for each bequest in |  | N  one or more of your children. If|
| U                                  |  | U  you do, the property will be managed|
| A  case your primary beneficiary fails| A  for the child until an age you |
| L                                  |  | L  specify (from 18 to 30).        |
|    to survive you by 45 days.      |  |                                    |
| P                                  |  | P  If you think you might want a   |
| A                                  |  | A  trust, read Part 7B of the manual|
| R                                  |  | R  before proceeding.             |
| T                                  |  | T                                  |
|                                    |  |                                    |
| 9                                  |  | 7                                  |
|                                    |  |                                    |
|                                    |  |                                    |
| --------------------------------30 |  | --------------------------------31 |
|  PRESS "RETURN" TO GO TO NEXT SCREEN| |  PRESS "RETURN" TO GO TO NEXT SCREEN|
| (F1=BACK  F2=QUIT  F3=DEF  F4=WHERE?)| (F1=BACK  F2=QUIT  F3=DEF  F4=WHERE?)|
+------------------------------------+  +------------------------------------+

+------------------------------------+  +------------------------------------+
| PERSON TO RECEIVE SPECIFIC PROPERTY |  |        DESCRIPTION OF BEQUEST      |
|                                    |  |                                    |
| S    Enter the name of a beneficiary| S Please enter a PRECISE DESCRIPTION of|
| E  to whom you wish to leave PERSONAL| E                                  |
| E  or REAL PROPERTY:               |  | E  the PROPERTY you want to leave to:|
|                                    |  |                                    |
| M                                  |  | M                                  |
| A   To name more than one beneficiary| A                                 |
| N  to jointly receive property you must| N      <NAME ENTERED BY USER>    |
| U  separate their names with + symbols.| U                                 |
| A  Use F3 or ? for help with this. |  | A   (If you use this screen to leave|
| L                                  |  | L      several items to one person,|
|                                    |  |        separate them with semicolons.)|
| P                                  |  | P  _____|
| A  _____|  | A  _____|
| R  _____|  | R  _____|
| T  _____|  | T  _____|
|                                    |  |    _____|
| 1                                  |  | 1  _____|
| 4                                  |  | 4  _____|
|            BEQUEST # 1             |  |            BEQUEST # 1             |
| --------------------------------32 |  | --------------------------------33 |
|  TYPE REQUESTED INFO.& THEN "RETURN"|  |  TYPE REQUESTED INFO.& THEN "RETURN"|
|         (F3=DEF  F4=WHERE?)        |  |         (F3=DEF  F4=WHERE?)        |
+------------------------------------+  +------------------------------------+

+------------------------------------+  +------------------------------------+
| WHAT IF BENEFICIARY PREDECEASES YOU?| | WHAT IF BENEFICIARY PREDECEASES YOU?|
|                                    |  |                                    |
| S  You have named more than one    |  | S  If the beneficiary you named to |
| E  beneficiary to receive the property| E  receive the property specified on|
| E  specified on the previous screen.| E  the previous screen fails to survive|
|    If a beneficiary fails to survive|  |    you by 45 days, you may choose to:|
| M  you by 45 days, you may choose to:| M                                  |
| A                                  |  | A                                  |
| N  1-have that person's share pass to| N  1-have the property pass in equal|
| U  his or her children in equal shares.| U    shares to the children of that|
| A  If there are no children, it passes| A    beneficiary; or             |
| L  equally to the other surviving  |  | L                                  |
|    beneficiary(ies); or            |  |    2-have the property pass to one or|
| P                                  |  | P    more alternate beneficiaries  |
| A  2-have that person's share pass |  | A    to be named in the next screen.|
| R  directly to the other surviving |  | R                                  |
| T  beneficiary(ies), in equal shares.| T                                  |
|                                    |  |       Enter 1 or 2 to make your choice.|
| 8                                  |  | 8                                  |
|  Enter 1 or 2 to make your choice. |  |                                    |
|                                    |  |                                    |
| ------------------- ------------34 |  | ------------------- ------------35 |
|   PLEASE ANSWER THE ABOVE QUESTION |  |   PLEASE ANSWER THE ABOVE QUESTION |
|         (F3=DEF  F4=WHERE?)        |  |         (F3=DEF  F4=WHERE?)        |
+------------------------------------+  +------------------------------------+
```

```
! ALTERNATE BENEFICIARY:BEQUEST # 1 !
! If nobody you have named to receive !
S                                     !
E      <NAME ENTERED BY USER>         !
E                                     !
                                      !
M                                     !
A  (nor any of their children)        !
N survives you by 45 days, name an    !
U alternate beneficiary:              !
A                                     !
L                                     !
                                      !
P                                     !
A  _____ !
R  _____ !
T                                     !
                                      !
8                                     !
!   TYPE "RETURN" IF YOU DON'T WANT TO !
! NAME AN ALTERNATE                   !
!-----------------------------------36!
!  TYPE REQUESTED INFO.& THEN "RETURN" !
!         (F3=DEF  F4=WHERE?)         !
```

```
!          REMAINING PROPERTY          !
!                                      !
S   It is essential that you name a    !
E  beneficiary to take your RESIDUARY  !
E  estate (any property not already    !
   disposed of by this will or other   !
M  estate planning devices).           !
A                                      !
N   Do this even if you beleive you    !
U  have disposed of all your property  !
A  through specific bequests, gifts,   !
L  and estate planning devices, such   !
   as joint tenancy, living trust, etc.!
P                                      !
A   To name a beneficiary for your     !
R  residuary estate proceed to the next!
T  screen.                             !
                                       !
9                                      !
!                                      !
!                                      !
!------------------------------------37!
!  PRESS "RETURN" TO GO TO NEXT SCREEN !
! (F1=BACK  F2=QUIT  F3=DEF  F4=WHERE?) !
```

```
!   LEAVING YOUR RESIDUARY ESTATE      !
!                                      !
S   Type the name of the beneficiary   !
E  for your residuary estate.  If you  !
E  name more than one, separate their  !
   names with the + symbol: e.g.:John  !
M  Doe;123 Elm St.;Ada, Ohio+Jan Roe;  !
A  456 1st St.;Pala, Utah              !
U                                      !
A                                      !
L                                      !
                                       !
P                                      !
A   _____  !
R   _____  !
T   _____  !
                                       !
9                                      !
!                                      !
!                                      !
!------------------------------------38!
!  TYPE REQUESTED INFO.& THEN "RETURN"  !
! (F1=BACK  F2=QUIT  F3=DEF  F4=WHERE?) !
```

```
! WHAT IF BENEFICIARY PREDECEASES YOU? !
!                                      !
S On the previous screen you named more!
E than one beneficiary to receive your !
E RESIDUARY ESTATE.  If a beneficiary  !
  for the residuary fails to survive   !
M you by 45 days, you have this choice:!
A                                      !
N 1-have that person's share pass to   !
U  his or her children in equal shares.!
A  It there are none, it passes        !
L  equally to the other surviving      !
   beneficiary(ies) just named.        !
P                                      !
A 2-have that person's share pass      !
R  directly to the other surviving     !
T  beneficiary(ies) for the residuary  !
   just named, in equal shares.        !
8                                      !
!  Enter 1 or 2 to make your choice.   !
!                                      !
!------------------ ----------------39 !
!   PLEASE ANSWER THE ABOVE QUESTION   !
! (F1=BACK  F2=QUIT  F3=DEF  F4=WHERE?) !
```

```
! WHAT IF BENEFICIARY PREDECEASES YOU? !
!                                      !
S  If the beneficiary you named on the !
E previous screen to receive your      !
E RESIDUARY ESTATE fails to survive    !
  you by 45 days, you have this choice:!
M                                      !
A 1-have the property pass in equal    !
N   shares to the children of the      !
U   beneficiary; if there are no such  !
A   living children the property       !
L   passes to the alternate            !
    beneficiary(ies)                   !
P                                      !
A 2-have the property pass to the      !
R   alternate beneficiary(ies)         !
T                                      !
                                       !
8  Enter 1 or 2 to make your choice.   !
!                                      !
!                                      !
!------------------ ---------------40  !
!   PLEASE ANSWER THE ABOVE QUESTION   !
! (F1=BACK  F2=QUIT  F3=DEF  F4=WHERE?) !
```

```
!  ALTERNATE BENEFICIARY: RESIDUARY    !
!                                      !
S   If nobody you have named to        !
E  receive your residuary estate       !
E  (nor any of their children)         !
   survives you by 45 days, name       !
M  an alternate beneficiary:           !
A                                      !
N                                      !
U                                      !
A                                      !
L                                      !
                                       !
P                                      !
A   _____  !
R   _____  !
T   _____  !
                                       !
8                                      !
!   TYPE "RETURN" IF YOU DON'T WANT TO  !
! NAME AN ALTERNATE                    !
!------------------------------------41 !
!  TYPE REQUESTED INFO.& THEN "RETURN"  !
! (F1=BACK  F2=QUIT  F3=DEF  F4=WHERE?) !
```

```
! ------------------------------------ !    ! ------------------------------------ !
!       TRUST FOR YOUR CHILDREN?      !    !    SET UP A TRUST FOR YOUR CHILDREN !
!  !                                  !    !  !                                   !
S  Are any of your children less than !    S     Do you want to set up a trust for!
E  30 years old? If so, you may want  !    E  any of your children?              !
E  to establish a trust under which   !    E                                     !
   property you leave to a child will  !      A full description of the trust, and!
M  be managed for the child's benefit !    M  what you can accomplish with it, is !
A  until he or she turns any age (from !    A  contained in manual Part 7B.       !
N  18 to 30) selected by you.          !    N                                     !
U                                      !    U                                     !
A   If you have minor children and have!    A                                     !
L  declined to name a guardian it is   !    L      IF YES TYPE "Y" AND "RETURN"   !
   particularly important that you     !                                         !
P  consider a trust if you have a      !    P      IF NO  TYPE "N" AND "RETURN"   !
A  substantial estate (see Manual part !    A                                     !
R  7B).                                !    R                                     !
T                                      !    T                                     !
                                       !                                          !
7                                      !    7                                     !
!  !                                   !    !  !                                   !
!  ------------------------------48!    !  ----------- ------------------49!
!    PRESS "RETURN" TO GO TO NEXT SCREEN!    !    PLEASE ANSWER THE ABOVE QUESTION !
!  (F1=BACK  F2=QUIT  F3=DEF  F4=WHERE?)!    !  (F1=BACK  F2=QUIT  F3=DEF  F4=WHERE?)!

! YOUR CHILDREN :                       !    !            NAME TRUSTEE              !
!1.FIRST CHILD                    !XX  !    !  !                                   !
L2.SECOND CHILD                   !XX  !    S                                      !
E                                      !    E                                      !
G                                 V    !    E                                      !
I  TYPE NUMBER OF 1ST CHILD YOU WANT   !    M                                      !
S  A TRUST FOR AND PRESS RETURN.   E   !    A                                      !
O                                 R    !    N  Enter the name of your first choice !
F                                 I    !    U                                      !
T                                 F    !    A  for trustee:                        !
/                                 Y    !    L                                      !
N                                      !                                           !
O                                 O    !    P                                      !
L                                 N    !    A  _____    !
O                                      !    R  _____    !
   __                                  !    T  _____    !
P                                      !                                           !
R                                      !    7   (THIS MAY BE THE SAME PERSON       !
E                                      !         YOU'VE SELECTED AS GUARDIAN)      !
S                                      !    !  !                                   !
S                                      !    !  --------------------------------51!
!  ------------------------------50!    !    TYPE REQUESTED INFO.& THEN "RETURN" !
        TYPE "Y" WHEN LIST IS OK        !    (F1=BACK  F2=QUIT  F3=DEF  F4=WHERE?)!

!           ALTERNATE TRUSTEE          !    !   NAME A PERSONAL REPRESENTATIVE     !
!  !                                   !    !  !                                   !
S  Enter the name of your choice for   !    S   Enter the name of your first choice!
E  alternate TRUSTEE in case           !    E                                      !
E                                 V    !    E  to be your PERSONAL REPRESENTATIVE  !
                                  E    !                                           !
M       <NAME ENTERED BY USER>    R    !    M  (executor) to see that your will is !
A                                 I    !    A                                      !
N                                 F    !    N  carried out. (This can be someone   !
U                                 Y    !    U                                      !
A  cannot serve:                       !    A  who receives property in your will.)!
L    (THIS MAY BE THE SAME PERSON O    !    L                                      !
      YOU'VE SELECTED AS GUARDIAN) N   !                                           !
P                                      !    P                                      !
A  _____       !    A  _____    !
R  _____   !    R  _____    !
T  _____   !    T  _____    !
                                       !                                           !
7                                      !    9                                      !
!  TYPE "RETURN" IF YOU DON'T WANT TO  !    !  !                                   !
! NAME AN ALTERNATE                    !    !                                      !
!  ------------------------------52!    !  --------------------------------53!
!   TYPE REQUESTED INFO.& THEN "RETURN"!    !   TYPE REQUESTED INFO.& THEN "RETURN"!
!  (F1=BACK  F2=QUIT  F3=DEF  F4=WHERE?)!    !  (F1=BACK  F2=QUIT  F3=DEF  F4=WHERE?)!
```

```
! NAME ALTERNATE PERSONAL REPRESENTATIVE !
!                                         !
S   Enter the name of your choice for an !
E                                         !
E   alternate PERSONAL REPRESENTATIVE in V
                                          E
M   case                                  R
A        <NAME ENTERED BY USER>           I
N                                         F
U                                         Y
A
L   cannot serve.                         O
                                          N
P
A   _____ !
R   _____ !
T   _____ !
                                          !
9                                         !
!   TYPE "RETURN" IF YOU DON'T WANT TO    !
!   NAME AN ALTERNATE                     !
!   ---------------------------------54!
!   TYPE REQUESTED INFO.& THEN "RETURN"   !
!   (F1=BACK  F2=QUIT  F3=DEF  F4=WHERE?)
```

```
!          REVIEW/MODIFY YOUR WILL:        !
!                                          !
!      BASICS:   1.Name/Social Sec. #      !
S                2.State                   
E                3.County                  V
E                4.Married?                E
                 5.Spouse's Name           R
M                6.Facts about Children    I
A                7.Pay Debts and Taxes     F
N                                          Y
U   BEQUESTS:    8.Property                
A                9.The Rest (Residuary)    O
L               10.Forgive Debts           N
                                           
P   NOMINATE:   11.Guardian                !
A               12.Trustee                 !
R               13.Personal Representative !
T                                          !
                                           
1   Type number of any item you want to    |
0    review or change:__ & "Return"        |
    ---------------------------------66|
    PRESS "RETURN" TO GO TO NEXT SCREEN
       F2=QUIT  F3=DEF
```

```
!        LIABILITIES OF YOUR ESTATE        !
!                                          !
!      Your estate is liable for:          !
S                                          
E  * Debts owed by you when you die        V
E                                          E
   * Expenses incurred after your death    R
M     (e.g., funeral and probate           I
A     expenses)                            F
N                                          Y
U  * Estate and inheritance taxes,         
A     if any                               O
L                                          N
     Your will can instruct your personal  
P   representative how to deal with        |
A   these liabilities--that is, which      |
R   assets to use or sell to pay them.     |
T   If your will doesn't do this, your     |
    state's law will dictate how payment   |
0   will be made.                          |
                                           |
!   ----------------_----------------55|
    PRESS "RETURN" TO GO TO NEXT SCREEN
       F2=QUIT  F3=DEF  F5=VFY
```

```
!             SEVERAL OPTIONS              !
!                                          !
!     WillMaker offers several options     |
S   for how your debts, expenses and       
E   taxes can be paid. These are           V
E   provided in the following screens.     E
                                           R
M   Note: WillMaker requires that debts    I
A   associated with all real property      F
N   left by your will (e.g, mortgages      Y
U   and taxes) be paid by the              
A   beneficiary who receives the           O
L   property.  See Manual Part 8,          N
    Section A.                             
P                                          |
A                                          |
R                                          |
T                                          |
                                           |
0                                          |
                                           |
!   ----------------_----------------56|
    PRESS "RETURN" TO GO TO NEXT SCREEN
  F1=BACK  F2=QUIT  F3=DEF  F5=VFY
```

```
!  YOU MAY CHOOSE METHOD OF PAYMENT        !
!                                          !
!    WillMaker allows you to choose one    |
S   method for payment of your debts and   
E   expenses (other than real property     V
E   debts) and another method for          E
    payment of your estate and             R
M   inheritance taxes.                     I
A                                          F
N     In the next screen(s) you can        Y
U   designate how you want your debts      
A   and expenses paid. Then you can        O
L   choose how you want your estate        N
    and inheritance taxes to be            
P   handled.                               |
A                                          |
R                                          |
T                                          |
                                           |
0                                          |
                                           |
!   ----------------_----------------57|
    PRESS "RETURN" TO GO TO NEXT SCREEN
   F1=BACK  F2=QUIT  F3=DEF  F5=VFY
```

```
!       CHOOSE METHOD OF PAYMENT           !
!                                          !
!     Each choice for payment of your      |
S   debts and expenses is well suited      
E   for some situations and not for        V
E   others. Please read Manual Part 8,     E
    Section A before you proceed. Then     R
M   enter the number of your choice:       I
A                                          F
N   1) Payment of debts and expenses       Y
U   from one or more designated assets     
A   (e.g., "my savings account with        O
L   X bank").                              N
                                           
P   2) Payment of debts and expenses       |
A   from your residuary estate.            |
R                                          |
T   3) Payment of debts and expenses       |
    according to the law of your state.    |
0                                          |
                                           |
!   ----------------_----------------58|
    PLEASE ANSWER THE ABOVE QUESTION
   F1=BACK  F2=QUIT  F3=DEF  F5=VFY
```

```
| WARNING...                    |        | DESCRIBE ASSETS FOR PAYMENT    |
|                               |        |                                |
|   Caution: You have chosen to |        |   Enter a PRECISE DESCRIPTION of the |
S designate a specific asset or assets  S asset(s) you wish to use for payment
E to pay your debts and expenses of  V  E of your debts and expenses. If you  V
E probate. As we point out in the  E  E list more than one asset, enter each E
  manual, this can be a wise choice  R    in the order you want it used.    R
M if you select liquid assets (e.g.,  I  M                                  I
A bank accounts, stocks). It may not  F  A Reminder: If an asset you describe F
N be so wise if you select non-liquid Y  N here has already been left as part Y
U assets (piano, jewelry, etc.), which    U of a specific bequest, it will go
A must be sold, often at a significant O  A first for payment of debts and    O
L loss, to raise the necessary money. N  L expenses. If you describe an asset N
                                            more than once when using WillMaker,
P If you wish to reconsider your       |  P describe it in exactly the same way. |
A selection, press F1. Otherwise,      |  A _____ |
R press Return.                        |  R _____ |
T                                      |  T _____ |
                                       |    _____ |
O                                      |  O _____ |
                                       |    _____ |
| ----------------_---------------59|  | ----------------------------------60|
     PRESS "RETURN" TO GO TO NEXT SCREEN      TYPE REQUESTED INFO.& THEN "RETURN"
  F1=BACK F2=QUIT F3=DEF F5=VFY             F1=BACK F2=QUIT F3=DEF F5=VFY
```

```
|    SELECT HOW TO PAY TAXES     |        | CHOOSE METHOD FOR PAYMENT OF TAXES |
|                                |        |                                   |
|   Now you may choose how your estate |    |   Here you choose how you want your |
S and inheritance taxes are to be paid.  S estate and inheritance taxes to be
E Estates worth less than $600,000 are V  E paid.  Before making this choice,  V
E exempt from federal estate tax and  E  E please read Manual Part 8, Section B.E
  the inheritance tax of most states.  R    Then enter the number of your choice:R
M If after reading Part 6 of the       I  M                                    I
A Manual you think that your estate     F  A 1) Payment of estate and inheritance F
N will not be subject to estate or      Y  N    taxes from one or more designated Y
U inheritance taxation, you may            U    assets (e.g., "my savings account
A reasonably decide not to make this    O  A    with X bank").                   O
L choice.                               N  L 2) Payment of estate and inheritance N
                                            taxes from all your taxable
P Do you want to specify how your       |  P    property on a pro-rata basis.    |
A estate and inheritance taxes will be  |  A 3) Payment of estate inheritance    |
R paid (Y/N)?  Enter N to skip the      |  R    taxes from your residuary estate. |
T estate and inheritance tax payment    |  T 4) Payment of estate and inheritance |
  option and continue with WillMaker.   |      taxes according to the law of    |
O                                       |  O    your state.                      |
| ----------------_---------------61|  | ----------------_---------------62|
     PLEASE ANSWER THE ABOVE QUESTION         PLEASE ANSWER THE ABOVE QUESTION
  F1=BACK F2=QUIT F3=DEF F5=VFY             F1=BACK F2=QUIT F3=DEF F5=VFY
```

```
|       WARNING...               |        |     REVIEW/MODIFY YOUR WILL:       |
|                                |        |                                   |
|   Caution: As we point out in Manual |  S   BASICS:    1.Name/Social Sec. #  |
S Part 8, Section B, designating the      E             2.State               |
E residuary to pay estate and          V  E             3.County              |
E inheritance taxes may greatly reduce E                4.Married?            |
  what your residuary beneficiary gets.R  M             5.Spouse's name       |
M It places the entire tax burden on   I  A             6.Facts about Children |
A the residuary beneficiary. People    F  N                                   |
N who receive specific bequests (or    Y  U BEQUESTS:   7.Property             |
U property outside of probate) won't      A             8.The rest (residuary) |
A be liable unless the residuary isn't O  L             9.Forgive debts        |
L large enough to cover the taxes.     N                                       |
                                          P NOMINATE:  10.Guardian             |
P If you wish to reconsider your       |  A            11.Trust                |
A selection, press F1. Otherwise,      |  R            12.Personal representative |
R press Return.                        |  T                                     |
T                                      |    Type number of any item you want to |
                                       |  1   review or change:   & "Return"   |
O                                      |  4               --                    |
                                       |                                       |
| ----------------_---------------65|  | ----------------------------------55|
     PRESS "RETURN" TO GO TO NEXT SCREEN     PRESS "RETURN" TO GO TO NEXT SCREEN
  F1=BACK F2=QUIT F3=DEF F5=VFY             <F2=QUIT  F3=DEF  F4=WHERE?>
```

```
:                CONGRATULATIONS                :
:  S            Your will is done!              :
:  E                                            :
:  E                                          V :
:     In order to:          Type:            E :
:  M  -----------           -----            R :
:  A Print your will        "P"              I :
:  N                           \             F :
:  U Quit                   "Q" \            Y :
:  A                             \             :
:  L Review your will       "R"              O :
:                                & "Return"  N :
:  P Erase your will        "E"  /             :
:  A  and start over             /             :
:  R                             /             :
:  T Display your will      "S"                :
:       on screen                              :
:                                              :
:  1                                           :
:  4                                           :
:                                              :
:     --------------------_-------------56:
:                       -                       :
```

```
:--------------------------------------------:
:      DO YOU WISH TO HAVE YOUR WILL          :
:                                             :
:   NOTARIZED IN ADDITION TO HAVING IT        :
:                                             :
:   WITNESSED?                                :
:                                             :
:   (WE RECOMMEND THIS IF YOU LIVE IN         :
:   THE STATE OF TEXAS.)                      :
:   ->SEE MANUAL PART 11A FOR DETAILS.        :
:                                             :
:   ENTER:                                    :
:   "Y" TO PRINT WILL WITH NOTARY FORM        :
:   "N" IF YOU DON'T WANT TO NOTARIZE         :
:                                             :
:                                             :
:                                             :
:>ENTER "R" TO RETURN TO MAIN PROGRAM         :
:>ENTER "Q" TO QUIT                           :
:                                             :
:  (DON'T FORGET "RETURN")                    :
:--------------------------------------------:
```

```
:--                                          --:
:                                              :
:                                              :
:                                              :
:                                              :
:                  TYPE:                       :
:                                              :
: "C" IF YOU HAVE CONTINUOUS PAPER             :
:                                              :
: "S" TO PRINT ONE SHEET AT A TIME             :
:                                              :
:                                              :
:>ENTER "R" TO RETURN TO MAIN PROGRAM          :
:>ENTER "Q" TO QUIT                            :
:                                              :
:  (DON'T FORGET "RETURN")                     :
:                                              :
:                                              :
:                                              :
:                                              :
```

```
:--------------------------------------------:
:                                            :
:                                            :
:                                            :
:                                            :
:CURRENTLY PRINTING  60  LINES PER PAGE:
:                                            :
:ENTER "Y" IF THIS IS OK                     :
:                                            :
:       "N" TO CHANGE TO ANOTHER VALUE       :
:                                            :
:>ENTER "R" TO RETURN TO MAIN PROGRAM        :
:>ENTER "Q" TO QUIT                          :
:                                            :
:  (DON'T FORGET "RETURN")                   :
:                                            :
:                                            :
:                                            :
:                                            :
:--------------------------------------------:
```

```
:--------------------------------------------:
:    WILLMAKER CURRENTLY ADDS 5 SPACES        :
: TO THE LEFT MARGIN SET ON YOUR              :
: PRINTER.                                    :
:                                             :
:   IF YOU WANT TO CHANGE THIS NUMBER         :
:   ENTER "N" TO INCREASE OR DECREASE.        :
:                                             :
:   ENTER "Y" TO USE THE CURRENT              :
:   VALUE OF 5 SPACES.                        :
:                                             :
:                                             :
:                                             :
:                                             :
:>ENTER "R" TO RETURN TO MAIN PROGRAM         :
:>ENTER "Q" TO QUIT                           :
:                                             :
:  (DON'T FORGET "RETURN")                    :
:--------------------------------------------:
```

```
:--------------------------------------------:
:                                            :
:                                            :
:                                            :
:                ENTER "Y"                   :
:                                            :
:       WHEN YOUR PRINTER IS READY           :
:                                            :
:       ENTER "N" TO RESET OPTIONS           :
:                                            :
:>ENTER "R" TO RETURN TO MAIN PROGRAM        :
:>ENTER "Q" TO QUIT                          :
:                                            :
:  (DON'T FORGET "RETURN")                   :
:                                            :
:                                            :
:                                            :
:                                            :
:--------------------------------------------:
```

PART 15

Glossary

---

abatement Cutting back certain gifts under a will when it is necessary to create a fund to meet expenses, pay taxes, satisfy debts, or to have enough to take care of other bequests which are given a priority under law or under the will. See Part 8, Section A.

ademption The failure of a specific bequest of property because the property is no longer owned by the testator at the time of his death.

administrator of an estate The distribution of the probate estate of a deceased person. The person who manages the distribution is called an executor if there is a will. If there is no will, this person is called the administrator.

adopted child Any person, whether an adult or a minor, who is legally adopted as the child of another in a court proceeding. See Part 7.

adult Any person over the age of 18. Most states allow all competent adults to make wills. A few, however, require you to be somewhat older (e.g., 19 or 21 to leave real estate). See Part 2. Competent adults may be left property without the need for appointing a guardian. See Part 2.

augmented estate A method used in a number of states following the common law ownership of property system to measure a person's estate for the purpose of determining whether a surviving spouse has been adequately provided for. Generally, the augmented estate consists of property left by the will plus certain property transferred outside of the will by such devices as gifts, joint tenancies and living trusts. In the states using this concept, a surviving spouse is generally considered to be adequately provided for if he or she receives at least one- third of the augmented estate. If she does not receive this much she may be able to go to court and demand a statutory share of decedents estate. See Part 5, Section D.

beneficiary A person (or an organization) receiving benefits under a legal instrument such as a will or trust. Except when very small estates are involved, beneficiaries of wills only receive their benefits after the will is examined and approved by the probate court. Beneficiaries of trusts receive their benefits as provided in the trust instrument.

bequest As used in WillMaker and this manual, the personal property and real estate left to a person in a will. Thus, when you leave property to someone, you are said to make a bequest of that property.

bond A document guaranteeing that a certain amount of money will be paid to the victim if a person occupying a position of trust does not carry out his or her legal and ethical responsibilities. Thus, if an executor, trustee or guardian who is bonded (covered by a bond) wrongfully deprives a beneficiary of his or her property (say by taking it on a one-way trip to Las Vegas), the bonding company will replace it, up to the limits of the bond. Bonding companies, which are normally divisions of insurance companies, issue a bond in exchange for a premium (usually about 10% of the face amount of the bond). Under WillMaker, executors and guardians are appointed to serve without the necessity of purchasing a bond. This is because the cost of the bond would have to be paid out of the estate, and the beneficiaries would accordingly receive less. Under WillMaker, you should take care to select trustworthy people in the first place.

children For the purpose of WillMaker, children are: 1) the biological offspring of the person making the will (the testator), 2) persons who were legally adopted by the testator, 3) children born out of wedlock if the testator is the mother, 4) children born out of wedlock if the testator is the father and has acknowledged the child as being his as required by the law of the particular state, or 5) children born to the testator after the will is made. See Part 7.

codicil A separate legal document that changes an existing will after it has been signed and properly witnessed. We do not recommend using codicils. Because a codicil is subject to the same formal requirements as the original will, we suggest that if you wish to make changes, you use WillMaker to make a new will and then destroy your old one. See Part 12. Do not allow two wills to exist at the same time, as confusion about your intentions might result after your death. See Part 11.

community and separate property Nine states follow a system of marital property ownership called *community property*. Very generally, all property acquired after marriage and before permanent separation is considered to belong equally to both spouses, except for gifts to and inheritances by one spouse, and, in some community property states, income property owned by one spouse prior to marriage. See Part 5, Section B for details.

In most marriages, the main property accumulated is a family home, a retirement pension belonging to one or both spouses, motor vehicles, a joint bank account, a savings account, and perhaps some stocks or bonds. So long as these were purchased during the marriage with the income earned by either spouse during the marriage, they are usually considered to be community property, unless the spouses have entered into an agreement to the contrary. If the property was purchased with the separate property of a spouse, it is separate property, unless it has been given to the community by gift or agreement.

If separate property and community property are mixed together (commingled) in a bank account and expenditures made from this bank account, the goods purchased will usually be treated as community property unless they can be specifically linked with the separate property (this is called *tracing*).

Under the law of community property states, a surviving spouse automatically keeps one-half of all community property. The other spouse has no legal power to affect this portion by will or otherwise. Thus, the property which a testator actually leaves by will consists of his or her separate property and one-half of the community property. To determine the net worth of an estate, therefore, a spouse should add half of the community estate (the sum total of the community property) to his or her separate property. See Part 5, Section B(1).

conditional bequests A bequest which only passes under certain specified conditions or upon the occurrence of a specific event. For example, if you leave property to Aunt Millie provided she is living in

Cincinnatti when you die, and otherwise to Uncle Fred, you have made a *conditional bequest*. WillMaker does not generally allow such conditional bequests. There is an exception, however. You can leave property to somebody on the condition that your primary beneficiary does not survive you by 45 days. Thus, you can leave your Leica camera to your friend Kenneth and then name Edith to receive the camera if Kenneth does not survive you by 45 days. You cannot, however, condition your bequest of the camera on Kenneth marrying your favorite niece. See Part 9, Section B.

debt An obligation to or by a testator that can be measured in money terms. Under WillMaker, debts owed at the time of death can be forgiven in the will (see Part 9 Section A). Debts owed by the testator at his or her time of death are to be paid first out of the residuary estate, and then according to state law (see Part 8, Section A).

devise An old legal term for real property that is transferred in a will. However, for ease of understanding, WillMaker uses the term *bequest* to refer to both personal and real property transfers by will.

dower and curtesy The right of a surviving spouse to receive or enjoy the use of a set portion of the deceased spouse's property (usually one-third to one-half) in the event the surviving spouse is not left at least that share and chooses to take against the will. Dower refers to the title which a surviving wife gets, while curtesy refers to what a man receives. Until recently, these amounts differed in a number of states. However, since discrimination on the basis of sex is now considered to be illegal in most cases, states generally provide the same benefits regardless of sex. See Part 5, Sections C and D.

encumbrances Debts (e.g., taxes, mechanic's liens, judgment liens) and loans (e.g., mortgages, deeds of trust, security interests) which use property as collateral for payment of the debt or loan are considered to encumber the property because they must be paid off before title to the property can pass from one owner to the next. Generally, the value of a person's ownership in such property (called the *equity*) is measured by the market value of the property less the sum of all encumbrances. See Part 5.

estate Generally, the property you own when you die. There are different ways to measure your estate, depending on whether you are concerned with tax reduction (taxable estate—see Part 6, Section C), probate avoidance (probate estate—see Part 6, Section B), or net worth (net estate—see Part 5, Section H).

estate planning The art of dying with the smallest taxable estate and probate estate possible while continuing to prosper when you're alive and yet passing your property to your loved ones with a minimum of fuss and expense. See Part 6, Sections C and D.

estate taxes Taxes imposed by the federal government on your property as it passes from the dead to the living. The federal government exempts $400,000 of property in 1985, $500,000 in 1986 and $600,000 in 1987 and thereafter. Also, all property left to a surviving spouse is exempt under the marital exemption. Taxes are only imposed on property actually owned by you at the time of your death. Thus, estate planning techniques designed to reduce taxes usually concentrate on the legal transfer of ownership of your property while you are living, to minimize the amount of such property you own at your death. See Part 6, Section C.

equity The difference between the fair market value of your real and personal property and the amount you still owe on it, if any. See Part 5, Section G.

executor/executrix The person specified in your will to manage your estate, deal with the probate court, collect your assets and distribute them as you have specified. If you die without a will, the probate court will appoint such a person, who is then called the *administrator* of your estate. It is common for married persons to name their spouse to this position. Also, however, it is a good idea to name two alternates to your original choice. The will produced by WillMaker refers to your executor as your personal representative. See Part 9, Section A.

financial guardian See *guardian*.

forgive a debt See *debt*

gifts Property passed to others for no return or substantially less than its actual market value is considered a gift when the giver (called the *donor*) is still alive, and a bequest, legacy or devise when left by a will. Any gift of more than $10,000 per year to an individual is subject to the Federal Estate and Gift Tax. A donor is required to take the Estate and Gift Tax credit for gifts over $10,000 and the amount of the credit thus used up will not be available when the donor dies. In other words, if enough property is given away in gifts over $10,000 during a donor's life, the full amount of the donor's estate may be subject to federal estate taxation. On the other hand, if gifts are kept within the $10,000 annual limit, the tax exemption available to the estate will not be adversely affected. See Part 6, Section C.

guardian An adult appointed or selected to care for a minor child in the event no biological or adoptive parent (legal parent) of the child is able to do so. If one legal parent is alive when the other dies, however, the child will automatically go to that parent, unless the best interests of the child require something different, or (in some states) the court finds the child would suffer detriment. However, many parents wish to control who will take care of their children if both parents die or if the surviving parent is unfit or doesn't wish to assume this responsibility. In addition to caring for the children, the guardian will usually be charged with managing all property belonging to your minor children, unless the property is placed in trust. WillMaker allows you to name a guardian or an alternate guardian. The probate court will then decide whether your choice of guardian should in fact be honored, taking into account the best interests of the children. Although the courts will normally honor your choice, there is no iron-clad guarantee of this. Sorry. See Part 7, Section A.

heirs Persons who are entitled by law to inherit your estate if you don't leave a will, or any person or institution named in your will.

Independant Administration of Estates Act This is a California statute that allows executors and administrators of estates to independently (without prior court approval) take all actions commonly required to properly handle an estate. California wills made by WillMaker simply refer to this statute instead of specifying the executor's powers (as is done by WillMaker for wills in other states).

intervivos trusts See *living trusts.*

intestate succession The method by which property is distributed when a person fails to leave a will. In such cases, the law of each state provides that the property be distributed in certain shares to the closest surviving relatives. In most states, these are a surviving spouse, children, parents, siblings, nieces and nephews, and next of kin, in that order. The intestate succession laws are also used in the event an heir is found to be pretermitted (i.e., not mentioned or otherwise provided for in the will).

joint tenancy A way to take title to jointly owned real or personal property. When two or more people own property as joint tenants, and one of the owners dies, the other owners automatically become owners of the deceased owner's share. Thus, if a parent and child own a house as joint tenants, and the parent dies, the child automatically becomes full owner. Because of this *right of survivorship*, a joint tenancy interest in property does not go through probate, or, put another way, is not part of the probate estate. Instead it goes directly to the surviving joint tenant(s) once some tax and transfer forms are completed.

Placing property in joint tenancy is therefore a common tool used in estate planning designed to avoid probate. However, when property is placed in joint tenancy, a gift is made to any persons who become owners as a result. Thus, if Tom owns a house and places it in joint tenancy with Karen, Tom will have made a gift to Karen equal to one-half the house's value. This may have gift tax consequences. See Part 6, Section B(3).

legacy An old legal word meaning a transfer of personal property by will. For ease of understanding, WillMaker uses the term *bequest* to refer to both real property and personal property transfers by will.

living trusts Trusts set up while a person is alive and which remain under the control of that person during the remainder of his or her life. Also referred to as *intervivos trusts*, living trusts are an excellent way to minimize the value of property passing through probate. This is because they enable people (called *trustors*) to specify that money or other property (called the *trust corpus*) will pass directly to their beneficiaries at the time of their death, free of probate, and yet allow the trustors to continue to control the property during their lifetime and even end the trust or change the beneficiaries if they wish. See Part 6, Section B.

marriage A specific status conferred on a couple by state. In most states, it is necessary to file papers with a county clerk and have a marriage ceremony conducted by authorized individuals in order to be married. However, in the thirteen so-called *common law marriage* states, you may be considered married if you have lived together for a certain period of time and intended to be husband and wife. These states are: Alabama, Colorado, District of Columbia, Georgia, Idaho, Iowa, Kansas, Montana, Ohio, Oklahoma, Pennsylvania, Rhode Island, South Carolina and Texas.

Unless you are considered legally married in the state where you claim your marriage occurred, you are not married for purposes of WillMaker. Accordingly, the person you may have lived with all of your life cannot inherit as your spouse. See Part 5, Section A.

marital exemption A deduction allowed by the federal estate tax law for all property passed to a surviving spouse. This deduction (which really acts like an exemption) allows anyone, even a billionaire, to pass his or her entire estate to a surviving spouse without any tax at all. This might be a good idea if the surviving spouse is young and in good health.

If the surviving spouse is likely to die in the near future, however, your tax problems will very likely be made worse by relying on the marital exemption. This is because the second spouse to die will normally benefit from no marital deduction, which means the combined estate, less the standard estate tax exemption, will be taxed at a fairly high rate. For this reason, many older couples with adequate resources do not leave large amounts of property to each other, but rather, leave it directly to their children so that each can qualify for a separate tax exemption. See Part 6, Section D.

minor In most states, persons under 18 years of age. A minor is not permitted to make certain types of decisions (e.g., enter into most contracts). All minors are required to be cunder the care of a competent adult (parent or guardian) unless they qualify as emancipated minors (in the military, married, or living independently with court permission). This also means that property left to a minor must be handled by a guardian or trustee until the minor becomes an adult under the laws of the state. See Part 7, Sections A and B.

net estate The value of all your property less your liabilities. See Part 5, Section G.

personal property See *property, personal and real*.

personal representative The person (often termed *executor* or *executrix*) who you name to administrate your estate when you die. See *executor*.

pretermitted heir A child (or the child of a deceased child) who is either not named or not provided for in a will. Most states presume that persons want their children to inherit. Accordingly, children, or the children of a child who has died before the person making the will (the *testator*) who are not mentioned or provided for in the will are automatically given a share of the estate unless such children are specifically disinherited in the will. WillMaker gets around this problem by providing every such child $1.00 in addition to any other gift. See Part 7, Section B.

probate The court proceeding in which: 1) the authenticity of your will (if any) is established, 2) your executor or administrator is appointed, 3) your debts and taxes are paid, 4) your heirs are identified, and 5) the property in your probate estate is distributed according to your will (if there is a will). Many people feel probate is a costly, time-consuming process which is best avoided if possible. Accordingly, instead of leaving their property in a will, they use a probate avoidance device, such as a joint tenancy, trusts (including savings bank, *living,* insurance and testamentary trusts), life insurance, etc. See Part 6, Section B.

However, even those who believe it wise to leave property outside of a will generally also recommend using a will too. This is because a person could inherit or accumulate property shortly before death and not have time to create an alternative plan to pass it on. Also, a will can accomplish such tasks as naming an executor, guardian and trustee, in addition to leaving property. In some states, very small estates are exempt from probate even if a will is used. See Part 6, Section A.

probate estate All of your property that will pass through probate. Generally, this means all property owned by you at your death less any property that has been placed in joint tenancy, a living trust, a bank account trust, or in life insurance. See Part 6, Section B.

probate fees Because probate is so laden with legal formalities, it is usually necessary to hire an attorney to handle it. Under the law of some states, an attorney handling probate is entitled to be paid a percentage of the overall value of the probate estate (i.e., your maximum potential probate estate). This can often mean that the attorney will take a large chunk of the estate before it is distributed to the heirs. If, for example, your sole estate consists of your home, whose market value is $900,000, it is this figure which will be used to compute the probate fees, even though you may only have an equity of $200,000. In such a case, the fees might easily equal $20,000, or 10% of your actual estate. High probate fees are one good reason to engage in estate planning techniques designed to pass your property outside of your will. Part 6, Section B.

property, personal and real All land and items attached to the land, such as buildings, houses, stationary mobile homes, fences and trees are considered *real property* or *real estate.* All property which is not *real property* is considered personal property. See Part 9.

proving a will Getting a probate court to accept the fact after your death that your will really is your will. In a few states this can be done simply by introducing a properly executed will. In others, it is necessary to produce one or more witnesses (or affidavits of such witnesses) in court, or offer some proof of the testator's handwriting. A will can be made self-proving (admissible on its face) by attaching a self-proving affidavit to it. See Part 11, Section A.

quasi-community property A rule in Idaho and California that requires all property acquired by people during their marriage in other states to be treated as community property at their death in the event the couple has moved to one of these states. See Part 5, Section B.

real estate A term used by WillMaker as a synonym for *real property*. See *property, personal and real.*

real property See *property, personal and real.*

residuary estate All the property contained in your probate estate except for property that has been left to specifically designated recipients. Thus, your residuary estate includes *the rest of your real estate* and the *rest of your personal property.* See Part 9, Section A.

self-proving will See *proving a will.*

separate property See *community and separate property.*

specific bequest As used in WillMaker, a bequest of a specific item, such as a car, a house, an amount of cash, or a family heirloom. See Part 9, Section A.

spouse In WillMaker, your spouse is the person to whom you are legally married at the time you sign the will. If you later remarry, you will need to make a new will if you wish to leave property to your new spouse. See Part 5, Section B.

taking against the will The ability of a surviving spouse to choose a statutorily allotted share of the deceased spouse's estate instead of the share specified in his or her will. In most common law property states, the law provides for a surviving spouse to receive a minimum percentage of the other spouse's estate (commonly between one-third and one-half). If the deceased spouse leaves the surviving spouse less than this in, or outside of, the will, the surviving spouse may elect the statutory share instead of the will provision (i.e., take against the will). If the spouse chooses to accept the share specified in the will, it is called *taking under the will.* See Part 5, Sections C and D.

taxable estate The portion of your estate that is subject to federal and/or state estate taxes. See Part 6, Section C.

tenancy-in-common A way of jointly owning property in which each person's share passes to his/her heirs. The ownership shares need not be equal. See Part 5, Section A.

testamentary trust A trust that comes into existance at the death of the person creating them (the trustor).

testator The person making the will.

trust A legal arrangement under which one person or institution (called a *trustee*) controls property given by another person for the benefit of a third person (called a *beneficiary*). The property itself is termed the *corpus* of the trust. WillMaker can be used to create a trust for the purpose of managing property left to your surviving children, but not for tax planning purposes. However, there are many ways to establish such a trust while you are still alive. See Part 6, Sections B and C.

trustee The person or institution responsible for managing a trust according to its terms. Under WillMaker the trustee has discretion to manage property for the benefit of one or more of your minor children until they reach the age you specify. See Part 7 Section B.

Uniform Probate Act A series of statutes which attempt to standardize probate procedures and which have been enacted into law in approximately half the states. See Part 5, Section F.

will A legal document in which a person states various wishes about what he/she wants done after his/her death.

About Legisoft

Legisoft was founded in 1983 by attorney Bob Bergstrom and scientist Jeff Scargle. Bob is a San Francisco attorney with a Ph.D. in Mechanical Engineering from Purdue and a law degree from Stanford. Jeff has a Ph.D. in Astrophysics from CalTech. They both have worked with computer systems for twenty years and during a discussion about law and order in the universe decided there was a need for high quality, interactive computer programs in the legal profession. Legisoft has just completed work on *California Incorporator* with Tony Mancuso and Nolo Press. Legisoft also publishes *Lawyer's WillWriter* and California *CourtFinder*.

About Nolo

Nolo Press is the leading publisher of self-help law books and software in the United States. A pioneer of the self-help law movement, Nolo was founded in 1971 by Charles Sherman and Ralph Warner with the resolve to make the law more accessible to ordinary people.

Over fifty titles later (with over 2,000,000 copies in print), Nolo has helped its readers save hundreds of millions of dollars in legal fees. Nolo Press has gained a reputation for producing unique legal books and software appreciated for their clarity and helpfulness by both lay people and lawyers.

About the Illustrator

Mari Stein is a freelance illustrator and writer. Her published work has been eclectic, covering a wide range of subjects: humor, whilsy, health education, juvenile, fables and Yoga. This is her fifth collaboration with Nolo Press; she has illustrated *29 Reasons Not To Go To Law School, Media Law, How to Copyright Software* and our *Incorporation* series.

Dear NOLO Reader,

Enclosed is your WillMaker disk. Included on this disk is the Microsoft BASIC runtime interpreter package (© Microsoft 1988). This software allows you to run the NOLO programs even if you do not already own Microsoft BASIC 2.0

To include the interpreter package on this disk, Mircrosoft requires the use of the licensing agreement below. Note that the words "the program" refer to the Microsoft BASIC runtime package and not to the NOLO programs contained on the disk. Please read the agreement before opening the diskette package, as opening the package constitutes agreement to its terms.

License Agreement

LICENSE

You may:

a. use the program on a single machine;

b. copy the program on a single machine readable or printed form for backup or modification purposes in support of your use of the program on the single machine.

c. modify the program and/or merge it into another program for your use on the single machine (Any portion of this program merged into another program will continue to be subject to the terms and conditions of this Agreement.) and,

d. transfer the program and license to another party if the other party agrees to accept the terms and conditions of this Agreement. If you transfer the program, you must at the same time either transfer all copies whether in printed or machine-readable form to the same party or destroy any copies not transferreed; this includes all modifications and portions of the program contained or merged into other programs.

You must reproduce and include the copyright notice on any copy, modification or portion into another program.

YOU MAY NOT USE, COPY, MODIFY, OR TRANSFER THE PROGRAM OR ANY COPY, MODIFICATION OR MERGED PORTION IN WHOLE OR IN PART, EXCEPT AS EXPRESSLY PROVIDED FOR IN THIS LICENSE. IF YOU TRANSFER POSSESSION OF ANY COPY, MODIFICATION OR MERGED PORTION OF THE PROGRAM TO ANOTHER PARTY, YOUR LICENSE IS AUTOMATICALLY TERMINATED.

TERM

The license is effective until terminated. You may terminate it at any other time by destroying the program together with all copies, modifications and merged portions in any form. It will also terminate upon conditions set forth elsewhere in this Agreement or if you fail to comply with any term or condition of this Agreement. You agree upon such termination to destroy the program together with all copies, modifications and merged portions in any form.

LIMITED WARRANTY

THE PROGRAM IS PROVIDED "AS IS" WITHOUT WARRANTY OF ANY KIND, EITHER EXPRESSED OR IMPLIED, INCLUDING, BUT NOT LIMITED TO THE IMPLIED WARRANTIES OF MERCHANTABILITY AND FITNESS FOR A PARTICULAR PURPOSE. THE ENTIRE RISK AS TO THE QUALITY AND PERFORMANCE OF THE PROGRAM IS WITH YOU SHOULD THE PROGRAM PROVE DEFECTIVE, YOU (AND NOT LEGISOFT/NOLO PRESS OR AN AUTHORIZED COMPUTER DEALER.) ASSUME THE ENTIRE COST OF ALL NECESSARY SERVICING, REPAIR OR CORRECTION.

SOME STATES DO NOT ALLOW THE EXCLUSION OF IMPLIED WARRANTIES, SO THE ABOVE EXCLUSION MAY NOT APPLY TO YOU. THIS WARRANTY

GIVES YOU SPECIFIC LEGAL RIGHTS AND YOU MAY ALSO HAVE OTHER RIGHTS WHICH VARY FROM STATE TO STATE.

Legisoft/Nolo Press does not warrant that the functions contained in the program will meet your requirements or that the operation of the program will be uninterrupted or error free. However, Legisoft/Nolo Press warrants the diskette(s) on which the program is furnished, to be free from defects in materials and workmanship under normal use for a period of ninety (90) days from the date of delivery to you as evidenced by a copy of your receipt.

LIMITATIONS OF REMEDIES

Legisoft/Nolo Press's entire liability and your exclusive remedy shall be:

1. the replacement of any diskette not meeting Legisoft/Nolo Press's "Limited Warranty" and which is returned to Legisoft/Nolo Press or an authorized Legisoft/Nolo Press Computer dealer with a copy of your receipt, or

2. if Legisoft/Nolo Press or the dealer is unable to deliver a replacement diskette which is free of defects in materials or workmanship, you may terminate this Agreement by returning the program and your money will be refunded.

IN NO EVENT WILL LEGISOFT/NOLO PRESS BE LIABLE TO YOU FOR ANY DAMAGES, INCLUDING ANY LOST PROFITS, LOST SAVINGS OR OTHER INCIDENTAL OR CONSEQUENTIAL DAMAGES ARISING OUT OF THE USE OR INABILITY TO USE SUCH PROGRAM EVEN IF LEGISOFT/NOLO PRESS OR ANY AUTHORIZED LEGISOFT/NOLO PRESS PERSONEL COMPUTER DEALER HAS BEEN ADVISED OF THE POSSIBILITY OF SUCH DAMAGES, OR FOR ANY CLAIM BY ANY OTHER PARTY.

SOME STATES DO NOT ALLOW THE LIMITATION OR EXCLUSION OF LIABILITY FOR INCIDENTAL OR CONSEQUENTIAL DAMAGES SO THE ABOVE LIMIATION OR EXCLUSION MAY NOT APPLY TO YOU.

GENERAL

You may not sublicense, assign or transfer the license or the program except as expressly provided in this Agreement. Any attempt otherwise to sublicense, assign or transfer any of the rights, duties or obligations hereunder is void.

This Agreement will be governed by the laws of the State of Washington.

Should you have any questions concerning this Agreement, you may contact Nolo Press, 950 Parker Street, Berkeley, CA 94710.

YOU ACKNOWLEDGE THAT YOU HAVE READ THIS AGREEMENT UNDERSTAND IT AND AGREE TO BE BOUND BY ITS TERMS AND CONDITIONS. YOU FURTHER AGREE THAT IT IS THE COMPLETE AND EXCLUSIVE STATEMENT OF THE AGREEMENT BETWEEN US WHICH SUPERSEDES ANY PROPOSAL OR PRIOR AGREEMENT, ORAL OR WRITTEN, AND ANY OTHER COMMUNICATIONS BETWEEN US RELATING TO THE SUBJECT MATTER OF THIS AGREEMENT.

SOFTWARE

willmaker

Nolo Press/Legisoft
Recent statistics say chances are better than
2 to 1 that you haven't written a will, even
though you know you should. WillMaker makes
the job easy, leading you step by step in a fill-
in-the-blank format. Because writing a will is
only one step in the estate planning process,
WillMaker comes with a 200-page manual
providing an overview of probate avoidance
and tax planning techniques.
National 3rd Ed.

Apple, IBM, Macintosh	$59.95
Commodore	$39.95

california incorporator

Attorney Mancuso and Legisoft, Inc.
About half of the small California corporations
formed today are done without the services of
a lawyer. This easy-to-use software program
lets you do the paperwork with minimum effort.
Just answer the questions on the screen, and
California Incorporator will print out the 35-40
pages of documents you need to make your
California corporation legal.

California Edition (IBM)	$129.00

the california nonprofit corporation handbook—computer edition with disk

Attorney Anthony Mancuso
This is the standard work on how to form a
nonprofit corporation in California. Included on
the disk are the forms for the Articles, Bylaws
and Minutes you will need, as wel as regular
and special director and member minute
forms. Also included are several chapters with
line-by-line instructions explaining how to
apply for and obtain federal tax exempt status.
This is a critical step in the incorporation of
any nonprofit organizaton and applies to
incorporating in all 50 states.
California 1st Ed.

IBM PC 5 1/4 & 3 1/2	$69.00
Macintosh	$69.00

for the record

Attorney Warner & Pladsen.
A book/software package that helps to keep
track of personal and financial records; create
documents to give to family members in case
of emergency; leave an accurate record for
heirs, and allows easy access to all important
records with the ability to print out any section
National Edition

Macintosh	$49.95
IBM	$49.95

how to form your own new york corporation—computer edition with disk

Attorney Anthony Mancuso
More and more business people are incorporating to qualify for tax benefits, limited liability
status, the benefit of employee status and financial flexibility. This software package
contains all the instructions, tax information
and forms you need to incorporate a small
business, including the Certificate of Incorporation, Bylaws, Minutes and Stock Certificates.
The 250-page manual includes instructions on
how to incorporate a new or existing business;
tax and securities law information; information
on S corporations; Federal Tax Reform Act
rates and rules; and the latest procedures to
protect your directors under state law. All organizational forms are on disk.
New York 1st Ed.

IBM PC 5 1/4 & 3 1/2	$69.00
Macintosh	$69.00

how to form your own texas corporation—computer edition with disk

Attorney Anthony Mancuso
This new software package not only contains all
the instructions, tax information and forms (on
disk) you need to incorporate a small business,
it also adds and important new element—forms
for director and share holder meeting minutes,
necessary for holding future meetings and transacting ongoing business. The computer edition
includes:

- The Certificate of Incorporation, Bylaws,
  Minutes and stock certificates
- Full instructions on how to incorporate a
  new or already existing business
- Tax, corporation and securities law
  information
- Complete information on electing S
  Corporation tax status
- Federal Tax Reform Act rates and rules
- The latest procedures to protect your
  directors under state law
- And minute forms necessary for director
  and shareholder meetings.

Texas 1st Ed.

IBM PC 5 1/4 & 3 1/2	$69.00
Macintosh	$69.00

the california nonprofit corporation handbook

Attorney Anthony Mancuso

This book explains all the legal formalities involved in forming and operating a non-profit corporation. Included are all the forms for the Articles, Bylaws and Minutes you will need. Also included are complete instructions for obtaining federal 501(c)(3) exemptions and benefits. The tax information in this section applies wherever your corporation is formed.

California 5th Ed. $29.95

how to form your own corporation

Attorney Anthony Mancuso

More and more business people are incorporating to qualify for tax benefits, limited liability status, the benefit of employee status and the financial flexibility. These books contain the forms, instructions and tax information you need to incorporate a small business.

California 7th Ed. $29.95
Texas 4th Ed. $24.95
New York 2nd. Ed. $24.95
Florida 1st Ed. $19.95

1988 calcorp update package

Attorney Anthony Mancuso

This update package contains all the forms and instructions you need to modify your corporation's Articles of Incorporation so you can take advantage of new California laws.
$25.00

the california professional corporation handbook

Attorney Anthony Mancuso

Health care professionals, marriage, family and child counsellors, lawyers, accountants and members of certain other professions must fulfill special requirements when forming a corporation in California. This edition contains up-to-date tax information plus all the forms and instructions necessary to form a California professional corporation. An appendix explains the special rules that apply to each profession.

California 4th Ed. $34.95

nolo's small business start-up

Mike McKeever

Should you start a business? Should you raise money to expand your already running business? If the answers are yes, this book will show you how to write an effective business plan and loan package.

National 3rd Ed. $17.95

marketing without advertising

Michael Phillips & Salli Rasberry

Every small business person knows that the best marketing plan encourages customer loyalty and personal recommendation. Phillips and Rasberry outline practical steps for building and expanding a small business without spending a lot of money.

National 1st Ed. $14.00

the partnership book

Attorneys Clifford & Warner

Lots of people dream of going into business with a friend. The best way to keep that dream from turning into a nightmare is to have a solid partnership agreement. This book shows how to write an agreement that covers evaluation of partner assets, disputes, buy-outs and the death of a partner.

National 3rd Ed. $18.95

the independent paralegal's handbook: how to provide legal services without going to jail

Attorney Ralph Warner

A large percentage of routine legal work in this country is performed by typists, secretaries, researchers and various other law office helpers generally labeled paralegals. For those who would like to take these services out of the law office and offer them at a reasonable fee in an independent business, attorney Ralph Warner provides both legal and business guidelines.

National 1st Ed. $12.95

getting started as an independent paralegal (two audio tapes)

Attorney Ralph Warner

This set of tapes, approximately three hours in all, is a carefully edited version of Nolo Press founder Ralph Warner's Saturday Morning Law School class. It is designed for people who wish to go into business helping consumers prepare their own paperwork in uncontested actions such as bankruptcy, divorce, small business incorporations, landlord-tenant actions, probate, etc. The tapes are designed to be used in conjunction with *The Independent Paralegal's Handbook*.

National 1st Ed. $24.95

how to file for bankruptcy

Attorneys Stephen Elias, Robin Leonard & Albin Renauer

Here we show you how to decide whether or not filing for bankruptcy makes sense and if it does, we give you step-by-step instructions as to how to do it. *How To File For Bankruptcy* covers the procedure for completing a Chapter 7 and includes a discussion of Chapter 13 to help you decide which process is appropriate for you.

National 1st Ed. $24.95

collect your court judgment

Scott, Elias & Goldoftas

After you win a judgment in small claims, municipal or superior court, you still have to collect your money. Here are step-by-step instructions on how to collect your judgment from the debtor's bank accounts, wages, business receipts, real estate or other assets.

California 1st Ed. $24.95

make your own contract

Attorney Stephen Elias

If you've ever sold a car, lent money to a relative or friend, or put money down on a prospective purchase, you should have used a contract. Here are clearly written legal form contracts to: buy and sell property, borrow and lend money, store and lend personal property, make deposits on goods for later purchase, release others from personal liability, or pay a contractor to do home repairs.

National 1st Ed. $12.95

social security, medicare & pensions

Attorney Joseph L. Matthews & Dorothy Matthews Berman

Social security, medicare and medicaid programs follow a host of complicated rules. Those over 55, or those caring for someone over 55, will find this comprehensive guidebook invaluable for understanding and utilizing their rightful benefits.

National 4th Ed. $15.95

everybody's guide to small claims court

Attorney Ralph Warner

So, the dry cleaner ruined your good flannel suit. Your roof leaks every time it rains, and the contractor who supposedly fixed it won't call you back. This book will help you decide if you have a case, show you how to file and serve papers, tell you what to bring to court, and how to collect a judgment.

California 8th Ed. $14.95
National 3rd Ed. $14.95

devil's advocates: the unnatural history of lawyers

Jonathan & Andrew Roth

This book is a painless and hilarious education on the legal profession from its rude beginning through its ruder history to its rudest present. Laugh or weep as you learn the historical underpinnings of how and why lawyers have solidly become their own worst enemies.

1st Ed.
$12.95

29 reasons not to go to law school

Ralph Warner & Toni Ihara

Filled with humor and piercing observations, this book can save you three years, $70,000 and your sanity.

3rd Ed. $9.95

poetic justice

Ed. by Jonathan & Andrew Roth

A unique compilation of humorous quotes about lawyers and the legal system, from Socrates to Woody Allen.

$8.95

for sale by owner

George Devine

In 1986 about 600,000 homes were sold in California at a median price of $130,000. Most sellers worked with a broker and paid the 6% commission. For the median home that meant $7,800. Obviously, that's money that could be saved if you sell your own house. This book provides the background information and legal technicalities you will need to do the job yourself and with confidence.

California 1st Ed. $24.95

homestead your house

Attorneys Warner, Sherman & Ihara

Under California homestead laws, up to $60,000 of the equity in your home may be safe from creditors. But to get the maximum legal protection you should file a Declaration of Homestead before a judgment lien is recorded against you. This book includes complete instructions and tear-out forms.

California 6th Ed. $8.95

the landlord's law book: vol. 1, rights & responsibilities

Attorneys Brown & Warner

Every landlord should know the basics of landlord-tenant law. This volume covers: deposits, leases and rental agreements, in-spections (tenants' privacy rights), habitability (rent withholding), ending a tenancy, liability, and rent control.

California 2nd Ed. $24.95

the landlord's law book: vol. 2, evictions

Attorney David Brown

Even the most scrupulous landlord may sometimes need to evict a tenant. In the past it has been necessary to hire a lawyer and pay a high fee. Using this book you can handle most evictions yourself safely and economically.

California 1st Ed. $24.95

tenants' rights

Attorneys Moskowitz & Warner

Your "security building" doesn't have a working lock on the front door. Is your landlord liable? How can you get him to fix it? This book explains the best way to handle your relation-ship with your landlord and your legal rights when you find yourself in disagreement.

California 10th Ed. $15.95

the deeds book: how to transfer title to california real estate

Attorney Mary Randolph

The Deeds Book shows you how to choose the right kind of deed, how to complete the tear-out forms, and how to record them in the county recorder's public records. It also alerts you to real property disclosure requirements and California community property rules, as well as tax and estate planning aspects of your transfer.

California 1st Ed. $15.95

dog law

Attorney Mary Randolph

WeThere are 50 million dogs in the United States—and, it seems, at least that many rules and regulations for their owners to abide by. *Dog Law* covers topics that everyone who owns a dog, or lives near one, needs to know about dispute about a dog injury or nuisance.

National 1st Ed. $12.95

the criminal records book

Attorney Warren Siegel

The Criminal Records Book takes you step by step through the procedures to: seal criminal records, dismiss convictions, destroy marijuana records, reduce felony convictions.

California 2nd Ed. $14.95

fight your ticket

Attorney David Brown

At a trade show in San Francisco recently, a traffic court judge (who must remain name-less) told our associate publisher that he keeps this book by his bench for easy reference. If you think that ticket was unfair, here's the book showing you what to do to fight it.

California 3rd Ed. $16.95

how to change your name

Attorneys Loeb & Brown

This book explains how to change your name legally and provides all the necessary court forms with detailed instructions on how to fill them out.

California 4th Ed. $14.95

how to do your own divorce

Attorney Charles E. Sherman
This is the book that launched Nolo Press and advanced the self-help law movement. During the past 17 years, over 400,000 copies have been sold, saving consumers at least $50 million in legal fees (assuming 100,000 have each saved $500—certainly a conservative estimate).

California 15th Ed.	$14.95
Texas 2nd Ed.	$12.95

california marriage & divorce law

Attorneys Warner, Ihara & Elias
For a generation, this practical handbook has been the best resource for the Californian who wants to understand marriage and divorce laws. Even if you hire a lawyer to help you with a divorce, it's essential that you learn your basic legal rights and responsibilities.

California 10th Ed.	$15.95

practical divorce solutions

Attorney Charles Ed Sherman
Written by the author of *How to Do Your Own Divorce* (with over 500,000 copies in print), this book provides a valuable guide both to the emotional process involved in divorce as well as the legal and financial decisions that have to be made.

California 1st Ed.	$12.95

how to adopt your stepchild in california

Frank Zagone & Mary Randolph
For many families that include stepchildren, adoption is a satisfying way to guarantee the family a solid legal footing. This book provides sample forms and complete step-by-step instructions for completing a simple uncontested adoption by a stepparent.

California 3rd Ed.	$19.95

how to modify and collect child support in california

Attorneys Matthews, Siegel & Willis
California has established landmark new standards in setting and collecting child support. Payments must now be based on both objective need standards and the parents' combined income.
Using this book, custodial parents can determine if they are entitled to higher child support payments and can implement the procedures to obtain that support.

California 2nd Ed.	$17.95

the guardianship book: how to become a child's guardian in california

Lisa Goldoftas & Attorney David Brown
Thousands of children in California are left without a guardian because their parents have died, abandoned them or are unable to care for them. *The Guardianship Book* provides step-by-step instructions and the forms needed to obtain a legal guardianship without a lawyer. The book covers:

- how to prepare, file and have your guardianship papers served
- how to get a guardianship hearing set in court
- what to say to the judge
- the legal responsibilities and duties of a guardian
- information about dealing with a variety of institutions and agencies
- alternative forms for use when a legal guardianship is not needed.

California 1st Ed.	$19.95

legal guide for lesbian and gay couples

Attorneys Curry & Clifford
In addition to its clear presentation of "living together" contracts, A Legal Guide contains crucial information on the special problems facing lesbians and gay men with children, civil rights legislation, and medical/legal issues.

National 5th Ed.	$17.95

the living together kit

Attorneys Ihara & Warner
Few unmarried couples understand the laws that may affect them. Here are useful tips on living together agreements, paternity agreements, estate planning, and buying real estate.

National 5th Ed.	$17.95

nolo's simple will book

Attorney Denis Clifford
We feel it's important to remind people that if they don't make arrangements before they die, the state will give their property to certain close family members. If there are nieces, nephews, godchildren, friends or stepchildren you want to leave something to, you need a will. It's easy to write a legally valid will using this book, and once you've done it yourself you'll know how to update it whenever necessary.
National 1st Ed. $14.95

plan your estate: wills, probate avoidance, trusts & taxes

Attorney Denis Clifford
A will is only one part of an estate plan. The first concern is avoiding probate so that your heirs won't receive a greatly diminished inheritance years later. This book shows you how to create a "living trust" and gives you the information you need to make sure whatever you have saved goes to your heirs, not to lawyers and the government.
National 1st Ed. $17.95

the power of attorney book

Attorney Denis Clifford
The Power of Attorney Book concerns something you've heard about but probably would rather ignore: Who will take care of your affairs, make your financial and medical decisions, if you can't? With this book you can appoint someone you trust to carry out your wishes.
National 2nd Ed. $17.95

how to probate an estate

Julia Nissley
When a close relative dies, amidst the grieving there are financial and legal details to be dealt with. The natural response is to rely on an attorney, but that response can be costly. With *How to Probate an Estate* you can have the satisfaction of doing the work yourself and saving those fees.
California 4th Ed. $24.95

legal research: how to find and understand the law

Attorney Stephen Elias
A valuable tool for paralegals, law students and legal secretaries, this book provides access to legal information. Using this book, the legal self-helper can find and research a case, read statutes, and make Freedom of Information Act requests.
National 2nd Ed. $14.95

family law dictionary

Attorneys Leonard and Elias
Written in plain English (as opposed to legalese), the Family Law Dictionary has been compiled to help the lay person doing research in the area of family law (i.e., marriage, divorce, adoption, etc.). Using cross referencs and examples as well as definitions, this book is unique as a reference tool.
National 1st Edition $13.95

patent, copyright & trademark: intellectual property law dictionary

Attorney Stephen Elias
This book uses simple language free of legal jargon to define and explain the intricacies of items associated with trade secrets, copyrights, trademarks and unfair competition, patents and patent procedures, and contracts and warranties.—IEEE Spectrum
If you're dealing with any multi-media product, a new business product or trade secret, you need this book.
National 1st Ed. $19.95

how to copyright software

Attorney M.J. Salone
Copyrighting is the best protection for any software. This book explains how to get a copyright and what a copyright can protect.
National 3rd Ed. $34.95

legal care for your software

Attorneys Daniel Remer & Stephen Elias
If you write programs you intend to sell, or work for a software house that pays you for programming, you should buy this book. This step-by-step guide for computer software writers covers copyright laws, trade secret protection, contracts, license agreements, trademarks, patents and more.
National 3rd Ed. $29.95

patent it yourself

Attorney David Pressman
You've invented something, or you're working on it, or you're planning to start...Patent It Yourself offers help in evaluating patentability, marketability and the protective documenta-tion you should have. If you file your own patent application using this book, you can save from $1500 to $3500.
National 2nd Ed. $29.95

the inventor's notebook

Fred Grissom & Attorney David Pressman
The best protection for your patent is ade-quate records. The Inventor's Notebook provides forms, instructions, references to relevant areas of patent law, a bibliography of legal and non-legal aids, and more. It helps you document the activities that are normally part of successful independent inventing.
National 1st Ed.
$19.95

H A L T

1319 F Street, NW
Suite 300
Washington, D.C. 20004
(202)347-9600

A law reform organization worthy of your support

HALT (Help Abolish Legal Tyranny)—An Organization of Americans for Legal Reform —is a nonprofit public interest group whose activities are primarily funded by its 200,000 individual members. Like Nolo Press, HALT advocates a number of changes in the legal system to make it possible for the average American to reasonably and affordably manage his or her legal life. To name but a few of their admirable activities, HALT lobbies to increase disciplinary sanctions against dishonest and incompetent lawyers, reduce probate fees and simplify procedures, increase the role of non-lawyer (independent paralegal) legal service providers, and expand small claims court. To keep its members abreast of major legal reform developments, HALT also publishes a quarterly magazine, holds law reform conferences, and publishes excellent position papers on legal reform issues.

Nolo Press supports HALT and its members and urges all interested citizens to join for a $15 annual membership fee.

The Power of Attorney Book

by Denis Clifford
$15.95

The Power of Attorney Book addresses some of those issues we would
rather not think about, but should plan for anyway:

- Who would make my medical and financial decisions if I were
  unable to?
- How can I avoid having my life artificially prolonged by the use
  of machines?

Using the durable power of attorney forms provided in this book, you can
authorize the person of your choice to make your medical and financial
decisions and let your wishes be known. By writing a durable power of
attorney before you are incapacitated, you save your family or friends the
time and expense of a court appointed conservatorship: You also insure
that your preferences will be considered. Since the durable power of
attorney takes effect only if you are incapacitated, it can act as an
insurance policy for any healthy person.

The ordinary power of attorney forms in this book can be used for more
prosaic matters; for instance, allowing someone to sign legal forms for
you while you are travelling. These can be as limited (the sale of a
house) or as open-ended as your like (the management of all your
financial assets).

Both the standard and durable power of attorney forms are valid in every
state. Complete instructions and tear-out forms are included.

INCORPORATION SOFTWARE FROM NOLO

California Incorporator
by Attorney Anthony Mancuso & Legisoft, Inc.
$129.95. Includes 250 page manual with disk
IBM

Under the new tax laws corporate profits of less than $185,000 are still taxed less than the same amount of individual income. Many successful business people simply can't afford not to incorporate. *California Incorporator* provides all the information and documentation necessary to incorporate a small business in California. By simply answering a series of questions on your computer screen, *Incorporator* software will provide to 30 or 40 pages of documentation required for forming a corporation including your corporate name reservation letter Articles of Incorporation, Bylaws, Minutes, and Securities Law waiver letters.

The California Non Profit Corporation Handbook
Computer Version With Disk
by Attorney Anthony Mancuso
$69.95. Includes 350 page manual with disk
IBM & Macintosh

This is the standard work on how to form a non profit corporation in California. Included on the disk are forms for the Articles, Bylaws and Minutes you will need, as well as regular and special director and member minute forms necessary for holding future meetings and transacting on-going business. Also included are several chapters with line-by-line instructions explaining how to apply for and obtain the federal 501(c)(3) tax exempt status. This is a critical step in the incorporation of any non profit organization and applies to incorporating in all 50 states.

How to Form Your Own New York Corporation
Computer Version With Disk
by Attorney Anthony Mancuso
$69.95. Includes 250 page manual with disk
IBM & Macintosh

How to Form Your Own Texas Corporation
Computer Version With Disk
by Attorney Anthony Mancuso
$69.95. Includes 250 page manual with disk
IBM & Macintosh

More and more business people are incorporating to qualify for tax benefits, limited liability status, the benefit of employee status and the financial flexibility. These software package contain all the instructions, tax information and forms you need to incorporate a small business including the Certificate (or Articles) of Incorporation, Bylaws, Minutes and stock certificates; full instructions on how to incorporate a new or already existing business; tax, corporation and securities law information; complete information on electing S Corporation tax status; Federal Tax Reform Act rates and rules; and the latest procedures to protect your directors under state law. All organizational forms are on disk.

FOR THE RECORD [T.M.]

IBM AND MACINTOSH SOFTWARE FROM NOLO PRESS

BY CAROL PLADSEN & RALPH WARNER

All of us know we should keep good personal, financial and legal matters records…but few of us do. **For the Record** makes it easy by collecting vital information about your property and many of your actual records in one place. With **For the Record** your records are easy to find and easy to retrieve.

Prompts you to record anything you might have forgotten

Through an extensive menu of 27 categories and over 200 sub-categories, **For the Record** prompts you to enter and keep track of:

- emergency information
- sources of income
- real estate
- business interests
- collectibles and other objects of value
- insurance and tax records
- credit cards
- medical information
- personal information and memorabilia and more…

Special on-screen notepads let you record any miscellaneous information that may be relevant to a particular entry. Cross-references help you find related information.

Allows you to share your records or keep them private

You can print out your **For the Record** files and give them to a relative or friend, or you can keep information private in a locked file in your computer with your own designated password.

More than a manual

The 200 page **For the Record** manual offers hundreds of legal and practical tips on record-keeping and financial planning on everything from where to store your will to how to shop for a credit card.

$49.95

 SELF-HELP LAW BOOKS & SOFTWARE

ORDER FORM

Quantity	Title	Unit Price	Total

Sales Tax (CA residents only):

7%   Alameda, Contra Costa, San Diego, San Mateo & Santa
        Clara counties
6 1/2% Fresno, Inyo, LA, Sacramento, San Benito, San Francisco
        & Santa Cruz counties
6%   All others

Subtotal _____

Sales Tax _____

TOTAL _____

Method of Payment:

☐ Check enclosed

☐ VISA   ☐ Mastercard

Acct # _____ Exp. _____

Signature _____

Phone (   ) _____

Ship to:

Name _____

Address _____

_____

Mail to:

**NOLO PRESS
950 Parker Street
Berkeley CA 94710**

For faster service, use your credit card and our toll-free numbers:

Monday-Friday 9-5 Pacific Time

US   1-800-992-6656

CA   (outside 415 area)   1-800-445-6656

      (inside 415 area)   1-415-549-1976

General Information   1-415-549-1976

Prices subject to change

Please allow 1-2 weeks for delivery

Delivery is by UPS; no P.O. boxes, please

ORDER DIRECT AND WE PAY POSTAGE & HANDLING!

WARNING: BEFORE INSTALLING WILLMAKER ON YOUR HARD DISK, READ THE INSTRUCTIONS IN PART 14.

Specifications

Requirements:	Apple II+ (64K), IIe, IIc, IIGS
	IBM: PC, AT, XT, PS/2 and compatibles running PC DOS 2.1 or later: 256K RAM **Note:** A 5 1/4" disk is supplied for the IBM and compatible machines. To obtain a 3 1/2" disk, see the coupon enclosed in the envelope (inside back cover).
	Apple: 64K RAM
	Macintosh: 512E, Plus, SE, XL (with Macworks™), II
	One disk drive
	A display device
	Apple/IBM: Any standard printer that works with the computer
	Macintosh: Imagewriter, Laserwriter, or comparable printer
Operating System:	ProDOS (Apple) — supplied with disk
	PC DOS (IBM) or MS DOS
	Macintosh — supplied with disk
Languages:	Compiled BASIC and Assembly
Copying/Editing:	WillMaker can be copied to a back-up diskette (or hard disk)
	All editing must be done through the program rather than another editing program
	WillMaker is a rule-based system using abstract data structures and a blackboard
Copy Protection:	WillMaker is not copy protected, but is protected by copyright and may not be used for commercial purposes